MAXTON

MAXTON

by

GORDON BROWN

MAINSTREAM
PUBLISHING

First published in 1986 by
MAINSTREAM PUBLISHING COMPANY (EDINBURGH) LTD
7 Albany Street
Edinburgh EH1 3UG

The publisher acknowledges subsidy from the Scottish Arts Council
towards the publication of this volume

ISBN 1 85158 042 5

British Library Cataloguing-In-Publication Data

Brown, Gordon, *1951*-
    Maxton: a biography
    1. Maxton, James
    2. Independent Labour Party – Biography
    3. Politicians – Great Britain – Biography
    4. Socialists – Great Britain – Biography
    1. Title
    941.082'092'4   DA566.9.M39/

    ISBN 1-85158-042-5

Typset in 10pt Century by Digital Publications Ltd, Edinburgh
Printed by Billing & Sons Ltd, Worcester

By the same Author:

Red Paper on Scotland (1975)
The Politics of Nationalism and Devolution (1980)
Scotland: The Real Divide (1983)

CONTENTS

Page

SECTION III: SOCIALISM IN OUR TIME

SECTION IV: SOCIALISM IN RETREAT

Introduction

The story of James Maxton and of the Clydeside MPs who descended on Westminster in 1922, has fascinated me since I was a teenager. This book has been almost twenty years in the making. I first wrote about Maxton while at University in 1967-68. For encouragement then and since I am grateful to Dr Paul Addison of Edinburgh Univeristy and grateful especially to his colleague Dr John Brown who guided me through the final stages of my PhD thesis on politics in the nineteen twenties from which much of this biography is drawn. Without his encouragement I doubt if my thesis, or this book, could ever have been completed.

Maxton is remembered by many who have outlived him. I have benefited from conversations on various occasions with Bob Edwards MP and Lord Carmichael. I have also discussed Maxton with Lady Lee and the late Lord Shinwell. The late Annie and Ada Maxton were generous in their help and advice. More recently Mr John Maxton MP has given me similar assistance and also permission to study the correspondence and documents contained in the Maxton Papers now deposited in the Strathclyde Regional Archive at the Mitchell Library, Glasgow. To the staff there, and to the staff of the National Library of Scotland and the British Newspaper Library at Colindale, I am grateful. I am grateful too to Mr James Dollan for providing me with access to the unpublished autobiography of his father and to the ILP for making available their records. I have also consulted the Labour Party records, now in Walworth Road, London and the ILP Glasgow records housed in the Mitchell Library.

This book could not have been completed without the help of my brother Andrew who volunteered his assistance in combing newspapers and periodicals for Maxton's speeches and writings.

Dr Colin Currie read my first draft and I am grateful to him for his advice and for the time he surrendered to suggest many improving amendments to the text.

Valuable comments came also from my brother John, from Ian Levitt, who is completing a book on Scottish social conditions in the inter-war years, and from Murray Elder. Janet Crook and David John helped in my searches through *Hansard*. Encouragement has come too from Russell Galbraith and Bob Cuddihy at Scottish Television, from Marion Caldwell, and, in this and other projects, from my friends and colleagues in the Dunfermline East Labour Party. Errors of fact remain my own responsibility.

Bill Campbell and Peter Mackenzie of Mainstream are not only publishers who have built up a considerable reputation for Scottish publishing in both Europe and America: they are friends of many years who encouraged me to write this book. I doubt if they ever believed that this book would be completed. I hope they do not regret encouraging me to do so.

This book is dedicated to my parents who have continued to support and encourage me not only through school and university, but also in more recent, and more controversial, activities.

Gordon Brown
1 May 1986

1

St Enoch Square November 1922

"Not since the Reform Act of 1832 had so much enthusiasm been evoked at a political demonstration," recalled Patrick Dollan of the events of the Sunday after the 1922 General Election. "Many veterans have since told me that it was the most inspiring hour of their life."[1]

Glasgow blazed red. Ten of the city's 15 constituencies had elected socialist MPs. The Prime Minister, Andrew Bonar Law, had only narrowly escaped electoral defeat in his Glasgow Central constituency.

The Conservatives were aghast. One of their defeated remarked that "one had to go back to Flodden before we would find a similar national disaster". Another complained that the three great qualities possessed by Scotland, "a love of liberty, a love of industry and a love of religion", were now lost.[2] At a Glasgow post-election meeting Conservatives labelled the results as "more like the voice of Bolshevik Russia or of Sinn Fein Ireland than of Glasgow".

Their reactions reflected the bitterness of the most keenly fought election this century. By the standards of today some of the punches were low. A Tory leaflet had stated that Labour, if elected, would nationalise women. One Tory poster spelt out the message: "Bolshevism is only socialism with the courage of its convictions", and another portrayed a bearded Russian with the caption: "He wants you to vote Socialist – Don't".

In the previous Parliament, Labour members accounted for only 61 seats. In 1922, their representation more than doubled, to 142 seats. 30 of these were Scottish, one-third of them in Glasgow, and another third from mining communities nearby. All the Labour leaders, with the exception of Mr Arthur Henderson, had been returned. Labour was now the official opposition. This was the election in which the fortunes of the Labour Party rose and those of the Liberals correspondingly fell. One of the Conservative

11

members, Walter Elliot was to recall that it was "in 1922 that the new line up in Parliament took place. The hard unyielding struggle has gone on since then. The political tenacity has been great and the changes slight."

On the 20 November 1922, the new MPs from Glasgow and the West of Scotland left on the night mail train for Westminster from St Enoch Station. In their ears rang the words of Psalm 124, sung by the massive and triumphant crowd around.

> Now Israel may say and that truly
> If that the Lord had not our cause maintained
> If that the Lord had not our right sustained
> When cruel men against us furiously
> Rose up in wrath to make of us their prey

Not sentiments widely heard in Bolshevik Russia, and the declaration issued earlier in the day owed more to the Bible than to Bolshevism, more to the traditions of the Scottish Covenanters than those of Soviet Communism. It pledged them to self-sacrifice to achieve international brotherhood. They would "abjure vanity and self-aggrandisement, recognising that they are the honoured servants of the people and that their only righteous purpose is to promote the welfare of their fellow citizens and the well being of mankind".

Two huge Red Flags glowed brilliant in the gleams of arc lamps above the station, as from the steps James Houston conducted the William Morris choir, and the crowd sang *The Red Flag*, the *International*, and *Jerusalem*:

> We will not cease from mental strife
> Nor let the sword sleep in our hand
> Till we have built Jerusalem
> In England's green and pleasant land

England would benefit too. The crowds in their thousands joined in. No-one knows how many were there. Some say 40,000, others 80,000, others still 120,000. They filled the station square and overflowed into Argyle Street and its side-streets. Processions which had marched from meetings in the new Labour constituencies all over Glasgow, and busloads of supporters from the rest of the West of Scotland, had descended on the station. Whatever the numbers present, they exceeded official anticipation and reinforcements of police had to be summoned.

Some of the new MPs addressed the crowd from the platform overlooking the square and, as Dollan recalls, they "were cheered like thunder". But who were they, these Clydesiders now out to make politcal history? What roads had they travelled to their triumph in St Enoch Square, and where were they going to take the socialist politics of the United Kingdom?

18 MPs were to travel down to Westminster together. Among them were Neil McLean, a mechanic who had become a trades union organiser before he won the Govan constituency in 1918; the Lanarkshire miner John Robertson, the victor of a famous Bothwell by-election of 1919; George Hardie, Keir Hardie's brother; James Muir, one of the leaders of the Clydeside industrial unrest in the Great War; Tom Henderson, a joiner in the shipyards who had become a Town Councillor; the Christian Socialist Captain John Hay, who had been a teacher in China and had been decorated for his service in the Chinese Labour Corps, and Jimmy Stewart, a hairdresser in the Royal Infirmary, who had graduated to the Chairmanship of Glasgow Town Council's Public Health Department. ("He used to shave and haircut patients at 5 a.m. so that he could get time off from business in the afternoon to attend Parish Council meetings," recalled Patrick Dollan.)

Emanuel Shinwell, the Chairman of the Trades Council, had been elected in the East of Scotland at Linlithgow, and the editor of the ILP's newspaper, *Forward*, Tom Johnston, had won West Stirling. Robert Nichol, Lachlan McNeill Weir, William Wright and Robert Murray joined them. But the central figures of the group soon to be known as the Clyde Brigade were to be John Wheatley, Campbell Stephen, David Kirkwood, George Buchanan and James Maxton.

George Buchanan had been a second, and late, choice as the Gorbals candidate. Labour leaders including Philip Snowden and Ramsay MacDonald had been mentioned as possible candidates, but Buchanan came to Westminster with the direct experience of Town Council debate behind him. As Dollan says, "He spoke about the grievances of the Gorbals in every oration he delivered."

Buchanan was only 32 at the time of his election. He was a patternmaker. His brother and sister had both been through university but there was no money to send him as well. He had been Glasgow's youngest councillor when elected in 1918 for the Hutchesontown ward. First in Pimlico, later in Battersea, he was to share lodgings with Campbell Stephen and Maxton.

13

Campbell Stephen was the new member for Camlachie. He had been born and raised in a tenement flat in Townhead in Glasgow, had started on a professional career as a minister in Ardrossan, and then become a teacher before qualifying at the English Bar as a barrister. He was to be "the infallible guide, the drafter of difficult questions on behalf of the Clyde Brigade and the man who avoided head on collisons with the speaker . . . a parliamentary slogger if ever there was one".

Stephen was a professional man who had adopted the Glasgow working class: David Kirkwood, the new member for Dumbarton, represented the skilled engineers, the industrial élite of the trades union movement. In the industrial struggles of the First World War Kirkwood had gained a national reputation as the chief shop steward at Glasgow's huge engineering works, Beardmore's. For his militancy he was deported to Edinburgh, although later he was reinstated as a foreman. In the Forty Hour Strike of 1919 Kirkwood was arrested for planning sedition as the Government sent tanks to the Clyde. Yet Kirkwood's extremism was much exaggerated. Now 50 years old, he was an admirer of Burns and the Bible, a total abstainer, and a down to earth practical union negotiator.

At 53, John Wheatley was the oldest and most politically experienced of the new MPs. Born in County Waterford in Ireland only weeks before his family emigrated to Baillieston in Lanarkshire, Wheatley had gone down the mines at the age of 13, and worked as a coal miner for 12 years. By a rigorous process of self-education – while a miner he had often walked 10 miles to study at the Glasgow Athenaeum – he had graduated from the pits to publican, shopkeeper, advertising manager for a Catholic newspaper, and finally became a publisher in his own right.

Well dressed, and rotund, with thick glasses, Wheatley looked more like a successful capitalist than a crusading socialist but it was Wheatley, more than anyone else, who had helped shift Glasgow's Catholics towards Labour. In 1906 he had formed the Catholic Socialist Society and, in a series of angry debates and encounters with Catholic traditionalists – including luminaries like Hilaire Belloc – and with Marxists, he had demonstrated how devout Catholics could also be practical socialists without sacrificing their religious convictions.

In 1912 Wheatley had joined the Glasgow Town Council, and had devised and then popularised a scheme to rid Glasgow of its tenement slums, replacing them with low-rent cottages on the edge of the city. His analytical mind, and his political skills, were to make him the Director General of the Clydesiders' Westminster operations and in 1923 he established his own weekly newspaper, the *Glasgow Eastern Standard*, to advertise his Parliamentary achievements and those of his colleagues.

Of all the Clydesiders, there was one that audiences loved best. On the day after his election, the Conservative *Glasgow Herald* newspaper described him as "one of the ablest speakers and lecturers in the Labour Movement". James Maxton – swarthy, lantern jawed, and intense with a huge lank forelock (definitely not for tugging) – not only preached the revolution but, as one commentator remarked at the time, looked it. Though only 37 when he went to Westminster, he had been first a teacher, then the Glasgow organiser for the ILP and a member of the local education authority. But he was best known as simply the most compelling platform orator of his day.

As Maxton reached the platform that night in St Enoch Square, his back was bruised and his hands were aching from the sheer physical enthusiasm of congratulations thrust upon him. From a truck, he addressed possibly the most enthusiastic audience he had ever faced. Such was the crowd, he said, that it had been more difficult for them to get to St Enoch Station than it was to get into the House of Commons. The huge crowd knew and trusted him. "Rely on us," he said, "as we rely on you."

And as ever there was fun and mockery. Bonar Law's election slogan, "Peace and Tranquillity", was taken from a hymn which Maxton paraphrased for the crowd.

> Bonar, seek not yet repose,
>   Cast the dream of rest away;
> Thou art in the midst of foes—
>   Watch and Pray

Perhaps sensing the huge crowd's doubts about the impact of their small band of heroes on the ancient might of the House of Commons, Maxton reassured them. "People talk about the atmosphere of the House of Commons getting the better of the Labour men," he said, "they will see the atmosphere of the Clyde getting the better of the House of Commons."

Not everything went smoothly that happy night. Another of the newly elected members, David Kirkwood, was unable to get into the station because of the crowd and had tried to get in via the St Enoch Hotel. Railway officials took him for just another reveller and turned him back. Undismayed, he recounted this to the crowd, reassuring them, "Don't mind, comrades. When we come back next time it will be our hotel."[3]

The 10.45 night mail duly left St Enoch Station to the sound of the singing of the *Red Flag*. It was the culmination of long years of propaganda and political activity, and of a jubilant day of rallies, meetings, demonstrations and celebrations.

In the afternoon, St Andrew's Hall and the City Hall had been packed to overflowing by services of dedication. In a touching blend of the triumphant and the devotional, the crowds had heard their heroes and cheered them, and sung hymns, and psalms and socialist inspirational songs, led by the Socialist Choristers and the William Morris Choir.

The meetings had been organised by the Glasgow Trades and Labour Council, who read out the Declaration issued by the Clydesiders to the people of Scotland. Expressing their "infinite gratitude to the pioneer minds of past generations who by their services and sacrifices have opened up the path for the freedom of the people", the Declaration promised "that they will urge without ceasing the need for providing houses for the people, suitable to enshrine the spirit of Home" and would "bear in their hearts the sorrows of the aged, the widowed mother and the poor that their lives shall not be without comfort".

The new MPs would fight for adequate wages, benefits and conditions in industry, "to eradicate the corrupting effect of monopoly and avarice". They would "have regard to the weak and those stricken by disease" and "for those who have fallen in the struggle for life". It was a political agenda but one that found resonance with humanitarian thought and the religious life of the nation. As a minister of the United Free Church of Scotland was to tell the *Glasgow Herald*, the declaration had its roots with the Covenanters, its nearest parallel the Solemn League and Covenant of the seventeenth century.

The new MPs set out simply to serve. As Maxton told the crowd, "when things were at their worst the spirit of Scottish people was to put a stout heart to a stey brae". The Labour Movement had taken that as its aim and object. In the House of Commons they would quite simply "work unceasingly". Though the Clydesiders would be new to Westminster, they would not be naîve. Previously they had worked in politics seven days a week and in their spare time. Now as full-time professionals, they would set a "hot pace in Westminster for the genial old Tories from the backwoods who would now earn their £400 salary by the sweat of their brows".

They knew they could not promise miracles, but they promised courage, hard work, and genuine and strenuous service.

For them the whole of 20 November had been a succession of meetings. Earlier in his new constituency of Bridgeton, Maxton spoke to more than 3000 people packed in the Olympia Theatre.

At the Metropole Theatre, where the Glasgow Independent Labour Party had held meetings for the last six years, thousands queued for what Chairman Patrick Dollan called "a splendid send-off". He told them of the fifty years since first a Labour candidate had stood for the Town Council. It had been a long struggle. In 1885 one Labour man had polled only 86 votes. In the little millenium of 1922, 160,000 all over Glasgow had voted Labour.

In the Metropole, too, James Maxton, organising secretary of the Glasgow ILP until only a few days ago, addressed the audience. "All the Labour Members from this city are personal friends. We are not leaving Glasgow as so many individuals, but as a team working towards a goal – and that goal is the abolition of poverty."[4]

However ecstatic Labour supporters felt at the time, it may not have turned out to be the Scottish equivalent of July 1789 in France, or October 1917 in Russia, but it still ranks as the Scottish Labour Movement's finest hour.

***

James Maxton was born in 1885 and died in 1946. He was the Member of Parliament for Bridgeton from 1922 to his death, and a central figure in the Labour Party and Independent Labour Party for more than 30 years. His political career spanned the great events which shaped modern Britain – two world wars, industrial unrest which many thought would bring revolution to Britain, mass unemployment in the twenties, the hunger marches in the thirties, and the rise, and eventual triumph of the modern Labour Party in 1945.

Maxton was involved in the intrigues, the controversies and the campaigns and agitations which surrounded all of them. Even before he reached Westminster in 1922, he had achieved prominence as a teacher sacked for his socialist beliefs, as a wartime conscientious objector imprisoned for sedition, and as a full time Labour organiser at the height of acrimonious debates over the Left's attitudes to Lenin and the Russian Revolution. In the years which followed he was the most consistent critic of the Labour Party leadership of the nineteen twenties and thirties and the leading sponsor of perhaps the most impressive left-wing prospectus which was published during the inter-war years and sought to achieve socialism with speed.

Maxton, like many Labour leaders, has suffered the condescension of posterity. He has been belittled and dismissed as "a beloved rebel", picturesque but peripheral. He was a politician who refused to be compromised by the allurements of Westminster, who refused the aristocratic embrace, who took socialism to the point of social intransigence, but he achieved little. A wasted life, wrote A J P Taylor. "He was a politician who had every quality – passionate sincerity, unstinted devotion, personal charm, a power of oratory – every quality save one – the gift of knowing how to succeed."[5]

Maxton never held Government office. No great legislative reforms bear his name. The Independent Labour Party which he dominated for 20 years dwindled eventually to nothing, even as his audiences grew larger. But at the height of his powers, in the 1920s, he threatened to change the whole course of politics by offering British socialism a third way between Labour gradualism and Communism.

Some of his contemporaries were great platform orators. Others were skilled House of Commons performers. Maxton was both. He was the man whom Churchill called, some said in envy, "the greatest gentleman in the House of Commons", the leader his own mentor John Wheatley described as "a new God", the socialist Tom Johnston described as "in direct line of succession from Keir Hardie". To Lord Brockway he was "a prophet" who "reached a height of creative inspiration matched by no one else". "The occasional talk with Maxton was an inspiration," wrote Harold Laski. Ellen Wilkinson described him simply as "the man most likely to lead the British people to socialism".

Maxton's style of oratory was unique. His appearance, the long black hair, and the dark, almost sinister, features, was dramatic and his gestures – the pointing finger, the beckoning forearms – made the most of it. His grim, even haggard, features broke easily into a smile. His humour, natural, pleasing and illuminating, was proverbial. "Maxton would have made a fortune on the stage," wrote Patrick Dollan: "He was irresistible, I cannot think of anybody who could make an audience laugh as easily."[6]

He was a compelling orator and he knew it. "I am here to preach the gospel of discontent," he once said. Speaking, he wrote in 1922, "calls out all the latent will power, character and intellect a man possesses. Reading and study are both essential if a man is going to be a first class platform speaker, but the only way to learn to speak is to speak and the experience of speaking will compel study."[7]

"I write with great difficulty," he once confessed. Maxton had no great socialist books to his name. He published a short biography of Lenin and a brief polemic, "If I were a Dictator" but he never wrote the promised biography of John Maclean[8] and a later project, a book provisionally entitled "Westminster From Within" was stillborn.[9] Despite offers to do so, Maxton refused to write any autobiography. In a letter to the editor of the *Scottish Daily Express* in April 1935, he responded to the biographical articles that had been comissioned on him. "I always think life should be completed before (it is) written about," he said. "For this reason I have refused to contemplate writing my own life or to cooperate with anyone who proposed to write it."[10]

Writing he found a painful and laborious duty anyway. In 1932 he was asked to write an ILP polemic against the Labour Party, but turned the request down. "When I have ground out my weekly *New Leader* article," he replied, "I feel I have done my painful duty in the journalistic field."[11] Although from 1926 to the 1940s he wrote several hundred words weekly on current issues, he never saw himself as a writer. "I have never been one of the writers of the movement, never want to be, and I am afraid I am incapable if I did desire it," he said. "Speech is my medium of expression."[12]

Maxton was never a Government Minister, and his failure to achieve any high office may have been the result of a proper disinclination on the part of a man who knew that his talents were inappropriate. He was accused by some of laziness. Once in the House of Commons, he referred to his own "well advertised mental lethargy".[13] The sheer volume of his propaganda efforts belies this. He read widely in the socialist literature, was a public speaker endlessly in demand and a pamphleteer productive over decades.

By the 1930s his influence had waned. Engulfed in the sectarian socialist controversies of the period, Maxton could have been dismissed as a fringe politician. But in the 1920s he offered British Socialism an alternative course and direction. *Socialism in Our Time*, the programme that he championed, was a proto-Keynesian programme to banish unemployment and poverty, and to create socialism quickly and without catastrophe. Socialists had predicted a crisis of capitalism, a point at which there would be no alternative to a move towards a socialist society. But most would be frightened into inaction by the economic hurricane which swept Britain between the wars. Maxton despaired of them. To him, it was as though the Salvation Army had taken to its heels on the Day of Judgement. The crisis was not an excuse for avoiding socialism, but the opportunity for implementing it in the form of *Socialism in Our Time*.

For the most of his career he was to be criticised for merely taking tales of the slums and the dole queues into Parliament, but he had greater concerns and visions too. As early as 1922, Maxton and his colleague John Wheatley had seen the fundamental economic problem. High unemployment was a consequence of low consumer demand and only by the raising of purchasing power could unemployment be made to fall again. To this proposition they had, by 1923, superimposed the idea that Free Trade was a mirage and its alternative, protection, protected only a few cartels. Instead Britain must plan its import and export trade. In 1924-5 they worked with others to fashion the idea of a "Living Income" – minimum wages in industry and family allowances at home. By 1926 they had formulated these various strands into a precise, practical and feasible alternative which they called *Socialism In Our Time*.

Socialism in Our Time was a political strategy for socialists, and an encompassing economic and social programme for the country. Maxton and his allies rejected the view that violence was the necessary midwife of the socialist society, arguing that socialism could be achieved with speed through Parliament. They resisted the temptations of gradualism, a policy that, they said, might create socialists – but not socialism. From then on, Maxton spoke, lectured, wrote, debated, argued and schemed to broadcast his plan, and to win for it the audience, the acclaim and the acceptance that he felt it deserved. Wheatley may have been the moving spirit and others in the ILP may have contributed both in terms of theory and of political organisation, but Maxton was the polemicist and the populariser, the man people came to hear and the man they listened to, the politician whose success or failure in the end mattered most.

The rightness of his proposals for solving unemployment cannot now be doubted; his challenge to the Labour leadership arose because he believed in them. He was neither an opportunist nor an adventurist, nor could he be reasonably accused of wild recklessness. He was simply a man with a mission. Maxton, wrote Patrick Dollan, was "convinced that a socialist society could be achieved within two decades and his activities are directed accordingly".[14] His job, as he saw it, was to convince people that his vision was attainable. "He walks the world and preaches socialism – a milleniary socialism to be fulfilled in our time – like some early Christian apostle," wrote Egon Wertheimer, a student of the Labour Party of the twenties. His audiences "await hourly the proclamation of the kingdom of God on earth".[15]

This new biography of James Maxton seeks to place his speeches and his political activities firmly in the context of his programme for socialism. With John Wheatley and others, Maxton proposed the most ambitious British socialist project of his time, seeking to demonstrate a middle way between the views of Ramsay MacDonald and Lenin. Their failure, the failure of the ILP and the Labour Party, foreshadowed the failure of a whole generation of British politicians to solve the problems of unemployment and poverty.

SECTION I: SOCIALIST IN THE MAKING

2

From Unionist to Socialist

Many early British socialists sprang from the industrial working class. James Maxton did not. The elder son of James Maxton, a schoolteacher, he was born on 22 June 1885 in the burgh of Pollokshaws, now part of the City of Glasgow. His mother, Melvina, who originated from Alva in Clackmannan, had also been a schoolteacher but by the time Jimmy was born had left teaching to look after the new arrival and his elder sister, Jessie.

The Maxtons at that time enjoyed comparative comfort. His father had risen by education, a typical Scottish "lad o pairts". Born in Crieff in 1843, the son of a mason, he had gradually ascended the hierarchy of the Scottish teaching profession. After serving as a pupil teacher in Perthshire, he had attended teacher training college in Edinburgh, where he had met the future Mrs Maxton, and had taught for three years in Wick before becoming, in 1877, an assistant teacher, and, in 1883, assistant headmaster, at Pollock Academy, one of the old parish schools of Scotland. He was then on a salary of nearly £2 a week. For the first five years of Jimmy's life, the family lived in a small three-bedroomed house in Pollokshaws.

In 1890, Mr Maxton the teacher became Mr Maxton the headmaster, at the newly built Grahamston School in Barrhead, four miles from Pollokshaws.

The family moved, and Barrhead, where he received his elementary education under the direct influence of his father, was to be Maxton's home for much of the rest of his life. He loved it, and once said that it was his own great regret that he had not been born there.

The new school at Grahamston was a day school with some 300 pupils. Its newly appointed headmaster, now on almost £3 a week (50 shillings a week, and a bonus of 5% of the fees he collected), had risen a little in the world. The Maxton family at this time could be regarded, by the standards of the day, as comfortably off.

There was little or nothing in this early background that would suggest that Maxton would become the best-known revolutionary socialist in Britain. Jimmy later described his father's politics as "Liberal Unionist", but politics for him were only a minor interest. His interests were in "education, recreation, literature and church work, not politics. I never heard political discussion at home."[1] Mr Maxton was devoted to his profession, his family, books and the Church. He was a great admirer of Thomas Carlyle and seems to have accepted his political philosophy. Interestingly, Jimmy Maxton too became interested in Carlyle's works in his later years. Mr Maxton, the headmaster, was also an elder in the local Presbyterian Church, and subsequently became its Sunday School Superintendent. Occupying these positions, all of considerable importance in Scottish church and village life, he was a man of some importance. The parental goals which emphasised social responsibility and the improving role of education never left Maxton.

Mr Maxton may have had strong religious beliefs but he was also broadminded. In later years, his son was consciously appreciative of this and wrote of "a very happy childhood". Though brought up in a believing household (at the age of nine, Maxton won the Glasgow Sabbath School Union junior scholars certificate with a score of 82% in a religious knowledge examination),[2] the young Maxton was encouraged to think for himself, and his family seems not only to have tolerated freedom of expression but encouraged it too.

Maxton's father, in addition to his church and professional commitments, was an early activist in the "Teachers' Union" that was later to become the Educational Institute of Scotland. For a period he was President of the Renfrewshire Branch. Both Jimmy and his sister, Annie, who was to become an Infants' Mistress in later life, were to follow in his footsteps in this work.

Although overtly political topics were not discussed in the Maxton family, there can be no doubt that Maxton grew up amid a strong, if unstated, tradition of service and social responsibility. The profession of both his parents and his father's church and union commitments meant that from the first Maxton must have been steeped in the liberating possibilities of education and an acceptance of the duties of leadership in the service of others.

At the end of the nineteenth century, Barrhead was a self-contained town, and the Maxtons' house was only ten minutes walk from the open countryside. Long walks in the country in the summers of his childhood gave Maxton an appreciation of rural life which lasted all his days. Following the various illnesses which beset his adult life, he sought the isolation of the hills and open spaces to convalesce.

The headmaster's family continued to expand. By the time Maxton was 12, he had two younger sisters, Annie and Ada, and a younger brother, John, All of them, and his older sister, Jessie, were to become teachers in later life.

In June 1897, his father signed Maxton's first lower grade leaving certificate, which was for English. His certificate in lower grade arithmetic, and a merit certificate, followed almost a year later. Now with a family of five, the headmaster might have found it difficult to provide the education he would have wished for his family. At the age of 12, Maxton did his bit by winning a Renfrew County scholarship to Hutchesons' Grammar School in the south of Glasgow. He became one of the 25% of boys there whose education was fully subsidised. At Hutchesons he joined a great educational tradition, famous in Glasgow and the West of Scotland for its academic standards and its record of solid achievement, and there he received a grounding in the basic educational disciplines upon which his later achievements rested.

The young Maxton was quick-witted and clever. In 1899 and 1900 he passed his leaving certificate examinations in English and Maths, in 1901 the higher grade examinations in Maths and the lower grade in Latin. He went on to achieve a further pass, this time in Greek.

He appears to have made light of routine school work and there is little evidence to suggest that he exerted himself greatly at Hutchesons, or indeed later at Glasgow University. His leaving certificate was annotated in his own hand with such comments as: "tomfoolery – honours, cheek – first class honours, intellectuality – failure, winching – honours advanced".[3]

If not an academic success, he was popular in other spheres. "I was rather a happy-go-lucky student," he later recalled, "in fact the only awards I gained were a few medals for swimming and prizes for fencing and drill." It was during these years that Maxton developed his keenness to entertain. At ILP Conferences and Summer Schools in the 1920s and 1930s, Jimmy was always "doing a turn". Dressing up as the "Pirate King" was one of his favourites, entertaining delegates during the social evenings that inevitably followed the long debates and discussions of the day on socialism. There was little or nothing in the way of mass entertainment in Jimmy's childhood and musical evenings at home or with friends at their homes were the social highlights.

Maxton remained at Hutchesons' Grammar School for only

three years. Although he could have continued on his scholarship and proceeded to Glasgow University he left in keeping with his father's wishes. He wanted to become a teacher and his father believed that teachers should start young, in the pupil-teacher role then widely accepted as legitimate teacher training.

The young Maxton moved to Martyrs' Public School. Qualifying for the post by a scholarship examination, Maxton, the pupil-teacher, acted as the general assistant to a qualified colleague part of his time, spending the other half in study at a central institute. His first salary amounted to £15 a year. The report he received said that he had proved himself a teacher of "good ability". His English and Greek were "good", his history "fairly good", his Latin "very good" and his mathematics "excellent". He passed his studentship examination in the "first class", and later collected his pupil teacher's certificate in March 1904.[4]

In the summer of 1902, Maxton's father died during their annual holiday in Millport. The young Maxton had been with his parents on their holiday but had returned to work in Glasgow three days before his father's death. (Maxton senior had suffered a heart attack on the beach at Millport after swimming and efforts at resuscitation had failed.) His mother descended abruptly from comparative prosperity to widowhood with the responsibility for five children. Ironically, pension rights for teachers had been one of the causes pioneered via the Educational Institute for Scotland by Maxton's father. Pension rights had just been introduced but too recently for Maxton's own family to benefit.

For the family there followed a period in straitened circumstances that Maxton talked of later as "the kind of poverty that is sometimes called genteel". Despite this, Mrs Maxton was determined that her children's education would continue. "We weren't quite penniless," Maxton wrote later, "and we could have managed very nicely if the older ones had been put out to wage-earning employment."[5]

Mrs Maxton, now the dominant figure in her elder son's life, insisted that his education must go on. "I cut short my career as a pupil teacher," Maxton later explained, "and went into the Training College for Teachers and Glasgow University at the same time."[6] There his specific courses included geometrical and fractional drawing.

In April 1903 Maxton passed university preliminary examinations in Latin, Greek and Dynamics and in October 1903 registered for Glasgow University courses in the Humanities, including Latin. Courses in English Language and Literature, and in Maths, were to follow in the 1904 session.

It was in his first weeks at Gilmorehill that the 17-year-old Maxton succumbed to an unserious aberration, "a political stain on his character"[7] which was to haunt him from time to time throughout his years as a socialist.

The occasion of his fall was the University Rectorial Election. Each of the four ancient Scottish Universities have a Rector who was then elected by the students every three years. The Rector, in name at least, is the Chairman of the University Court, its governing body. Although the character of the office has changed recently, with more incumbents more likely to exercise their right to chair the Court, traditionally the Rector's role was largely symbolic and his election the occasion of high jinks and convivial violence.

Although the two candidates in the Rectorial election of 1902 were a Liberal and a Unionist, the political content of the student campaigns run on their behalf was negligible. The Unionist, George Wyndham, Chief Secretary for Ireland and a well-known politician, and his Liberal opponent, John Morley, were simply figureheads of opposing student factions.

There are good reasons to believe Maxton was virtually apolitical when he went up to University just as the Rectorial campaign was gathering steam. Enrolling as a student, he was confronted by representatives of the two factions. In his own words, "I was challenged as to whether I was a Liberal or a Tory. I honestly did not know the difference. In that respect I have made no real progress since. I declared myself a Tory."[8] So Maxton recounted the incident in 1932. He was compelled to refer to it because the rumour was then in circulation to the effect that he had been an active member of the Tory Party for some time, and doubts were being cast on the sincerity of his socialist convictions.

In the election campaign, Maxton took the Tory label, but it should be clear that the campaigning involved was, in today's phrase, more about personalities than about issues. Intellectual arguments were not deployed. Campaigning was traditionally rough, with bad eggs and bags of soot being exchanged by the contesting parties. Maxton entered vigorously into the spirit of the occasion, and according to his own account never shirked his share of the conflict. Kidnapping was regarded as a legitimate tactic, and by the end of the campaign Maxton was in a position of sufficient trust to be on sentry duty to detain an official of the Liberal Club imprisoned in a cellar.

Another incident was the siege and capture of the Tory headquarters, in defence of which Maxton was to be found. On polling day itself, 25 October 1902, the Unionists blockaded one of the halls where votes were to be cast. This was regarded as unfair even by the standards of a Scottish Rectorial election, and an appeal was made to the university authorities, but too late to prove effective.

Maxton was later to dismiss the whole episode as youthful high spirits without political significance. He recounted it mainly in terms of farce. "Fortunately for me it was not a battle of brains," he wrote. "I never shirked my share of the conflict, earned distinction indeed and was trusted to do sentry-go over an official of the Liberal Club who was imprisoned."[9] In the event the Unionist candidate, George Wyndham, was elected by the narrow margin of 674 votes to 645. "It was the only occasion on which a Tory ever got support from me – and it did not last long," Maxton was to say in later life. "I have no regrets about it all," he used to joke, "I said no word for Conservatism but hurled many eggs and much soot, which was well worth doing, politics apart."[10]

His brief connection with Glasgow University's Unionist Association led eventually to his joining the 1st Lanarkshire Rifle Volunteers. Soon, however, it appeared that his reading and studies had led to an emergent radical political awareness. Halfway through his 12-month attachment to the Volunteers, he requested a transfer from his rifle platoon to the ambulance section, which he considered non-combatant. He was adjudged to be "satisfactory and efficient" in the administration of first aid and in May 1905 received a Royal Army Medical Corps certificate from the 1st Lanarkshire Rifle Volunteers.[11] His anti-war sentiments developed steadily from this period.

In these years Maxton also took his first University classes for the Master of Arts degree. In the 1903 session he had studied Humanities. In the following year he enrolled for English Language and Literature and Maths, but from the beginning of his second year at University Maxton took a much greater part in University life. In sport he fulfilled the promise he had shown at Hutchesons' Grammar, specialised in middle distance running and gained a place in the University team. He also developed an interest in student politics and was elected to the Students Representative Council, another aspect of the democratic nature of the Scottish universities, more serious than Rectorial shinnanigans and established by Act of Parliament to represent the students to the University's governing body. He remained a member of the SRC until he left the University, and was also elected to the editorial committee of the Glasgow University magazine published by the SRC.

His political views were beginning to develop and take shape. This, it seems, was largely the result of contact with other students, including Tom Johnston, who was to become the first editor of the *Forward* newspaper, and another man four years older than Maxton and more influential than anyone else in turning his mind to socialism. The man was John Maclean, who was to become the great folk hero of Scottish socialism a decade later. Maclean was a member of the Social Democratic Federation. This austere and revolutionary group spurned and was spurned by the Labour Representation Committee, the forerunner of the modern Labour Party, which itself had been formed only three years previously. Maxton seems to have been drawn not by the narrowly cataclysmic politics of the SDF but to Maclean himself, its most charismatic leader.

Maxton and Maclean were both natives of Pollokshaws. They seem to have travelled together by train quite frequently. From these chance meetings Maxton's interest in socialism developed beyond the impression gained from a few pamphlets. It was Maclean who led Maxton to the works of Karl Marx. Maclean, Maxton was to say later, was "the best teacher of the Marxian system I have ever met in Britain".[12] The works of Marx, Maxton found, he later admitted, "difficult and unreal" but Marx, discussions with Maclean, and such books as Robert Blatchford's *Merrie England* and *Britain for the British* together with occasional attendances at socialist meetings where Maclean spoke, finally convinced Maxton of the virtues of socialism.

By 1904, Maxton, at the age of 19, regarded himself as a socialist although he had not yet joined any organisation. In that year he attended a meeting at the Paisley Hippodrome and heard Philip Snowden, the pioneering socialist and later the first Labour Chancellor of the Exchequer.[13] The convert became a recruit. Maxton joined the Independent Labour Party. It was the start of a life-long association and the beginning of his dedication to an enduring cause.

3

Educate, Agitate and Organise

The Independent Labour Party that Jimmy Maxton joined in 1904 had been in existence for only 11 years. Although small, with no more than 10,000 members throughout Britain, it was an active proselytising force still bearing the stamp of its founder, the Lanarkshire miner Keir Hardie.

Until the 1880s, Keir Hardie and most other Scottish miners had been supporters of the Liberal Party. Hardie's break with the Liberals dated from the Mid-Lanark by-election of 1888, where he was refused nomination as a Liberal candidate and chose to stand instead as the candidate for independent Labour. Undismayed by his modest total of 617 votes, he went on to found the Scottish Labour Party later in the same year and the Independent Labour Party, for Britain as a whole, in 1892.

Hardie himself never prospered politically in Scotland, and was never elected to any office there. He won his first parliamentary seat in London in 1895, but parliamentary representation by the ILP in Scotland remained elusive. For the next 20 years Scotland was electorally unrewarding for the ILP and the newly emerging Labour Party.

The problem was that Scotland was Liberal, and Liberalism spoke for Scotland. In the 1860s Marx had called the Liberal Party in Britain the most progressive party in the world and as late as the 1890s Engels called the Scottish Liberals the most advanced bourgeoisie in the country. Liberalism dominated the electoral geography of Scotland. The Liberals prevailed in every Scottish election from 1832 to 1914 with the exception of the General Election of 1900. Thereafter, in 1906 and in the two elections of 1910, the party polled 58%, 56% and 53% of the Scottish vote.

For years miners' candidates tried to unseat local Liberals in Lanarkshire and in the mining communities, but with little success. The Liberal programme in Scotland at least was more radical and for the large Irish community there the party was seen as the one most likely to offer Home Rule to Ireland. Gladstone's personal following was also a major factor in the persistence of Liberal support north of the border. Hardie himself, long after his own break with Liberalism, was sufficiently moved by the death of his former leader to write a lengthy obituary.

Liberalism appeared to offer workers the prospect of economic progress and social improvement and several Scottish Liberal Members of Parliament were radical social reformers, like the flamboyant R.B. Cunninghame Graham who represented North West Lanark. Perhaps even more important was the Liberal view of society which sought to show how industrial progress would, in time, benefit the ordinary working man. Liberalism offered a view of society not divided by class but linked by communal bonds. People gained their identity through their churches, friendly societies, trades unions, and voluntary organisations such as the Temperance Orders and even the Freemasons. They were not primarily workers but members of a variety of local organisations and societies. This was Gladstone's vision and he had preached it to the nation as early as 1879, in his famous Midlothian campaign.

It was the deadweight of this tradition of politics, emphasising the limitations both of the state, and of the potential of political activity, which is central to explaining the widespread indifference of the working-class voter, the psychological obstacles to political organisation and the early socialists' failure to create a political consciousness among the working class. If there was an enemy it was not the capitalist business classes but the landed aristocracy. The persistence of Liberal support well into the second decade of the twentieth century was based on hostility to the great landed estates. The Liberal Party was seen as the party of land reform.

The ILP that James Maxton joined sought to propagate the socialist message, and secure Labour Members of Parliament. Until 1918 it was to be the main vehicle through which individual socialists joined the new Labour Party. In 1904 it had no more than 40 branches in Scotland. At the 1900 Conference of the UK-wide Independent Labour Party in Glasgow, only 13 of the 75 delegates were Scots. At the 1905 Conference, there were 11 out of 153. If Labour was to flourish in Scotland workers must see themselves primarily as workers, identifying with each other and organising with each other. This in turn was only possible through trades union organisation.

Perhaps surprisingly, trades unions had made little real progress in Scotland. Even after the first wave of New Unionism in Scotland there were in 1892 only 147,000 trades unionists. Two-thirds of trades unionists were in the engineering and shipbuilding, or mining and construction industries, and most were concentrated in the West. Four manual workers out of every five had no union connection. Only in the years from 1911 onwards did Scottish trades unionism secure a firm foothold.

ILP progress was therefore slow but in 1897 the Scottish Trades Union Congress voted for independent Labour representation, and a Scottish Workers Parliamentary Election Committee was formed in 1899. These efforts were aimed at securing working-class representation in the 1900 and subsequent General Elections, but to little avail.

Maxton joined the ILP's Barrhead branch, which was probably typical of the scattered and struggling organisations round the country. It had been formed in November 1894 with the grand objectives of securing Labour Representation in Parliament and on local councils, and of achieving "the abolition of class privilege, monopoly and oppression". It took on these responsibilities with an initial membership of only ten, rising to 26 during the campaigns over the "Right to Work" in the mid-1890s. Thereafter it declined and had been resuscitated as the Barrhead Socialist Society at a meeting in November 1902, with 11 present.[1]

The early history of the ILP is the story of unsung local heroes – Tom Maguire in Bradford, William Small and Robert Smillie in Lanarkshire, and Robert Murray in Barrhead. In the first months of its revival, the local branch, still only 21 in number, revolved around the bookshop in Main Street which Murray ran and where the new branch met. No record exists in the Barrhead branch's minute books of Maxton's application and subsequent membership in 1904, and some accounts suggest that it may have been 1906 or 1907 before he finally was recruited. At any rate he was quickly elevated, as he recalled later, to the "lofty eminence" of Literature Secretary. Soon the new branch felt confident enough to seek permanent premises and took out a lease on an ante-room in the public halls, intending to make it a local social centre. On offer there were draughts and dominoes, playing cards, books and pamphlets, lectures, open air propaganda, and even a rambling club. But at heart the branch was a debating society. Papers were read and discussed at meetings and political organisations, even the Liberal Party, were invited to send speakers. Once again the little organisation faltered with Fabian Society affiliation impossible by the summer of 1904, and the lease of the room renewed for only a year.

What had brought Maxton into the ILP? Individuals had influenced him. The evangelical socialism of Philip Snowden's Paisley meeting of 1904, and Maxton's frequent contacts with John Maclean had both contributed, but it was, according to Patrick Dollan, "the poverty he saw among children that made him a revolutionary agitator",[2] and Maxton himself later recalled how as a teacher he had wanted to develop young peoples' individual talents and found that social conditions limited any such possibility. "I started out to solve what I thought was a very small and limited problem, how to get these fifty children who came to me each day to be developed, and supplied with the material necessities that precede physical and mental development," he wrote in 1927. "As a very young teacher I discovered how individualism and their individualities were cramped, distorted and destroyed by poverty conditions before the child was able to react to its environment. That was a deciding factor in bringing me into the socialist and labour movement."[3]

Jimmy's early involvement with the ILP soon transformed the domestic routine of family life in Barrhead. All his sisters, and his brother John, ten years his junior, were to become teachers or lecturers and, under Jimmy's influence, all were to become both socialists and members of the ILP. It was to be a most political family. As daughters and sons joined up, so too did their mother, serving in her later years as an ILP Parish Councillor.

Jimmy's oldest sister, Jessie, was an early woman graduate of Glasgow University and one of the first women to lecture in teacher training on the staff of what is now Jordanhill College of Education. She married the Rev John Munro, a socialist and a pacifist who later stood as a parliamentary candidate for the ILP. More active politically was his younger sister Annie, a teacher and leading member of the Educational Institute of Scotland, who eventually became the dominant force in the Barrhead and Scottish ILP. Their younger sister, Ada, later a headteacher in a Glasgow school, joined up too, and John was to be a wartime conscientious objector, being imprisoned in Wormwood Scrubs, and would later stand in as an ILP organiser in Glasgow in 1922 before setting out on a brilliant academic career. He became Professor of Agricultural Economics at Oxford University. John married within the ILP. His wife was the daughter of James Alston who had been one of the earliest ILP councillors in Glasgow and the sister-in-law of Bob Nichol, who was to become the ILP MP for East Renfrewshire in the famous Labour landslide of 1922. John's son has continued the family tradition into a second

35

political generation. Since 1979 he has been the Labour MP for the Glasgow constituency of Cathcart.

As Maxton, the socialist, joined the ILP, so Maxton, now an agnostic, deserted the traditional church. Yet the outlook of the ILP in the 1900s blended well with the traditions of service which characterised a family of teachers who had been brought up in a church-going home. The Independent Labour Party contained Marxists, advanced Liberals, land reformers and Christian socialists, but its outlook at this stage remained dominated by the views of its founder, Keir Hardie. Hardie, Maxton later wrote, was "more Marxist in practice than those who paid great deference to Marxist theories" but although Hardie had come to socialism through the Marxist teachings of Scots socialists like William Small, his socialism in practice owed more to religion than to economics. Almost every speech or article of Hardie's endorsed this view. Socialism was "at bottom a question of ethics or morals", he wrote. It was "a handmaiden of religion and as such entitled to the support of all who pray for the coming of Christ on Earth".

Scottish socialists inherited a distinctive tradition. "The Scottish Labour Movement was not founded on materialism," David Lowe recorded in his *Souvenirs of Scottish Labour*. "The instinct for freedom and justice which animated the Covenanters and Chartists also inspired the nineteenth-century pioneers. Their teachers and prophets were Jesus, Shelley, Mazzini, Whitman, Ruskin, Carlyle and Morris. The economics took a second place. The crusade was to dethrone Mammon and to restore spirit, and to insist that the welfare of the community should take precedence over the enrichment of a handful."[4]

Despite the evangelical zeal of its national leaders and local recruits, the Barrhead branch of the party made little progress in the early years of the decade. By the summer of 1904, the branch was in financial trouble and had to agree to let out its room to the Liberals for a meeting. Not until 1906 could they afford the affiliation fees of the national ILP. Much of their discussions revolved around proposed meetings with some of the best-known labour speakers, like Hardie, and Smillie, and later they spent much time trying to organise a union amongst the local laundry workers. The initial meeting was, they reported, very successful but after a second rally only one woman had offered to join a trade union. When the Barrhead branch eventually joined the national ILP in April 1906 they recorded their official membership at only 18. Although the branch entered into discussions with other Renfrewshire branches about fielding a General Election candidate, they were unable to join the fight. With an election on the way, they decided in January 1906 that "we support neither of the two candidates but those who thought it advisable might go to the polls".[5]

The years before 1914 were, as an early historian of the Scottish ILP recalled, "a struggle with adversity". Only two Scottish parliamentary seats were won by Independent Labour representatives in the Liberal landslide at the General Election of 1906, and only one of these in the West of Scotland. Alexander Wilkie took Dundee with the support of the Jute Workers Union, but had benefited from the attempt of the Liberals to impose a London lawyer on Dundee. He benefited too from the city's two-member constituency which allowed electors to vote Liberal and Labour simultaneously and from the transferable vote system that operated there. As the historian of the Labour Movement in Dundee has suggested, "his election was a confirmation of Dundee's liberalism rather than a challenge to it. Wilkie did not outpace Churchill: indeed in 1910 he recommended the second vote to him."[6] Only the Blackfriars, or Gorbals, constituency of Glasgow returned a Labour representative. This was possible because in Blackfriars Barnes managed to attract Irish support.

Maxton's first documented speech on behalf of the ILP was given in 1904 at his teacher training college, the Glasgow United Free Church Training College. He took a subject which he pursued throughout his subsequent political career – unemployment. The meeting took the form of a mock parliamentary debate and, due to chance, ambition or prescience Maxton spoke in the role of the Leader of the Independent Labour Party.

At the debate was George Dallas, the Secretary of the Scottish Division of the ILP. There is some evidence to suggest that Maxton's rhetorical talents were spotted that night, because from then on he became one of the ILP's little band of stump orators who appeared tirelessly, night after night and weekend after weekend, in the open air propaganda effort by which the ILP became known in Scotland.

Maxton still had to earn his living. In 1905, having completed his teacher training but not his degree, he left University, evidently for financial reasons. His mother still had the three younger children to bring up. From April 1905 Maxton taught at the Sir John Maxwell School in Eastwood where he took charge of the qualifying class. His headmaster found him "punctual and always ready to oblige", a teacher of "earnestness and spirit", and he was congratulated for his voluntary extra-curricular work in preparing pupils for elocution and athletic contests.[7]

Maxton also worked with apprentices in continuation classes at Pollok Academy where from 1905 to 1909 he taught English, Arithmetic and Maths. His headmaster recorded after three years of working with Maxton that he had been "of the greatest assistance to me in many ways, exercised a kindly discipline, gets good work out of his pupils and is invariably very popular among them".[8] As a teacher he was "an invariable favourite". After five years of these night school classes with apprentices he was described as "one of the few teachers who can manage a class in the continuation school in such a way as to retain their interest, attention and personal liking".[9]

Around this time, while teaching at evening classes, Maxton met up again with John Maclean. A consequence of this was to be the first of Maxton's many conflicts with authority. They were agreed about the need for an evening class designed to further the socialist cause, and took up to a headmaster an evening class course entitled "Citizenship and Social Science". The classes, *Forward* newspaper explained, offered an "elucidation of basic economic principles, but also a criticism of the various schools and theories of economics, domestic and foreign, a brief history of economics and a skeleton course of industrial society from primitive society up to the present day. Attention to the development of trades unions and cooperation will form special features."[10] The set text turned out to be *Das Kapital*. Quite soon the Education Authority reacted by bringing the course to a sudden end.

Maxton had originally intended to take spare time classes at University to finish his degree, but it appears that his outside commitments impeded his progress, and he was not to complete his Glasgow University degree until 1909. In 1903, 1904 and 1905 he had successively taken classes in Humanities, including Latin, English Language and Literature and Maths, and then Roman Law. In the years after 1906 he planned to finish off his degree and enrolled for Constitutional Law and Moral and Natural Philosophy classes. His work as an agitator proved so absorbing that he spent less and less time on University work. However, with a degree a necessary precondition of progress in teaching, he attended classes at Gilmorehill throughout 1908 and 1909, fitting them around his day school work, and eventually completing his Master of Arts degree. Also in 1909 he passed his final teaching exams and was admitted to membership of the Educational Institute, his father's old union, a year later.

In 1908 Maxton transferred from the still semi-rural outer suburb of Eastwood to St James School in Bridgeton in the heart of East End Glasgow. It was the beginning of another life-long association, and Maxton was to represent Bridgeton at Westminster for nearly a quarter of a century.

4

Children's Champion

"Even in mid winter so many naked little feet, not in the streets only but in the very schools." So wrote the astonished author of *Child Slaves in Britain* when he visited Glasgow in 1905.[1] European witnesses were even more surprised. Two German observers found in the Glasgow of 1904 "masses of ragged, barefooted unwashed and uncombed people, evidently injured by the misuse of alcohol – women as well as men – such as we have never met with before in our lives".[2]

Such was the social deprivation in Glasgow that confronted Maxton, the young teacher. In the first decade of the century, Glasgow was the most densely populated city centre in Europe, with little of a working-class suburbia and most of the industrial labour force packed into the heart of the city. "The citizen of Glasgow had less of the earth's surface than any citizen of the realm," concluded Glasgow's Public Health Administrator Dr D J Russell in 1905. In some congested communities such as Bridgeton where Maxton now taught almost a thousand men, women and children lived and slept huddled together in one acre, an area of land not much bigger in size than a football pitch. 40% of Glasgow and Lanarkshire was officially deemed to be "overcrowded". Although the numbers living in one-roomed houses fell from 40% of the population in 1870 to 18% in 1911, over 80% of West of Scotland families lived in houses of one to three rooms.

About 20,000 houses were so prone to overcrowding that they were "ticketed" with official limits set on the number of inhabitants and regular inspections ordered to prevent the worst excesses of overcrowding. One inspection in 1903 of some of the worst of Glasgow's city centre tenements found "both men and women concealed in every corner . . . hidden in the cupboard, in presses, under the bed and even on the housetops. In the worst case . . . we took 7 off an adjoining roof, 11 adult persons being found in the house which contained only 880 cubic feet."

Glasgow was, as one of the city's historians has remarked, Manchester and Liverpool rolled into one – with a port linked to trade in coal and iron, and a textiles centre with a chemicals industry that had evolved to meet the needs of the textiles factories. With an influx of immigrants from the Scottish Highlands and from Ireland its population had doubled from half a million in the 40 years before 1914, passing the three-quarters of a million mark in the 1890s and the million mark just before the outbreak of the First World War. During these 40 years shipbuilding output quadrupled and steel output increased more than twentyfold.

Shipbuilding and marine engineering were the pivot of the West of Scotland economy, lying at the centre of a complex concentration of coal, iron and steel and engineering and finishing trades. In Govan and Glasgow 60,000 skilled and unskilled workers were employed in the shipbuilding and engineering trades alone. By 1913 the city's 40 shipbuilding firms produced more than the whole of Germany, and launched three-quarters of a million tonnes – one-third of the entire British shipbuilding output.

There were distinct geographical barriers – the Port to the west, and the Clyde Valley to the east – which set limits to Glasgow's physical expansion, and led to the concentration of closely knit housing developments in the central and eastern areas of the city. By 1914 there were more people packed into the three square miles of Glasgow than in any other area of Europe. Small villages – Govan, Maryhill and Gorbals – had already been drawn into the city, and the middle class had already moved west. The worst congested areas of all were the districts of Townhead, Bridgeton, Tradeston and Anderston in the east of the city.

The tenement was at the heart of the problem. From the outside the visitor would have been impressed by the expensive stone structure. When the Royal Commission on Housing reported in 1917 they acknowledged that the tenement was solidly built, warmer than cottage-style housing, and housed the worker close to his place of work. Once inside, a different picture emerged. The tenement was normally built around a hollow square with an enclosed back court which excluded ventilation and light. Such was the rush to produce multiple rents from the smallest plot of ground that behind one row of five or six-storey tenements on a main street often there would be another set of tenements built in what were called the "backlands", so creating a city behind a city. So appalled were the Housing Commissioners that they wrote of "the clotted masses of slums" in "the congested backlands and ancient closes". Only the barest of sanitation was

41

available, with in many cases only communal earth toilets for each stairway.

In more than half the Glasgow homes – nearly 100,000 dwellings – there were two or more people living in each room, a rate of overcrowding that was eight times worse than industrial England. When an enquiry was carried out in 1904 it was found that a quarter of the homes had more than three people sharing each room and in the worst tenth of the houses, there were four persons or more to each room. In England less than 1% of homes experienced such overcrowding.

It was common for four families to share the use of a toilet. The result was inevitable: in the first years of the century the Glasgow death rate was 28 per 1000 and the infant mortality rate was 149 per 1000, a third higher than the rest of Scotland. In one-roomed houses disease claimed one in every five of children born, an infant mortality rate of 210 per 1000.

Maxton was now employed in one of the most congested and poverty-stricken areas of slum tenements in the city. At St James School in Bridgeton he was the assistant master, "an earnest and capable man", his headmaster recalled, with special interest in "sociological and economic problems".

There is little doubt that the poverty, squalor and overcrowding of Bridgeton in 1908 advanced Maxton's socialism from the abstract to the practical. No one faced with a class of pale, stunted tenement-dwelling slum children could have remained unmoved, and from then on Maxton's own brand of socialism – fiery, humanitarian and of necessity revolutionary – began to take shape. "I always feel guilty when I have something denied to the majority of my fellows," Maxton later explained. "What socialist worthy of the name does not feel in his heart a tremendous pity, a tremendous desire to relieve immediately the sufferings of the victim?"[3]

Maxton's speeches in Parliament and elsewhere often referred to the conditions in the schools where he had taught. Classrooms were overcrowded and underventilated – cold and stuffy in the winter, hot and stifling in the summer. Teachers today might justifiably complain if class numbers reach 40. In Maxton's day anything up to 80 children might face the teacher in one classroom.

It was the sheer poverty of those he taught which moved Maxton. Children were small and emaciated because of inadequate diet. They were inadequately clad, most often in family hand-me-downs. If they had boots and shoes they were likely to be secondhand and ill-fitting. The children were malodorous and sometimes verminous simply because of the appalling conditions in which they lived. Rickets, the inevitable result of living almost without sunlight and on a diet deficient in Vitamin D, was common, the resultant softening of the bones producing deformed chests and pathetically distorted limbs. The Scottish Education Department introduced a new scheme of physical education, and when Maxton took his class to the drill hall he found "thirty out of sixty youngsters could not bring both heels and knees together because of rickety malformations".[4] Because of all this, Maxton saw the task of socialism not as the eventual production of a dim and distant better world but as a remedy, immediate if at all possible, to the hideous problems he saw every day in children he taught and loved. Most of his early speeches, according to Patrick Dollan, were appeals for fair play for the young. Even then he was known as the "Children's advocate". He came to the conclusion that education was not enough in itself, that the problems of poverty, unemployment, inadequate housing had all to be eradicated before education took its proper place in a civilised society.

Concerned as he was with the condition of his pupils, he did still struggle to improve the conditions of his colleagues. Like his father before him, he joined the Educational Institute of Scotland as soon as he was a registered teacher. That happened in July 1910. The system of public education in which he worked was provided by education authorities consisting largely of businessmen. It was a paternalist system designed to provide education for the masses and still reflecting the grudging system of charity. It ran on the cheap, paying most teachers between £50 and £80 per annum, a meagre salary even by the poor standards of the day.

As part of the fight to improve conditions, Maxton and others including John Maclean, formed the Socialist Teachers' Society. As well as being a member of the EIS, Maxton joined the Scottish Class Teachers' Association, and in a very short time had been elected to the National Councils of both organisations.

The teachers' campaign provided Maxton with his first political fight. Conditions in the Renfrewshire and Paisley School Board area were regarded as worse than those in surrounding areas, and because of this teachers did not stay long. To counteract this drift the Renfrewshire and Paisley Board reached an agreement with other boards in the area that none would appoint a teacher from any of the other boards during the first year of that teacher's service.

To Maxton this was blackmail, and with the support of the

43

Socialist Teachers' Society, he undertook to fight it. Not only were conditions bad, wages were low, and he compared the Paisley Board to "any other sweating employer ... exerting its collective brain to discover some means whereby it might keep its teachers and still pay them low wages". There was some public sympathy for the teachers and Maxton set out to enlarge it. He condemned the methods employed by the Paisley Board as akin to the local firm of Coates & Clark, the thread manufacturers, around which Paisley had been built. He castigated the local authority as "a miserable slave-driving, charity-ridden imitation of a third-class Scottish burgh. They have only copied the methods which certain groups of colliery owners in Scotland adopted in dealing with the colliers. The colliers would not have it. Perhaps the teachers will. If they do, they have even less of the spirit of independence in them than I imagine them to possess."

Maxton's first political skirmishings on behalf of the teachers were at least partially effective. The cartel arrangement between the boards started to break up and there was some improvement in local conditions. However, in the longer term, his work on behalf of the teachers met with only limited success. The changes he pressed for were slow to come and many did not occur in his lifetime.

One change which was made by the Glasgow Education Authority was considered by Maxton to be a dubious benefit. The summer holiday was extended from six weeks to two months. Teachers benefited more from this than did pupils in the most deprived areas. For them it meant "the children of the poorest parents living in the most squalid disticts will be driven out of the schools to spend their holidays between their filthy homes, amidst unlovely ideas and unlovely sounds, which will sink into their consciousness and form part of an unlovely personality in the future".

Perhaps the worst effect of the change was in the long term. Maxton commented that "children who will put up with these conditions when they are at school will put up with any conditions of labour and housing when they are men and women – and we want rebels".

Maxton had more constructive ideas about how his schoolchildren should spend summers. He proposed to the Glasgow School Board that it should run summer schools in public parks and in nearby country areas such as those he had loved in his childhood. His proposal was worked out in some detail, and called for the use of the city's tramways for transport, the erection of marquees as classrooms and the special recruitment of teachers for training and supervision. His suggestion was rejected. Similar schemes, however, became acceptable and were implemented in the 1930s and 1940s.

At this stage in his life Maxton seems to have been a happy and fulfilled young man, full of enthusiasm for teaching and for the children he taught, and full too of energy and enterprise in the cause of socialism. By day he taught children the basics of a Scottish education, in the evenings and at weekends he taught the social gospel, and all the time he was learning too.

It was during his four years at St James School that Maxton first spoke to the Bridgeton ILP when he deputised for William Stewart as a speaker at a Burns supper. "That was Jimmy's first introduction to Bridgeton," his agent Jimmy McKimmie later recalled.[5]

He was much in demand as a speaker at the ILP's popular open air meetings. With the backing of George Dallas, the ILP's Scottish Secretary, he spoke widely in Glasgow on week nights and, at weekends, further afield. As a travelling speaker he was accommodated overnight by ILP area members, and was happy to discuss politics after the day's meetings were over and far into the night.

William Stewart, a later Scottish Secretary of the ILP, evokes an early Maxton speech and, incidentally, some gruesome Scottish holiday weather:

I first met James Maxton on a wintry summer day 9 years ago, I think, perhaps 10. It was summer by the calendar, winter by the weather glass. Maxton was in Ayr on holiday. I was on holiday also but with propaganda designs upon the pleasure seekers. It was mid-July Glasgow Fair Sunday but there was snow on the Arran hills and showers of sleet driving across Ayr Low Green. That is why I remember it so vividly. I intended to hold a meeting. Maxton introduced himself and I persuaded him to take the chair. His oratorical elements attracted a considerable crowd of frost-bitten hardened holiday makers.

In the ILP at the time aspiring speakers ascended a strictly controlled ladder. They started, as Maxton had, in the virtually superogatory role of Chairman at an outdoor meeting. Next came promotion to speaking outdoors. A further step led to the Chairmanship of an indoor meeting, the highest rank, that of main speaker at an indoor meeting, being achieved by only a few. After just five and a half years in the ILP, Maxton's talents had, by 1910, taken him from the lowest step to the highest. The teacher who had been converted to socialism by the plight of his poorest pupils had already made a name as the Children's Advocate. The politician who would take their plight to Westminster had begun to make his mark.

5

"Sowing the Seeds"

"The Scottish worker of literature and history is commonly depicted as a man dour, dogged, honest, hard-working and superlatively thrifty," wrote Maxton in 1914 in his first published article which presumed to review the state of the Scottish Labour Movement. It is a piece of considerable length and variable interest.

The propagandist of ten years speculates on why his countrymen have been less enthusiastic about socialism than he is himself. After a shallow historical introduction Maxton analyses the strengths and shortcomings of the Scottish character in relation to socialism. The Scot, he says, is "the ideal worker from the sweater's point of view. His eagerness and capacity for labour raises his productive power to a maximum. His honesty renders the cost of supervision very low, while his thriftiness, frugality and simple way of life induce his wages to the lowest possible point."

Maxton blamed schools and churches for the Scot's pedestrian acceptance of society as it is. "It is his training, his schooling and his national atmosphere that tends to dwarf the average Scot's imagination, and in the working class as in other fields of activity this state of affairs tends to hold good. Modern Scotland does not initiate." But there was hope for change. Although Scots believed that individuals by their own efforts might rise by education, "the idea of attempting to raise the status of the working classes as a whole did at last gain foothold among the workers but it has to be remarked that Scotland did not initiate this reform. Rather it is a product imported into our country from outside, particularly continental sources."

Given all that, Maxton conceded that progress would be slow, but he and a few like him strove in the years before 1914 not with the immediate expectations of socialists winning power but to create a culture in which socialist ideas would flourish. The Labour Movement, Maxton explained, could not "expect to reap where it has not sowed".[1]

47

Under the ILP umbrella, there flourished choirs, newspapers, pamphlets, speakers' classes, lectures, and even cycling clubs and socialist Sunday schools. The early Glasgow socialists were a remarkable group, a curious amalgam of journalists, lawyers, lecturers and Sunday school teachers. The party's industrial recruits were, primarily, skilled workers. "You take my branch of the ILP when I first joined it," Harry McShane was later to recall. "I don't think there was a labourer in it: [they were] mostly engineers."[2]

Among many of the young ILP members, most of whom were teetotal, there blossomed a café culture in the Glasgow of the early years of the century. Many of the professional recruits, including Maxton, came together at informal socialist meetings held in Cranston's "art nouveau" tearooms in Glasgow's Renfield Street or in Craig's tearoom in Gordon Street. It was at such meetings that many of the socialist intellectual arguments were thrashed out and some of the Clydeside's most famous Labour MPs owed much of their political development to this café tradition.

Among the ILP's older leaders was William Stewart, who had started working life in the 1880s in the linen mills of Dunfermline and who had quickly become disillusioned with the philanthropic works of the town's most famous emigrant Andrew Carnegie. "Philanthropy may degrade, it cannot unite," he wrote. "Carnegieism in its later money dispensing phase can never undo the evil of its earlier money getting phase." Fired by his new socialist convictions, Stewart, now a local shopkeeper, was elected as the first socialist member of the Dunfermline Parish Council and then moved west to become, in 1899, the Scottish correspondent of the ILP newspaper *Labour Leader*. He was the moving spirit behind the creation of the Scottish Divisional organisation for the ILP in 1906, and was the principal ILP leader who encouraged the young Maxton in his propagandist activities.

Another who moved quickly to the fore in the Glasgow ILP was Patrick Dollan who was in 1908 persuaded by his Catholic friend John Wheatley to join the ILP. A Scots-born son of an Irish miner, Dollan had been brought up in a miners' row in Baillieston, Lanarkshire, and was, in turn, a rope worker, a shop assistant, a shop manager, and then himself a miner before becoming a journalist and industrial correspondent for Catholic newspapers and then *Forward*, whose full-time reporter he became on a salary of thirty shillings a week in 1910, and then, in 1912, assistant editor.

His editor was the ILP's leading socialist pamphleteer, Tom Johnston, a Kirkintilloch licensed grocer's son who became a socialist while a student contemporary of Maxton's at Glasgow University. At University he had joined the Fabian Society and become the President of the Socialist Society. After issuing a few socialist tracts on women's suffrage, banking and railway nationalisation, Johnston published, in 1909, *Our Noble Families*, a famous attack on the Scottish landed classes. But his greatest journalistic achievement was the creation in 1906 of the Scottish ILP newspaper *Forward*. More than anything else, *Forward* fostered a distinctive West of Scotland socialist culture.

"We came 'cause we had to. Our coming, we believe, is the psychological moment," said *Forward's* first edition in October 1906. Forward Printing and Publishing Company had been set up to run a weekly newspaper and printing press with a nominal capital of only £1,000 in £1 shares. It was "a mad hare-brained enterprise", Johnston later explained. The initial resources, he recalled, "would not have run to the stocking of a fried fish shop".[3]

Forward attempted to be both evangelical and ecumenical in its approach to socialist propaganda. "We shun sectarianism as we shun smallpox," wrote Johnston as *Forward* attempted to bring socialists together under one banner, and promised to open its columns to anyone who wanted to speak out. In addition to ILP writers, the Marxist John Maclean was a regular contributor, as was the Irish nationalist James Connolly. Its contributors had, as Tom Johnston later recalled, "been influenced by Ruskin, William Morris, Robert Blatchford and the Fabian Society but we had a De Leonite and a Marxian or two in our entourage".[4]

By 1911 *Forward* was selling 20,000 copies a week. *Forward*, wrote Harry McShane, one of its early readers, was "different . . . it was a very lively paper with lots of attacks on the landlords and on the big capitalist propagandists. It carried marvellous exposures all the time." With *Forward*, Sunday schools, youth clubs, cultural societies, and political activity, the ILP offered much more than simply politics. "This romantic type of socialism almost became a religion in itself," as Harry McShane recalled.

The ILP may have prospered amongst a minority, but Liberalism was still in the ascendant in Scotland. Aware of its dependence on working-class support, the 1906-1914 Liberal Government introduced some of the elements of a welfare state in school meals for children, old age pensions, and later national insurance provision for sick and unemployed workers. Such reforms put the ILP on the defensive, forcing Maxton at one point to write an essay addressing the question of whether or not Lloyd George was a socialist.

Liberals promised economic progress and social improvement. For a year or two the dream of the Edwardian summer afternoon held, but in 1908 a major depression brought the worst unemployment for thirty years to Scotland. Even relatively prosperous skilled tradesmen in the shipyards, traditionally Liberal supporters, were not immune. By September 1908 60,000 Glasgow men were out of work, and one tradesman in every five was unemployed. As the Liberal promise fell apart, socialist propagandists such as Maxton saw their chance. Weekly demonstrations were held on behalf of the unemployed in 1908. The ILP helped organise local Unemployed Workers Committees, and in Westminster Keir Hardie introduced a Right to Work Bill. As Harry McShane, who joined the ILP in 1908, later wrote, "the agitation about the 1908 unemployment transformed the labour movement in Glasgow. A number of new people joined the different socialist organisations."[5]

The unemployment campaign brought Maxton to the fore and his first documented appearance at a major indoor ILP rally took place during 1908 at the Paisley Hippodrome. His previous street-corner experience had made him an accomplished orator, and Maxton had already acquired many of the skills that were to make him famous. According to a close colleague, John McNair, he began by assuming that the members of his audience were ordinary, decent people. He spoke with great directness and simplicity. His speeches were always substantial but never crowded with arguments. He sought to give his audience their due measure of content, but it was his golden rule never to include more than three or four main points in his speeches. He was never boring, and almost always worth hearing. Even in his later Parliamentary career, when his political significance had faded, the House would fill as Members heard he had risen to speak.

Maxton's appearance was almost as dramatic as his rhetoric. Hollow cheeks, olive-complexioned, and with a lank forelock which added further visual interest to his already compelling features, he simply had to be noticed. His presence was irresistible and the huge range of his platform style, from heartbreak to high comedy with everything else between thrown in for good measure, an endless attraction.

In the open-air meetings of these early years, in parks and on street corners, he drew crowds. In only a few minutes he could quickly warm an audience up with a joke or two, and an immediate demonstration that he understood them and they would understand him. A little crowd around his chosen platform, fruitbox, tree stump or park bench, quickly grew to a larger one, and the combination of his reputation and performance soon ensured a worthwhile audience, silent and packed close to hear his every word. That was his effect on people. They wanted to listen. Every phrase seemed directed to every one of them. His face, his posture, his eyes and his hands all contributed as his theme developed. Magically, he could bring an audience to the verge of tears as he spoke of poverty they knew in the language they could understand and then, as quickly, he could move them to smiles and laughter. But always the message was socialism, and socialist utopia. The new world of all the people seemed much, much nearer as his speech drew towards its climax.

For the hundreds of meetings at which he spoke every year, Maxton received no financial reward. Any of the little organisations he spoke for could not have paid him anyway. On other occasions, travel expenses would be offered, but he never accepted them. He had a New Testament naîvety about and indifference to money, and while he was on a teacher's salary amidst so much poverty, to accept any more from any source would have been against his conscience.

He was already a heavy cigarette smoker. Most of the pictures of Maxton from his early propagandist days in the 1900s until his death in 1946 show him with a cigarette in his mouth or his hand. He was virtually a chain smoker.

He did not drink much. Most of the early socialists had seen the social damage that alcohol did and were total abstainers, but reports that Maxton was a teetotaller were an exaggeration. He himself was quite averse to the label and wrote in later life that he always took care to have at least one drink in the course of a year simply to avoid the stigma of total abstinence and the aura of kill-joy bigotry which it conveyed.

If the more visible struggles of the early socialist propagandists were against capitalism, another struggle, against sectarianism, was also going on. Sectarianism divided the city, Catholic from Protestant, East End from West End. Maxton hated it and was thus brought into contact with a new comrade, John Wheatley.

In 1891 the Pope had issued an encyclical entitled *Rerum Novarum*. It was known as the "Workers' Charter" but explicitly condemned socialism. Wheatley and others ignored this and founded the Catholic Socialist Society which ran regular meetings on a Sunday afternoon in a hall near Glasgow Cross. The more

51

reactionary clergy condemned these and created open hostility to Wheatley among Catholic workers. An effigy of Wheatley was burnt outside his home by right-wing opponents, but the meetings went on and Maxton took his stand on the platform beside Wheatley, the beginning of a bond of friendship that was to last until Wheatley's sudden and early death in 1930.

There were other encounters with sectarianism. On one occasion, a meeting attended but not addressed by Maxton was broken up by a group of Orangemen, and the platform smashed. In the face of this assault by extreme Protestants, a series of groups in Glasgow – the ILP, the Social Democratic Federation, the Socialist labour party, the Glasgow Trades Council and the Clarion Scouts – decided after discussions to hold a joint meeting. This opened with the singing of the *Red Flag*, as a gang of the Orangemen mustered in the side street. A huge ring of socialists formed to surround and protect their meeting. The Orangemen attacked and fighting broke out. Maxton was among those who received rough handling before the police restored order.

Over this period Maxton became well-known in Glasgow and the West of Scotland generally, and eventually, through the ILP office in Glasgow and his friendship with the ILP Scottish leaders, William Stewart and George Dallas, he came into contact with socialists of national acclaim such as Ramsay MacDonald, Philip Snowden, Bob Smillie and Keir Hardie himself.

1909 saw Maxton and others engaged in the campaign against the Osborne judgement, a ruling in favour of railwaymen who did not wish to pay into the union's political fund, then subscribed to the Labour Party. There was widespread agitation for a change in the law and eventually the Asquith Liberal Government introduced a bill which legalised the political levy. Unwittingly, the Liberals had created by law a firm financial base for the Labour Party which was, within only a few years, to replace the Liberal Party as the principal alternative to the Tories.

Maxton was still at this stage a teacher at Bridgeton. In 1912 he thought of moving job and applied to become an Inspector for the Government's new Health Insurance Commission, but was unsuccessful. Instead he moved within the teaching profession, being appointed an assistant master at Haghill School in Dennistoun. By this time socialist propagandist activities were placing ever greater demands on the young teacher. He was sufficiently well-known in the socialist movement to be elected Chairman of the Scottish Council and subsequently Scottish representative on the National Administrative Council of the ILP. The NAC he joined included all the great names of the movement – Keir Hardie, the undisputed leader, Ramsay MacDonald, Philip Snowden, Margaret Bondfield, Bruce Glasier and Willie Anderson. As long as there was an ILP of any significance Maxton remained at the heart of it almost without interruption.

Maxton seems to have been on friendly terms with the other leading figures. Keir Hardie was certainly more than simply a comrade and colleague. It was a source of great pride in Maxton's political life that Tom Johnston's article on his election as Chairman of the Independent Labour Party in 1926 referred to him as being in direct line of succession to Keir Hardie himself. Maxton could have been paid no greater compliment.

Few records of Maxton's views or speeches during these years survive, but around 1910 Maxton sought to write a pamphlet on the distinction between social reforming Liberalism and socialism. It was entitled "Is Lloyd George a Socialist when Chancellor" but never got past the stage of a first draft in which Maxton offers a description of his beliefs. "A socialist is a man who believes that the means of production, distribution and exchange should be owned by the whole people for the benefit of the whole people," he wrote, "he is not simply a sentimentalist who sees the social evils of poverty, debt, unemployment, overwork and adulterated food, and longs to do something to remove these evils."[6]

Most of all Maxton criticised the landlord, who enjoyed rent capital and interest "by virtue of mere ownership and has consequently no claim to a share of the wealth produced". Maxton echoed Tom Johnston's view of *Our Noble Families*, writing that "the prosperity of many of the wealthy families was founded on robbery, swindling or vice and historical records bear out this contention".

The industrial unrest of the period, wrote Maxton, was a manifestation of "deep rooted disease underneath", and the escalation of that industrial unrest after 1910 transformed the socialist movement yet again. Trades union membership soared – even among hitherto unorganised groups such as the Scottish Farm Workers. To Maxton this was "the most striking and interesting of recent developments",[7] and the ILP moved closer to the aspirations of both skilled and unskilled workers. With their increasing numbers, trades unions sought to demonstrate their new found bargaining strength. In 1910 the ILP offered its support as Glasgow match girls went on strike in Neilston. In 1911 the seamen, dockers, railmen and then transport workers were involved in national stoppages. In Clydebank the sewing workers at the giant Singer's factory struck also, and *Forward* newspaper ran a series of articles urging a boycott of Singer sewing machines, while claiming that the company was "picking out every known socialist in its employ for victimisation". In 1912 it was the turn of the miners.

Maxton's national reputation was confirmed in the aftermath of that year's Tonypandy episode, in which soldiers had been deployed against miners on strike for a minimum wage in South Wales. Troops despatched by the then Home Secretary, Mr Winston Churchill, clashed with miners and riots broke out with tragic results. Hardie, by now in Parliament, claimed the Government's use of force to assist coal owners in the protection of blackleg labour amounted to intimidation. He pointed out that in areas where no such outside interference had occurred there had been no rioting. To this day the incident is enshrined in the history of the Miners Union and the Labour Movement. Maxton, now a leading ILP speaker campaigning throughout the country in the wake of the disturbances, became a national, not simply a Scottish figure.

During the years from 1910 the industrial unrest unleashed yet another factional controversy within the embryonic socialist movement. For a time syndicalism – the view that industrial activity alone was necessary to achieve revolutionary change – became fashionable. Long debates between the ILP who advocated a reformist policy, using Parliament and local government to create socialism, and Maclean and revolutionary socialists, took place. Maxton had worked with Maclean in his evening classes in Pollokshaws and remained a life-long friend but their differences came to the fore in this debate.

Maclean advocated the use of Parliament only as a propagandist platform from which to preach revolutionary politics at the workplace. Maxton, who accepted the Marxist theory of labour value, and the inevitability of a class struggle, did not accept Maclean's full-blooded version of dialectical materialism, and refused to go along with him when he moved party after 1910 and called on ILP socialists to desert the Labour Party. There was a bitter controversy which surfaced in the columns of *Forward*. Maclean advocated elections only as a propaganda vehicle for socialist ideas and industrial action as the means to achieve socialism. Maclean argued that the Labour Party was "a miserable caricature of Marxism", working against socialism, while Johnston countered with the argument that syndicalists and socialists could be part of Labour, but that socialists required the mass support of trades unionists if they were to succeed. Some ILP members, including Harry McShane, responded to John Maclean's call to leave the ILP and join his new Social Democratic Party, later the British Socialist Party, but Maxton refused to join. He agreed with Tom Johnston that an ideological faction which could not take "the average man with it, will peter out in a brilliant rainbowed futility".[8]

Instead Maxton and the ILP put their faith in the painfully slow process of winning political support at the ballot box. Although by 1914 he still predicted "no great immediate results" from the ILP's propagandist activities, he could at least demonstrate some progress. A third Scottish Parliamentary seat, alongside the Gorbals and Dundee, went Labour in December 1910. In West Fife the miners' leader William Adamson defeated the Liberals in a straight fight after the Conservatives had withdrawn from the contest.

Some local election successes were recorded and by 1914 there were probably 200 Labour representatives on parish councils, school boards and town and county councils. On the Glasgow Town Council Labour now held 18 seats, but only in one Scottish district, Carmichael, did the party hold outright majority power. A report to the Labour National Executive Committee noted "the political organisation of Scotland is not as good as it might be ... the steady and persistent work of the local Labour Parties is not as marked as in England".[9] Socialism, the Glasgow ILPers recognised, had made little headway among the poorest. "We see no revolutionary ardour in the Cowcadden slums but we do see it among the better fed and more leisured working districts," Johnston was later to recall. There was, he said, "a huge jungle of prejudice and inertia and ignorance to be cleared away".[10]

Maxton was undismayed by the difficulties that lay ahead and in 1914 became the Parliamentary candidate for the constituency of Montrose Burghs. He was a popular choice, and in his selection speech promised unceasing propagandist activity. "In Jimmy Maxton," Forward reported, "the Montrose Burghs have got a good candidate, a likeable candidate, with no airs or gold watch chains about him; a first-rate speaker, with a keen sense of humour; a hard worker, willing to take the donkey's share of the toil; a man who will do the cause of Socialism credit at all times and in all circumstances ...". Ever optimistic, Maxton told the Scottish ILP that "the one thing I shall regret about this candidature is that I shall win Montrose Burghs, and that will take me, to some extent, from my rounds of street-corner agitation, from my tussles in the teachers' organisations, and from the more intimate associations that I have with hundreds of good people in the Glasgow district".

By now, as Keir Hardie had warned for years, the prospect of war loomed closer. International events increasingly absorbed Maxton's attention after a holiday trip he made throughout Europe with his Glasgow socialist friends George Dallas and James Houston during the summer of 1912. For the most part the group roughed it, camping and even sleeping in the outdoors. They travelled from Rotterdam and Amsterdam through Holland, to Germany, where they stopped off at Dusseldorf and Cologne, and on to Belgium and France. Maxton kept a diary of his journey. Its contents were mainly personal – "slept in wood between Hague and Leyden", "Camp on roadside – no tent, sheet, blanket and coats. Up at 6 o'clock" – but notes in it include his comments on the strengths and weaknesses of the European socialist movements in the countries he visited or about which Europeans spoke. Sweden, he was told by Belgian comrades, had the best socialist movement, but the Belgian socialist movement was "not powerful". His teaching counterparts in Belgium, he found, suffered worse conditions. In Brussels they were told by trades unionists they met that Belgian socialists thought universal suffrage was the key to their eventual success.[11]

But there was to be little unity amongst the workers of the European countries when war eventually threatened. The ILP, at that time a member organisation of the Labour and Socialist International, was represented at its 1913 Congress by Keir Hardie. That Congress, switched from Vienna to Glasgow at the last moment because of the threat of war, heard Keir Hardie along with his French and German comrades, plead for action to prevent hostilities. The Congress pledged itself to an international General Strike if war broke out.

The ILP was unequivocally against war. By 1914 ILP protests and demonstrations were taking place throughout the country, Maxton being prominent in the Scottish campaign. As the manifesto *An Appeal to the Working Class* by Keir Hardie and Arthur Henderson put it in August 1914:

Men and women of Britain, you have now an unexampled opportunity of showing your power, rendering a magnificent service to humanity and to the world. Proclaim that for you the days of plunder and butchery have gone by. Send messages of peace and fraternity to your fellows who have less liberty than you.

Down with class rule! Down with the rule of brute force! Down with war! Up with the peaceful rule of the people!

It was unavailing. War broke out and in neither Britain, Germany nor France did the working class respond with a General Strike. The great slaughter had begun.

6

War Abroad: Struggle at Home

"There's no chance of me volunteering," Maxton wrote on 25 August 1914 to his new girlfriend, Sissie McCallum, a fellow teacher at Haghill school. "I'm working for peace for all I'm worth".[1]

Attitudes to the war created a new dividing line in left-wing politics in Britain. Like Maxton, the ILP had immediately made clear its total opposition to the war. With the fighting only days old, the National Administrative Council of the ILP, of which Maxton had now been a member for two years, issued an uncompromising statement condemning hostilities. They warned across "the roaring of the guns" that much blood would be spilt, that deprivation would be the result, that Germans, as much as French and Belgian workers, were the comrades of British workers. The statement ended with this ringing note:

> In forcing this appalling crime upon the nations, it is the rulers, the diplomatists, the militarists who have sealed their doom. In tears and blood and bitterness, the greater Democracy will be born. With steadfast faith we greet our future; our cause is holy and imperishable, and the labour of our hands has not been in vain. Long live Freedom and Fraternity! Long live International Socialism!

But the issue of war split the Labour Party. Ramsay MacDonald resigned his Chairmanship of the Parliamentary Labour Party to join the opponents of war but Arthur Henderson who had signed, along with Keir Hardie, the declaration of the British Section of the Internationalist Socialist Bureau against war only a year earlier, joined the Asquith Government. Other Labour leaders followed him, including J.R. Clynes.

In Scotland, Maxton moved to the forefront of the opposition to war. In the first week after the declaration, he addressed anti-war meetings in the Montrose constituency, spoke in Forfar, Brechin, Arbroath and Carnoustie, and then visited Manchester. He returned to join Keir Hardie as a platform speaker in a major

Edinburgh rally and had then gone to Glasgow and Clydebank to speak. "This war has made me hop around a lot and given us a lot of work and worry," he explained to Sissie.[2]

Few punches were pulled in the ILP attack on Labour leaders who had joined the War Government. Maxton was especially critical of Arthur Henderson, who had become a "distinguished recruiting agent along with Messrs Bonar Law and Asquith". He was speaking on this occasion at a "Workers' War Conference" held in Glasgow on 20 February 1915. The Labour Party, he declared, should have been preparing for the position which had now arisen instead of blindly identifying themselves with the war which had given the speculators their golden opportunity.

But the opponents of war faced a rising tide of public hostility as the country was gripped by a mood of jingoism. In Scotland, miners and industrial workers were among the most enthusiastic of early recruits to the armed forces and by February 1915 20% of Scots miners had enlisted. Though generally hostile to the war, the ILP's broadsheet *Forward* felt it necessary to carry a pro-war column alongside its anti-war propaganda. Meetings were rowdy and sometimes could not take place. The ILP Annual Conference of Easter 1915 could not be held at its pre-arranged meeting place because of local opposition, and would have been cancelled but for the late intervention of a broad-minded minister who provided the use of a church hall.

It was the last ILP conference Keir Hardie was to attend. He was by now a broken, sick, old man. He had seen his hopes of avoiding war dashed, and the movement which was to prevent war split down the middle. It is said that latterly, because of his staunch opposition to the war, many of his old friends would ignore him or refuse to shake his hand. On 26 September 1915, Keir Hardie died. Tom Johnston wrote in his obituary tribute that Hardie had died of "a broken heart". The war itself had claimed the life of a man who had been dedicated to preventing it.

In the months immediately prior to Keir Hardie's death, it had already become difficult for the ILP to operate. The Defence of the Realm Act had been passed by Parliament, giving wide powers to the authorities to enable them to suppress opposition to the war. To the ILP, the most galling aspect of this legislation was its acceptance by Labour Ministers in the new War Government.

Maxton stepped up his anti-war efforts. He believed that the Germans would soon seek a negotiated settlement and in meetings in Lanarkshire in the summer of 1915 he was to be heard addressing the question of possible peace terms. The ILP was adamant in its anti-war stance. It told its supporters that "if advice is to be given to the workers it should come from our own platforms, preserving the character and traditions of our movement, and we refuse to take our stand with the militarists and enemies of labour with whose outlook and aims we are in the sharpest conflict".

The ILP weekly newspaper, *Labour Leader*, had been at the forefront of the campaign against the war and in favour of peace terms. In August, when they published a peace manifesto from the German socialist party, the authorities decided to intervene. They seized the newspaper and closed it down. The manager, Edgar Whiteley, and the editor of the paper, Fenner Brockway (who was to become a colleague of Maxton's in later years), were arrested under the Defence of the Realm Act. The evidence against them and the newspaper was unconvincing, the charges were withdrawn and within four weeks it was on the streets again. During these weeks, Maxton had taken up the cause of *Labour Leader* and, although the authorities had not been successful on this occasion in suppressing the peace campaign, it was just the first shot in the battle at home, while the war raged on the fields of France.

The anti-war campaign was not the ILP's only initiative. Property owners on the Clyde had issued notices of rent increases. In response the ILP launched a campaign aimed at controlling house rents and called for a rents strike. With the influx of war workers to the Clyde munitions yards and factories, rents had been pushed up by as much as 20% in some areas.

In November 1915, 20,000 tenants went on rent strike and 4,000 industrial and munitions workers stopped work to support them. Much of the propaganda centred on landlord exploitation of soldiers' wives. One of many women who led the agitation told the *Glasgow Herald* that women "were not asking for charity, but justice". Glasgow tenants "respected all law that was just and fair" but did not "respect the law which allowed increases in rents at the present juncture". The rent strike, organised by the ILP and John Wheatley, was to be one of the most successful agitations of the war – and it brought the Rent Restriction Act of 1915. The free market in urban housing rents was permanently destroyed. The Clydeside socialists may have been unpopular for their anti-war activities but their campaign for rent restriction brought them considerable public support.

Meanwhile in the shipyards and workshops of the Clyde another struggle began. As early as December 1914, the engineers on the

Clyde had served notice on their employers demanding an increase of two pence per hour. The aim was to raise the Clyde rates up to the level of those being paid in other areas. However, the official trades union leaders failed to push their case effectively and, after a compromise settlement on wages, of 1 pence an hour, the engineers, and their shop stewards, formed the Clyde Workers' Committee.

The Clyde Workers' Committee soon found itself in sharp conflict with the Government. The Minister of Munitions, Lloyd George, had tightened up the operation of the Munitions Act and the Dilution of Labour Act. Workers were now prohibited by law from leaving one job to go to another without first obtaining the permission of the employer. Any worker who disregarded this became subject to military law. These measures, along with the use of unskilled workers in skilled trades, were strongly contested by the Clyde Workers' Committee.

The convenor of the Committee was David Kirkwood, who in later life was to become a Parliamentary colleague of Maxton's. When Lloyd George came to Glasgow in December 1915 to win the support of the engineers for these regulations he found that he required police protection. The Lloyd George meeting was packed with many ILP supporters and anti-war demonstrators. Kirkwood introduced the Minister of Munitions to the assembled engineers:

> This, fellow workers, is Mr Lloyd George. He has come specially to speak to you and I have no doubt that you will give him a patient hearing. I can assure him that every word he says will be carefully weighed. We regard him with suspicion because every act associated with his name has the taint of slavery about it.

Somewhat taken aback by this, Lloyd George addressed the meeting, advocating the use of unskilled labour to do the work of skilled labour so that the war effort could proceed.

Kirkwood asked him if he was prepared to give the workers a share in the management of the works. Lloyd George asserted that the workers were not capable of managing factories. Kirkwood then made clear that the shop stewards had the confidence of the workers, and that they had already led the men out on strike themselves, and back to work again. "Who run the workshops now?" he asked. Lloyd George considered workers' participation a revolutionary proposal and pointed out that Labour leaders now in Government, such as Arthur Henderson, who was present, shared responsibility for the Munitions Act. "We repudiate this man, he is no leader of ours," Kirkwood responded. "If you, Mr Lloyd George, want to know the mind of the workers don't go to such men. If you wish to do away with the discontent in the workshops, then do away with the cause." At this point, to the accompaniment of *The Red Flag* sung by a chorus of shop stewards, Lloyd George left the meeting.

In December 1915 pressure against anti-war rebels mounted. A demonstration in support of free speech and against conscription was organised for the St Andrew's Hall in Glasgow. When permission was refused, the meeting was switched to George Square. When that venue was also refused, a crowd of two thousand assembled in North Hanover Street to be addressed from a lorry by Shinwell, Maclean, Maxton and Gallacher. There was "no overcrowding or jostling or disturbance", Shinwell later told the police, but Maxton and the other speakers were arrested for causing an obstruction.[3] The offence under the Police Act of 1866 carried only a twenty shillings fine, or ten days imprisonment, but the episode was one of the events that led the Glasgow School Board to start proceedings against Maxton.

Maxton's anti-war activities had led to his being absent from school. The last straw was his decision in January 1916 to attend the annual Labour Party Conference in Newcastle. Maxton was slow in asking for the necessary permission to be absent. He was told that his application for leave of absence had arrived too late to come before the appropriate committee and that leave of absence could not therefore be granted. He decided to attend the conference anyway and told the School Board he had arranged for a fully qualified teacher to take his place. The substitute he proposed was John Maclean, who had already been dismissed from the Board for his socialist activities and who was clearly unacceptable to the authorities.

Maxton was disciplined. At the end of January he was called before the School Board officials, accused of absenteeism, and was then reprimanded, dismissed from his post in Dennistoun, and transferred to Anderston to become a teacher at the Finnieston School. Maxton was put on a final warning that any future misbehaviour would lead to his dismissal.

But political life was making even greater demands on Maxton and his anti-war allies. When the Glasgow socialist weekly *Forward* published a full account of the meeting at which Lloyd George had spoken, the issue was suppressed, its offices raided and the newspaper did not appear for four weeks. The Clyde Workers'

Committee issued a newspaper of its own called *The Worker* but it, too, was suppressed after four issues. The chairman of the committee, William Gallacher, the editor, John Muir, and the publisher, Walter Bell, were arrested and imprisoned. Bail was refused. Immediately thousands of workers downed tools and, as a result of this pressure, the men were released pending trial on charges of sedition.

The increasingly repressive Government policy had a clear objective: to speed up the production of weapons for the Western Front, more semi-skilled and unskilled workers, including women, had to be brought in to the munitions factories, and to achieve that, the power of the Clyde Workers' Committee had to be broken. In its more general political propaganda, the ILP posed no real political threat to the Government but the industrial action, with which many sought to associate themselves, was another matter. The Clydeside contribution of guns, munitions and ships to the war effort had to be maintained and vigorous action against militant elements was seen as essential to the national interest.

The ILP posed no real political threat to the Government but the industrial action, with which many sought to associate themselves, was another matter. The Clydeside contribution of guns, munitions and ships to the war effort had to be maintained, and vigorous action against militant elements was seen as essential to the national interest.

Association with industrial unrest in effect promoted the ILP, and socialist agitators, from fringe politics. Its war aims – no conscription and an immediate peace – now had to be taken seriously, at least to the extent of locking up the most militant political activists.

By this time, the manpower needs of a mass army on the Continent had led to the introduction of conscription against which the ILP had campaigned since the outbreak of hostilities. With thousands of others Maxton was called up. He was determined to claim exemption as a conscientious objector and faced a Tribunal, set up under the new legislation, in Barrhead in March.

He conducted his own case and asked the chairman if he would be allowed to call witnesses. Never one to do things by halves, Maxton had ten witnesses standing by on his behalf but offered to compromise by calling only four. Faced with the prospect of an all night sitting Provost Millar allowed only three. It was very much a local affair. A Mr Weir, on the Tribunal, asked, "Now, Mr Maxton, we know you and you know us. Do you not think that you could trust in our belief in your integrity?" "No," said

Maxton emphatically, "I cannot accept that solution. My position in the ILP gives my case an interest which is not merely local and confined to this court. I must insist that the whole of the procedure be gone through."

Maxton began by explaining that he had been an active worker in the socialist movement for many years. As a member of the ILP he had gone about the country speaking on behalf of the party in its pre-war campaign against armaments and militarism. He had spoken against German capitalists running British armament firms just as he had spoken against British firms dabbling in German armaments because the inevitable consequences were such events as the Dardanelles campaign in which his fellow countrymen had been slaughtered by arms provided to the Turks by British capital and British labour. He had protested publicly against the idiocies of diplomacy and the futility of war. He had fought the idea of conscription before the war began and had simply continued to oppose it.

> I am not going to change my attitude now. There comes a time when a man must judge what his duty as a citizen is and what it demands of him and what is demanded by his own conscience. I have made up my mind and would consider myself a shirker to my party, a shirker to the beliefs I have been promulgating for years, if I altered in the least the stand I have taken.

Immediately he finished speaking, he was asked why the Glasgow School Board had not pleaded on his behalf, as it had in the case of some teachers. Maxton explained the reason: he had his dismissal note in his pocket.

The Tribunal then disputed the need for witnesses. Mr Weir put it to Maxton, "We know that you hold these views sincerely." Maxton replied, "You agree, then, that I have established my conscientious objection? You are willing to give me absolute exemption now?" Mr Weir interjected, "But you cannot establish a man's conscience." Maxton agreed and added "this is one reason why it is absurd to expect a tribunal to be able to say whether a man has a conscience or not". Then the Tribunal agreed to allow only three witnesses. Maxton enquired, "You don't mean to say that I cannot be allowed ten minutes of your time when you are proposing to deal with my time and liberty for the next three or four years?"

William Stewart, John Maclean and Councillor Robert Murray all spoke on Maxton's behalf. Afterwards, Maxton was asked if he would agree to joining the Royal Army Medical Corps. His reply was an emphatic negative: "It's all part of the game, and you know it," he said.

The Tribunal then retired to consider their verdict. On their return, the Chairman announced that the case would be carried over for a fortnight so that instructions could be obtained from London on the Tribunal's powers. William Stewart then produced a letter which offered information regarding the Tribunal's powers. The Tribunal would not allow it to be read on the basis that it was new evidence and should have been produced before the case was completed.

Maxton then asked if this meant that he had established his position as a conscientious objector. One of the Tribunal, a Mr Tait, said, "Yes", and no one disagreed at the time, but the verdict was left open for two weeks. Maxton felt he had done relatively well and was quietly confident of the outcome. "I got a good show," he reported in a letter to Sissie.[4]

But within a few days the situation was to change dramatically as the Government took decisive action against the shop stewards of the Clyde. To succeed in their "dilution" policy the Government had to break the Clyde Workers' Committee and so seized on a series of strikes in mid-March as the pretext for deporting David Kirkwood and eight other shop stewards. They were arrested on 25 March and removed to Edinburgh. The Clyde left, already angered by the arrest of John Maclean and the staff of the *Worker*, held a protest demonstration at Glasgow Green on 26 March.

Maxton shared a platform that March Sunday with James MacDougall, another socialist propagandist who had become closely identified with Maxton in his anti-war activities. He had been available as a witness at Maxton's Tribunal but was not called. MacDougall addressed the crowd and called for strike action as a response to the arrests and deportations. Maxton was just as forthright.

It is now for the workers to take action and that action is to strike and down tools at once. Not a rivet should be struck on the Clyde until the deported engineers are restored to their families. In case there are any plainclothes detectives in the audience I shall repeat that statement for their benefit. The men should strike and down tools.

Undercover policemen were indeed present and were taking down his every word, but he was not arrested immediately. Life went on as usual and on the following Thursday evening he went to visit his old friend, John Maclean, now out on bail pending trial.

Maxton was arrested by four detectives on his doorstep at midnight on his return from his visit to Maclean. He went quietly, even restraining his dog Karl (called after Liebnecht, the social democrat, not Marx, the communist) from attacking the policemen. MacDougall had also been arrested and the two were taken to the Central Police Station in Glasgow where they spent the rest of the night.

Next day the two prisoners appeared in Court and were remanded for trial in the High Court. They were charged with attempting to cause mutiny, sedition and disaffection and with impeding, delaying and restricting the war effort. For the next few weeks, they were detained at Duke Street Prison in Glasgow.

On Maxton's arrival at Duke Street, a warder requested the usual details for the prison files. Maxton was asked his religion. "I'm a socialist," was the reply. "It's your religion I want, not your politics," retorted the warder. "I'm sorry but it's the only religion I've got," replied Maxton. The warder persisted, "Are you a Catholic?" "No," came the reply. "Then you must be a Protestant. Were you born in Scotland?" "Yes," replied Maxton. "Then you must be a Presbyterian," said the warder finally. Maxton duly became a prison Presbyterian.

However, a day later when Maxton discovered that one of his friends, the Rev John MacBain, who was a Labour member of the Glasgow Parish Council and an Episcopalian Minister, was chaplain at the prison, he applied to the Governor to have his religion changed. The Governor thought this request preposterous. "We can't change a man's religion for a whim," he said. Maxton duly replied, "Well one of your officials gave me a religion yesterday for a whim, so I don't see why I shouldn't have another today for a whim." As he reported to Sissie, he had been at church and was now trying to become an Episcopalian.[5]

Maxton and MacDougall applied for bail but despite efforts by the Labour Party and the ILP their application was turned down. When they appealed against the decision, Lord Ormidale dismissed their request and described their offence as "grave, dangerous, cowardly and of the most outrageous nature".

Maxton's imprisonment meant for once he was unable to attend the annual conference of the Independent Labour Party. Instead, he wrote a letter of apology, which was read to the assembled delegates on 24 April 1916:

I am very sorry indeed that I am not able to be with you at Newcastle – and it is only the fact that I am confined to my room (laughter) that prevents me being with you. I am in the best of health and spirits and view the future with the greatest equanimity whatever it has in store. People in the movement here have done everything they could to make me as comfortable as possible. The prison officials have been very decent and have shown every respect and consideration. It is a valuable and instructive experience (laughter) and everyone should have at least ten days in prison annually for the good both of their health and their immortal souls. I hope you will have a first class conference and that the year upon which we are entering will be a prosperous one for the party and that the people of all lands will set their minds upon the establishment of truth, justice and prosperity for all.[6]

The humour masked a more serious reality. The prison chaplain, John MacBain, reported to Maxton's mother that while he was "on the whole comfortable... what was grieving him was any reflection that might come upon you". In January Maxton's younger brother John had been court martialled and imprisoned in Wormwood Scrubs in London as a conscientious objector to the war. Even after Maxton's arrest, his faithful dog, Karl, had been stoned, no doubt by patriots, and Maxton feared for his family. In a letter home on 31 March, Maxton advised his mother, "if you're going to suffer much inconvenience at home to shut up shop and the three of you women clear out – out of the country if necessary or down to England or over to Ireland". He would make any necessary financial arrangements. He was worried about Sissie's reaction too. "I fancy she'll be pretty sick about this," he told his mother.[7]

Maxton was to write to Sissie on 4 April that he was "happy and contented" in prison, and was to request a new book on education and social problems for his prison reading. The warders he said were "very decent, a bit gruff and peremptory at times". He was even growing a beard. But there was anxiety over the likely length of his sentence. "I suppose I deserve about twenty years," he joked to Sissie. He had expected to be given a year in prison but felt that if there was more unrest or if there were German air raids, the courts "would increase it to something like Maclean's dose".[8] (Maclean had received a three year sentence.) Then, as he told her, there "will be a struggle to get something like a reasonable employment".

Personal matters were very much on his mind. On 17 April, when Sissie visited him in prison, he proposed marriage. They were both 30 years old. Sissie was two months older than her fiancé. She had blue eyes, brown hair and a ruddy complexion. She had been a teaching colleague at Haghill school and he had known her for four years. Despite the unpromising circumstances, they decided they would announce their engagement while he was still in prison. "I would like to think of it as having been agreed on under the circumstances as they were," he wrote to Sissie. Although their conduct, he conceded "would look very foolish to others", he was "very happy and very proud".[9]

Maxton's mother and sisters had known little of his liaison with Sissie. His mother was informed by letter of the existence of Miss McCallum and that "we have been very intimately associated for about four years. Now and during the last year the intimacy has developed into something deeper. It would probably have remained at that for some time if it had not been for this trouble." His sisters had to be mollified because Sissie was not, as yet, such a committed socialist. "Like Annie I would prefer her to be socialist but she has got the fundamentals necessary, pluck and the sportsman's instincts," he confided to his younger sister Ada in a letter.[10]

Some conventions had to be observed, and a ring was bought. A friend, James Houston, was ordered by Maxton to hand Sissie the money to buy a ring.[11] Prison had separated them physically – but emotionally brought them closer together. He wrote to Sissie that he had "absolutely nothing but my love to give you in return. You have got all that I think you know without me repeating it but this I think has made it deeper and more intense."[12] Promising to "make up to you for every sorrow you've suffered", Maxton wrote again on 4 May, "I've only realised in the last four weeks what a woman's love means. I never believed it possible that any woman would have done what you've done for me so loyally through thick and thin."[13] Twenty years later Maxton recalled his engagement for a newspaper profile:

> My life was so uncertain at that time that I warned her of the difficulties that would inevitably crop up when we were married. She fully realised how difficult would be the life of a woman married to a professional propagandist – for that was the career I had chosen then – but she was staunch and decided to take the risk. I did not tell her, however, there was a possibility of me being a jailbird for life.[14]

They were not to be married for three years, but from the beginning

Sissie was aware of his unshakeable political commitment. From prison he wrote that there was no turning back and that he had mapped out his future as a professional propagandist.

On 1 May 1916 socialist prisoners in Duke Street were cheered by the singing of *The Red Flag* and the *Internationale* from the annual May Day parade on Glasgow Green. On 3 May, Maxton appeared with MacDougall before Sheriff Lyall at Glasgow Sheriff Court. The charge was one of "attempting to impede, delay and restrict the production of munitions by statements which they made during a demonstration on Glasgow Green". Both tendered pleas of "Not Guilty" and were remitted for trial at the High Court in Edinburgh. Maxton was moved from Duke Street Prison to Calton Jail in Edinburgh. In the streets of Glasgow supporters were still singing the anti-war song he had written.

"Oh, I'm Henry Dubb
And I won't go to war
Because I don't know
What they're all fighting for

To Hell with the Kaiser
To Hell with the Tsar
To Hell with Lord Derby
And also GR

I work at munitions
I'm a slave down at Weir's
If I leave my job
They'll give me two years

To Hell with the sheriff
To Hell with his crew
To Hell with Lloyd George
And Henderson too

I don't like the factor
His rent I won't pay
Three cheers for John Wheatley
I'm striking today

To Hell with the landlord
I'm not one to grouse
But to Hell both with him
And his bloody old house.[15]

7

Prison

In 1916 the ILP Scottish Secretary, William Stewart, who had followed and encouraged Maxton's political evolution over ten years, wrote a brief portrait of Maxton. It was later published in his book, *Wartime and Other Impressions*.

"I have been associated with him a good deal during recent years and have seen him change," Stewart wrote. "He is the same Maxton I met on Ayr Low Green ten years ago and yet he is not the same. He is humorous, pleasantly cynical as ever in intimate intercourse with friends and companions, but in council or on public platforms he evinces a consciousness of responsibility which grows with his increasing knowledge of his own growth of influence." Maxton, he wrote, was popular, "finding friends everywhere ... in every corner of Scotland" but Stewart now saw him "growing and developing in mental vigour" as he evolved from part-time street-corner orator to professional politician. Ten years on, Maxton now possessed "a knowledge and potency of appeal that has its source in his sincerity" and he had become "a very serious earnest man for all his seemingly light-hearted, even boyish, quips and jests".

Already Maxton was earmarked by Stewart as a future Member of Parliament. Maxton "has not chosen a career – the career has chosen him. When people say that in going to prison he has spoiled his career they understand neither the man, nor his conception of life."[1] If others had already mapped out a Westminster future for the 30-year-old Maxton, he himself still had to face the rigours of a High Court trial and a stiff prison sentence.

The trial of James Maxton and James MacDougall took place on Thursday 11 May 1916 in the High Court of Edinburgh in Parliament House on the Royal Mile. Both decided to accept legal representation. Counsel for the defence was Mr Alexander Duffes, who was assisted by the Glasgow socialist lawyer, Rosslyn

Mitchell, who defended many other socialist activists accused during this period.

On Mitchell's advice Maxton had already decided that to minimise the sentence he should plead guilty. "I was, and it's quite obvious that we're not going to get a show in the courts," he explained to his mother on 18 April. "All our statements would be twisted and contorted to bear the worst possible appearance."[2] MacDougall pled guilty too. Many of their friends, including David Kirkwood and John Wheatley, attended the court but there was little other public interest in the trial. War news from the Western front was far more important.

The defence emphasised the youth of the two accused, and their public standing. They were, Duffes said, men of education – Maxton a school-teacher and MacDougall for some time the member of a School Board. Strength of feeling about the arrest and removal of other Labour men from Glasgow had coloured their utterances at the meeting on Glasgow Green. "They meant what they said at the time," declared Duffes, "but they were induced to say it by the state of their feelings and they now regret it."

The defence counsel pleaded for leniency pointing out that Maxton and MacDougall had already been in detention for six weeks and because "they asked me to express to his Lordship their regret at their quite inexcusable action on the occasion in question".

When the Lord Advocate, Mr Robert Munro KC, presented the case for the prosecution he said the gravest feature of the offending speeches was their timing. The munitions strike in Glasgow was a matter of grave national concern and the accused had sought to broaden it in response to the "deportation" of the ring-leaders. The Lord Advocate continued: "The news of their deportation must necessarily have been known at that meeting on the Sunday afternoon and I cannot accept the view that the speeches were occasioned by reason of the unexpectedness of the information."

The meeting, he contended, was in fact selected for the purpose of advising munition workers to commit a crime against the law of the land by striking. He then argued that the prisoners knew that by going on strike the munition workers would incur a penalty and that penalty would fall upon the hearers and not upon the speakers. This was the core of the prosecution argument, that knowingly they had incited the workers to strike. Being educated men "aggravates rather than palliates the offence and it is no fault of theirs that their advice to strike was ineffective".

The Judge, Lord Strathclyde, began his summing up by emphasising the gravity of the offence. Addressing Maxton and MacDougall directly, he said:

> As you very well know, the flower of our British manhood has gone abroad cheerfully and willingly to fight the battle of their country. The prisoners well knowing the meaning of the words they used and realising too their true significance, actually and with deliberation advised the workers on munitions to do everything in their power to deprive the brave defenders of our country not only of the means of winning the war – your war as well as theirs – but also of defending themselves from the murderous attacks of a ruthless foe.

Lord Strathclyde found great difficulty in believing that the prisoners fully realised "the dastardliness and cowardliness of the offence which they had committed". However, in his next remarks he made it clear that he was not going to deal with the prisoners with undue severity. "I am very willing to believe that your expression of contrition is genuine and I trust that the leniency which I am disposed to show will not be misunderstood." He reminded the prisoners that any future offences by them would result in stiff prison sentences and that if they had been in the armed services when they committed this offence, the death penalty might have been imposed.

Maxton was relieved when he and MacDougall were sentenced for only one year, to run from the date of their arrest. With a smile and a wave to their friends, they left the court.

Maxton returned to Calton Jail in Edinburgh to serve the remainder of his sentence.

Then about a hundred years old, the prison occupied the slope of Calton Hill overlooking the main Edinburgh-London railway line and vaguely resembled a castle, so that Maxton was later to refer to it as "my ancestral home". Not long afterwards it was demolished, yielding the site and indeed its stone to the Scottish Office, St Andrew's House.

Even by the standards of 1916 it was a dreadful place, its cells tiny and dungeon-like, its sanitation primitive and its amenities practically non-existent. Its conditions made a lasting impression on Maxton, and although he did not in later years talk much of his time in jail he became, and remained, a strong advocate of prison reform.

Maxton's fellow-prisoner, Arthur Woodburn, in his unpublished autobiography recalls Calton as "the poorhouse of all prisons" that had the "cold chill of a grim fortress".[3] While prisoners in Duke Street Jail had mattresses, the first 30 days in Calton Jail were spent on bare boards. Maxton immediately complained, pleading, eventually with success, that his sentence had started from the date of his arrest six weeks before and that he should be issued with a mattress.

The only books available were the Bible and a hymnbook. Breakfast consisted of six ounces of oatmeal and half a pint of buttermilk. The midday meal was two pints of broth and twelve ounces of dry bread. Supper was eight ounces of oatmeal and three-quarters of a pint of buttermilk. Maxton ate only two of the three meals, joking in letters to Sissie that the "only fault" with the food was that there was "too great a quantity".

Maxton's life was made more bearable by the letters he received daily from Sissie. It was, he wrote to her, "the brightest spot in the day".[4] He asked for a photograph of her for his cell and was permitted it, and was allowed to send her one letter every week. Throughout the year Sissie wrote every evening, anxious for news, and informing him of what she had been doing. She made repeated enquiries through intermediaries like the prison chaplain, Rev John Munro – who happened to be Maxton's brother-in-law – about Maxton's health.

The engagement of Mr James Maxton to Miss Sissie McCallum was formally announced on 19 May but the length of the separation stretching before them depressed both of them. Sissie wrote, "I am afraid I shall not get reconciled to the idea", and in almost every letter counted the weeks and the days until his release. Sissie's uncertain health and repeated illnesses made things worse for both of them.

As a socialist in Calton Jail Maxton was not alone. John Maclean, William Gallacher, James MacDougall and John Muir were serving sentences in 1916, but there was little opportunity for contact and none at all for their customary discussions. Each worked in his own cell, prisoners meeting each other only during the statutory hour in the exercise yard, and even then under close supervision.

After only two months James MacDougall suffered a mental breakdown and still had not fully recovered on his release eight months later. Arthur Woodburn recalls, "he went berserk and had to be removed shouting and roaring having cracked under the strain".[5]

Maxton withstood prison better than most. Perhaps his sense of humour, or his unshakeable socialist faith, or simply his unconquerable optimism and his gift for friendship even under the most unpromising circumstances, explained his resilience. Maxton was popular both with prisoners and with warders. Arthur Woodburn recalls him as "the warders' pet" but it should be clear that this involved him in no compromises. He persuaded some of them to form a branch of the Police and Prison Warders' Trade Union and even inveigled a few into the ILP.

Maxton's first prison work was the familiar sewing of mail-bags but he was eventually promoted from this to joinery, and did minor furniture repairs in a cell overlooking Waverley Station, still on his own but with more to look at. Gallacher, who had also acquired special status, in a maintenance job that effectively gave him the freedom of the prison, was evidently able to visit his comrade from time to time.

Visitors from the outside world were rare, and Maxton's quota was taken up by his fiancée, his family and his political friends from Glasgow. As an enforcedly inactive political activist Maxton craved political and war news. The authorities allowed him one daily and one weekly newspaper. Eventually, by special dispensation, he was also allowed some books brought in by his family, who had initially offered to restock the prison library.

In prison Maxton lost his most distinctive physical characteristic – his hair. When he reached Calton Jail, it was cropped to the scalp. Perhaps to his surprise, his fiancée liked it that way and suggested in a letter "we won't have it long any more".[6] Maxton was less enthusiastic and having perused the regulations discovered that he could have retained at least a few inches. Not surprisingly he soon became an expert on prison regulations.

However hard the régime and the pain of confinement was for them, Maxton and his friends were sustained as few prisoners were by a knowledge of the support they enjoyed outside. Sometimes that support materialised in the form of a socialist choir on Calton Hill, which overlooked the exercise yard. For whatever reason, and perhaps because of Maxton's unfailing good humour and popularity, warders present occasionally turned a blind eye to these demonstrations. Kirkwood wrote "when it was discovered that we were sending greetings, the officers found something to distract their attention. They all loved Jimmy Maxton."[7]

In later life Maxton talked sparingly about prison, usually in private and always to make a point. "I have come into the closest contact with all sorts and conditions of people," he once told an

ILP colleague. "I have known convicts and Cabinet Ministers and really the difference in ability between them is so trifling as to be almost negligible." Prisoners, Maxton found, were "mostly nice fellows" although they were "much too respectable, conventional, and patriotic" for him to retain as personal friends.

On Friday 2 February 1917 Maxton was taken to Duke Street Prison in Glasgow. On the following morning he was released and made straight for his home in Barrhead where he was welcomed by over a hundred West of Scotland socialists. In the evening he was the star guest at a "Welcome Home" social organised by Barrhead ILP. He was surrounded by friends and colleagues. His old friend, William Stewart, the Scottish Organiser of the ILP, Tom Johnston, editor of *Forward*, and P. J. Dollan, who was to become one of the great socialists in local government in Scotland, were all present and spoke.

In his reply Maxton thanked them and reiterated his belief in socialism and his conviction that it was the only cause worth working for. He talked without bitterness and referred to the kindness he had received at the hands of the prison authorities. As Dollan remarked, "I marvelled at his lack of complaint".[8]

William Stewart described his return in the following week's edition of *Forward*. He had arrived back "a little paler and a little thinner" but when he spoke "his voice was as steady and musical as before, his laugh was as spontaneous and infectious, and his eyes as full of sparkling fire as in the days before he left us". Stewart went on to relate that Maxton had much to tell about the "curious community in which he had been living", and that his friends had much to tell him.

In the same issue of *Forward*, Maxton himself contributed an article entitled "A Convict's Reminiscences". In it he confessed to finding it difficult to put his thoughts into writing because he was so overjoyed at being released from prison. So, rather than the intended message to Scottish socialists, the article became light-hearted. William Gallacher, the Communist agitator, was due to be released soon after and Maxton speculated that "Gallacher might have been liberated on Saturday but refused to go out till Monday so that he would not miss the Sunday Bible Class".

John Wheatley had organised a fund to assist those imprisoned or deported for their anti-war stance, and was able to arrange a period of convalescence for Maxton, Gallacher, Muir, MacDougall and Kirkwood at the Moffat Hydropathic. "Hydros", of which a few still survive, were peculiarly Victorian institutions which placed great faith in the powers of local waters. They functioned somewhat as health farms do today, providing healthy cosseting for the middle classes. Maxton and his colleagues had never experienced such luxury. At the Hydro they enjoyed Turkish baths and regular walks, and Maxton made up for his year of isolation by talking politics far into the night with Kirkwood, MacDougall and Gallacher. MacDougall had still not entirely recovered his mental health, and Maxton experienced symptoms perhaps related to the stress of prison. He became ill during his stay at the Hydro, "hiccoughing incessantly", as he reported in a letter to Sissie.

The local GP, one Dr Park, was summoned. For some reason, perhaps only his patient's accent, Dr Park began to talk about the Glasgow socialists then in the news. Unaware of whom he was examining, he described, according to Kirkwood, Maxton as a vagabond and Kirkwood as "a traitor of the deepest dye". Kirkwood wrote, "We kept back our laughter with difficulty. As we were saying our good-byes, Jimmy said, pointing to me: 'This is the traitor of the deepest dye.' 'And this,' I said, 'is the vagabond, though he's mair like a scarecrow than a Russian revolutionary.'"[9] Dr Park related Maxton's symptoms to his stomach, not, as was feared, to his heart. As Maxton later reported to Sissie, he had been found "organically sound in every way but wanted toning up".

After five days at Moffat, Maxton returned to Glasgow and shared a platform with William Gallacher on the Sunday at a packed meeting at St Mungo Hall. Gallacher spoke of the need to rebuild the shop stewards' movement. Maxton followed him and couldn't resist having a go at his friend and colleague. "You know," he told the audience as if in confidence, "I made a discovery down at Moffat Hydro. An argument with Gallacher isn't so much a question of intellectual ability as it is a test of physical endurance. If you don't believe me, try it sometime."

Again, Maxton thanked his supporters and friends for the kindness he had received in prison. In a letter to *New Leader* on 8 February 1917, he confessed that he had been reading Thomas Carlyle (his father's favourite author) while in prison. He recalled Carlyle's work on the French Revolution, and the experience of one of his characters, Madame de Stael, who had been imprisoned in the Bastille. Within its walls, she said, she had found the nearest approach to liberty in her experience. Maxton had, he recalled, felt exactly the same way. "My mind was absolutely free to roam over the most fruitful realms of thought untrammelled by the Defence of the Realm Act and uninfluenced by Northcliffe."

But Maxton's health continued to cause anxiety. He referred to himself as "an advertisement for an Indian Famine Fund" and on his return to Glasgow he became ill again and was ordered to stay in bed.

8

Working on the Clyde

Maxton's period in prison coincided with a sharp shift to the left in Scottish politics, and Scottish public opinion, which had resented Maxton's anti-war propaganda in 1915, had, by the end of 1916, begun to reflect war weariness if not to demand peace. On the left, the newly constituted Scottish Advisory Council of the Labour Party, first meeting in December 1916, had opposed compulsory conscription by a vast majority and gone on to vote in favour of peace negotiations. On the domestic front, Labour demanded "a Right to Work Bill" and action to deal with housing shortages and high rents. These resolutions reflected much of public opinion. Official reports confirmed all this. A Government Commission on Industrial Unrest, taking evidence in Scotland during 1917, reported "an acute need" for action on housing and warned that there remained amidst the deprivation "a revolutionary element".

After a convalescence Maxton returned to the centre of the Scottish political stage. He spoke at a joint Labour Party-Trades Union Conference in March 1917 only days after the first Russian Revolution. The Tzar had been overthrown. As Maxton remarked it left him "dumbfounded . . . it was what all socialists told us should take place, but it had come sooner than we expected".

When the Labour Conference assembled in March conscription was again the issue. A motion expressing reservations about it was considered by Maxton and the ILP to be too modest. He moved an amendment that "no form of compulsory military service will be acceptable to the workers of the country". His intervention led to the defeat of the platform and later the Labour Party in Scotland came out against all conscription for the war and demanded that the Parliamentary Labour Party leave the Coalition Government.

Arthur Henderson was to resign from the War Cabinet in July 1917, and in December Labour published its *Memorandum on War Aims*, calling for peace by negotiation, but the leftward drift of Scottish Labour, strongly encouraged by Maxton and the

ILP, caused considerable anxiety to Labour leaders in London. The disquiet was mutual. Scottish Labour Party Secretary Ben Shaw was compelled to report to the UK headquarters that "no leaflet north of the Tweed would find acceptance ... unless it contained an attack on the policy of the party at headquarters not to mention its personalities".[1] For Scottish socialists the UK party was not socialist enough.

A Londoner, Fenner Brockway, who had visited Scotland regularly from 1915 onwards, and had worked with the Clydeside socialists, was impressed also by the north-south differences. Of the Scots he later recalled, "they were speaking a different language from the English ILP'ers. Whilst we were exposing the duplicity of the foreign policy which had led to the war and advocating a peace of no conquests and no indemnities, they were denouncing rent increases and profiteering and the speed-up and long hours of munition workers. We concentrated on peace. They concentrated on the class struggle."[2]

The first Russian Revolution did a little for solidarity on the left throughout Britain. Several trades unions got together with the British Socialist Party and the ILP and proposed "a Workers' and Soldiers' Convention" to be organised in Leeds. The Leeds Convention called for the setting up of Workers' and Soldiers' Councils, based on the example of their Russian comrades, and the calling of local conferences in support. It was at this convention that Maxton first met Ernest Bevin, then a trade unionist, later Foreign Secretary in the 1945 Labour Government.

The first of the local conferences called for was arranged for St Mungo Hall in Glasgow. The Co-operative Board which owned it was under considerable pressure to cancel the booking. Comparisons with Russia evoked much public concern which in turn had been built up by the press. The meeting took place despite anti-left demonstrations outside. Ramsay MacDonald, then the leading peace campaigner, spoke to a packed hall. Maxton took on the responsibility for protecting the meeting from threatened violence and organised stewards from the Clyde Workers' Committee to good effect.

More regular employment eluded the recent ex-prisoner. Immediately on being sentenced to jail he had been asked to resign as a teacher but had refused to do so. He had been summarily dismissed from the employment of the School Board, being paid only for the time until he was sentenced. He was now without regular financial support.

The threat of conscription still hung over him. Prison had

only temporarily averted it. Maxton was again called before the Barrhead Tribunal. His lawyer, again Rosslyn Mitchell, sought to temporise and secured a two-week postponement on grounds of Maxton's ill health, assuring the Board that for a fortnight his client "must be protected against all forms of excitement". Maxton was anxious to avoid further imprisonment and considered applying to the Tribunal for exemption from war work on grounds of ill health. In a letter from Moffat Hydro Maxton had explained to Sissie that he had "a notion to try and get a doctor to give me a certificate of unfitness". When he was pronounced fit for general service he confessed to Sissie that he was "very grateful in one way but very annoyed in another".[3]

In the event Maxton was lucky: he came before a more sympathetic Tribunal, who granted him an exemption from active war service as long as he undertook work at home of national importance. Again he refused to undertake any work in connection with the making of munitions or ships for the navy, and as a result found himself unemployed for the first time in his life. He confided to a friend, Gilbert Macallister, the persecution he felt he was suffering and the hardship it was inflicting upon those who were dearest to him.

By July 1917 he had found a job. With the help of a socialist friend, John Scanlon, he started as a plater's helper at the "dry-land" shipyard of Alley and Maclellan in Polmadie. This was one of the few shipyards on the Clyde not engaged in war work. It produced barges for neutral countries. "I got into close relations with the manual workers," Maxton later explained, "and was able to participate in the struggles at that time as one of themselves." Within the shipyard Maxton moved from job to job and although he had never earned his living other than as a teacher he was in turn a general labourer, a carpenter's mate and a shipping clerk. This progression may reflect upon his physical fitness.

"The threat of overtime is becoming more definite," he wrote to Sissie. "I shall be glad to have the extra money but strongly object to the further curtailment of my limited spare time."[4] His opportunities for ILP propaganda work were severely restricted. Still he carried on. That winter he travelled 15 miles from Glasgow on an open-top tram to speak at an evening meeting in Wishaw. He arrived shivering with cold and discovered that he had left his bag on the tram. "I wouldn't have minded about the loss of the bag," he recalled to Sissie, "but it happens to contain my working shirt."

At another meeting, a Sunday night session in a Glasgow theatre, a man in the pit asked Jimmy why the ILP held its meetings on the Sabbath day. Maxton replied that "in order to answer that question, my friend, I shall require to go back to the time when the Lord was on the earth. And, if you will remember, a certain man came to the Lord on the Sabbath day who had allowed one of his asses to fall into a pit. He asked the Lord whether it were better to pull the ass out on the Sabbath day or leave it there till the Monday morning. The Lord replied that it was far better to pull it out on the Sabbath day." Leaning forward from the stage to address his questioner, he concluded, "My friend, there are still many asses in the pit!"

Sissie too felt the strain of Maxton's propaganda work. Maxton realised this. "You are a little hurt with me for having all my time occupied and nothing left for you. Compare yourself with the girl whose lover is at the front," he wrote to her. "In these times I always feel that I have got to work my hardest in the socialist movement to keep my self-respect." A socialist "who doesn't take his share in opposing war is a coward. There are cowardly socialists . . . but I am not one. I'll lose your respect as well as my own if I dodged my responsibility."[5]

Maxton's responsibilities now included a Parliamentary candidacy in a winnable seat. In 1916, while he was still in prison, the Bridgeton Labour Party wrote to the Montrose Burghs Labour Representation Committee, who had adopted Maxton as their candidate in 1914, requesting that he be allowed to stand instead in Bridgeton. He was endorsed as Parliamentary candidate for Bridgeton shortly after his release from prison. At the end of May a propaganda drive with the slogan "Bridgeton for Socialism" was organised to introduce the new candidate to the electorate. The National Chairman of the ILP, Dick Wallhead, covered the constituency with Maxton, addressing many meetings. Large crowds turned up.

No election would be held before the end of the war but industrial unrest at home and the astonishing events in Russia had put socialist ideas into the middle of public debate. Maxton and others in the Glasgow ILP now set out to draw up a socialist election programme. A Special Emergency Parliamentary Committee drew up proposals for a manifesto which they hoped would gain the support of Clydeside workers.

The ILP rejected "patchwork reforms", and its "minimum programme" included nationalisation under workers' control, new housing with interest-free rents and free education for all. There were disagreements between those who favoured the syndicalist position of Soviets and outright workers' control and those who believed in "control of the workshop by the worker subject to the will of the community as expressed in their national councils".[6] This was the beginning of the split between Parliamentary socialists and syndicalists. On this occasion as later, Parliamentary socialists prevailed and the ILP's election manifesto, completed in 1917, called for a "people's parliament".

Before the war the Scottish ILP had won only a handful of town council seats. Now their ambitions reflected their new confidence and every seat was to be fought. It might cost £3,000 and involve recruiting 25,000 helpers but both figures were now within the bounds of possibility.

By the end of the year Maxton – still a full time shipyard worker – was active, as Chairman of the Scottish Divisional Council of the ILP, in several campaigns. He had been one of the first in the ILP to recognise the importance of women in politics and was a keen supporter of the Women's Peace Crusade. If the ILP could win the women, he said, they could win the peace. He also supported Wheatley's housing campaign, which aimed first to control rents and then to provide decent individual houses for workers for rent at £8 a year, the equivalent of £12 per month today.

By now Maxton was also a member of the Labour Party's Scottish Executive, and soon to be a member of the Labour Party's National Executive. As a Scottish representative during both 1917 and 1918 in delegations to the National Executive Committee, he was Scottish Labour's leading spokesman in a bitter battle over the extent of the Scottish say in the future direction of the national party. In bold and controversial proposals of December 1917, the Scottish Executive sought to change the Scottish party's name from " Scottish Advisory Council of the Labour Party" and to reintroduce Keir Hardie's title of 1888, " Scottish Labour Party". They also sought automatic Scottish representation both on the party's National Executive and at the National Conference, and the right to endorse Scottish Parliamentary candidates and to draw up a Scottish programme. In acrimonious debates with the party's secretary, Arthur Henderson, and national agent, Egerton Wake, Maxton argued the Scottish case. Later Maxton represented the Scottish Executive at a delegation to the National Executive in May and September 1918. An uneasy compromise, not ratified until January 1919, agreed that there should be a Scottish programme, increased Scottish financial assistance from the national party, and a Scottish right to send deputations directly to the National Executive Committee.[7]

The politics of wartime industry reached a crisis in January 1918 as the Government sought to harness almost every able-bodied male for combat or war production. The Manpower Bill, promptly labelled the Manslaughter Bill by Maxton, met widespread opposition which was strongest in Sheffield (where there had been a major strike of engineers in 1917) and Clydeside. A Government Minister, Sir Auckland Geddes, was despatched by Lloyd George to Clydeside to persuade workers to support the Bill. At a mass meeting on 28 January he was first shouted down, then given a hearing and finally seen off by the adoption by the meeting of a resolution which declared that Clydeside would "do nothing at all in support of carrying on the war but to do everything we can to bring the war to a conclusion". Maxton, a genuine industrial worker, seconded the motion. The meeting proceeded to George Square and went on till midnight.

The aim of the shop stewards' committee had been a national strike against the war. For most of the country, and even for most of Clydeside, this had little appeal. The shop stewards soon recognised this and concentrated on preparing for peace. The May Day demonstration which included a mass strike on a nominal working day took place in George Square and, with estimates of the attendance varying from 70,000 to 110,000, was one of the biggest ever seen in Glasgow. The subsequent rally passed a resolution sending greetings to workers of all lands, to the newly-formed Soviet Union, and to the workers of Germany, with whom Britain was still at war.

Maxton spoke to the rally, declaring that "the workers of all lands want to live in peace, peace and brotherhood. The people of Glasgow want peace; they have demonstrated their desire today in a manner that will shake the war-makers. Peace, yes, peace, is our insistent cry, the people want peace and the world wants Socialism." According to one observer the cheers for Maxton were "thunderous. It was Glasgow's greatest May Day and a great day for Maxton."

In September 1918 Maxton represented the ILP at an international conference. In a letter to Sissie he described many "stormy scenes" and "big differences ... it will be impossible ... to secure unity".[8] In June he had met Kerenski, the Russian social democrat and the last pre-Bolshevik Russian leader. His motives for visiting Britain, it seemed to Maxton, were largely to do with national politics in the Far East. He was seeking support for Japanese intervention in the war.

As his political commitments again increased, Maxton's shipyard job finally became impossible. He wrote to Sissie that there was "nothing to be contented about in my position just now. I have almost made up my mind to apply to the Tribunal for a change in job. It's too risky being in this one and taking the number of days off that I require and there's absolutely no headway to be made in the shipyards."[9]

He was still negotiating a change of job as the war drew to a close. On 11 November 1918, Maxton was in London. In a letter to Sissie he wrote, "it's fine that we've got peace now and also that the German socialists are in power there. That ought to give us a lift after the people have got over their war jubilation." London has "gone daft over the peace and the political world is in turmoil".[10]

The General Election the ILP longed for was now in sight and Maxton prepared for the campaign in Bridgeton. "Now that the election is on we want to enthuse our own crowd as much as possible."[11]

SECTION II: SOCIALISM INTO PARLIAMENT

9

"Petrograd of the West"

"The Petrograd of the West" was how Lenin described the Glasgow of 1918. The socialist writer William Morris was probably nearer the truth when 30 years previously he had called Glasgow "the devil's drawing room". In the 1920s its dark squalor and its destitution was to earn it the reputation of the "city of the dreadful night".

Peace was to bring mass unemployment to a society which, even under conditions of war-time full employment, already suffered mass poverty. Glasgow, and Scotland, now faced a housing and public health crisis of staggering proportions. War, one writer remarked, had not "created the hell but heated it beyond endurance". Such dispassionate observers as the members of the Royal Commission on the Housing of the Industrial Population catalogued in their report of 1917 "insufficient supplies of water, unsatisfactory ... drainage, grossly inadequate provision for the removal of refuse ... the unspeakable filthy privvy midden in many areas ... gross overcrowding and huddling of the sexes together in the congested villages and towns".[1]

By 1918, through the influx of war workers, Glasgow had to house at least 100,000 more men, women and children than in the pre-war years. Two-thirds of the population now lived in dwellings found to be "inferior to the minimum standards of the Board of Health". Glasgow was, one observer remarked, "an uncomfortable city in the centre with a measureless circumference of uncommunicative tenements". 40,000 people still inhabited one-bedroomed houses. In all, 112,000 lived in no more than "a room and kitchen". 13,000 of these houses were "officially condemned", what Maxton and the ILP called "human slaughter houses". On average three of a family shared the one-roomed tenement flats and a score of people shared use of the standard tenement stair toilet. One Glasgow woman who had given evidence to the Royal Commission on Housing told Commissioners that "if decency at the beginning of life is made difficult decency at the end is made impossible. The beloved dead is laid on the bed and all the usual domestic duties have to be done with ever that still pale form still before them."[2]

The slums bred ill health. Every year a thousand or more died of tuberculosis in Glasgow. One child in every seven born died before reaching the age of one. Deaths amongst infants rose in the first two years after the war. Medical improvements reduced that statistic to one child in ten during the 1920s but whereas before the war proportionately fewer Scots children died in infancy than in England, the relative Scottish position was to worsen dramatically. By 1923 the Scottish death rate amongst young babies was 40% worse than in Britain as a whole and in some of the poorest areas of Glasgow the death rate was three or four times higher than in the middle-class areas. Sickness, ill health and disability forced thousands into receipt of Poor Law assistance. In Bridgeton alone, 40% of the population were on the disabled roll alone. Glasgow, James Stewart, one of Maxton's colleagues, was to say, had become "earth's nearest suburb to hell".

Over the next four years, rising unemployment, poor housing and general squalor were to propel Labour Councillors into office and Labour MPs into Parliament. Gladstonian Liberalism had promised continuing economic progress and a fairer distribution of the material rewards of industry. As conditions worsened and expectations fell, the Trades Councils and ILP branches – infrastructures of socialism gradually built up since 1910 – received increasing support.

It was the ILP which benefited most. During 1917 and 1918 the number of Scottish ILP branches had almost doubled – from 112 to 201 (there had been only 96 in 1914) – and party membership had trebled (from 3,000 to just under 10,000), with half of these members in Glasgow and Lanarkshire. While in Scotland the ILP led the way in securing converts, at a national level Maxton was involved, as an ILP representative on Labour's National Executive Committee, in discussing far reaching changes in the Labour Party constitution. These were to alter dramatically the position of the ILP. The ILP was, primarily, a propagandist party, an advance guard for socialism that concentrated on education and street-corner agitation. Until 1918, it was also the principal route by which individuals joined the Labour Party. No formal Labour Party structure existed and more often than not in local constituencies the ILP was the Labour Party.

The new Labour Party constitution of 1918 committed the party to common ownership, popular democracy and a philosophy of "economic, social and political emancipation" for working people. It also established the party as a federal organisation of trades unions and individual constituency organisations, with individual Labour Party members, branch parties, and trades union rights of affiliation. Constituency branches now offered a direct route to party membership: no longer did individuals need to join the ILP in order to be part of the wider Labour Party.

For the next few years local Labour Parties were slow in emerging and, in Scotland especially, the ILP retained its predominance as the principal socialist grouping in the country but the change of 1918 questioned the rationale for the existence of a separate body with its own individual membership, national structure and policy-making role, and led inevitably to charges that the ILP was now "a party within a party". Ten years later Maxton recalled the wide-ranging discussions that had then taken place on the future direction for the ILP. Some thought the ILP should now become a research body like the Fabian Society, he explained. Others felt the ILP's international links made it eminently suitable to be a body primarily concerned with foreign affairs. The decision, which he supported, to maintain a full-blooded party, meant that ILP members had to operate "with a dual personality" and made inevitable many of the clashes between ILP leaders and Labour leaders which were to dominate future years.[3]

For the moment the maximum possible unity was essential. At the beginning of November 1918 the Prime Minister, David Lloyd George, announced the first General Election for eight years. Tentative approaches were made to retain Labour's support for a continuation of the Coalition Government. The ILP would have none of it. From his position on the National Executive Maxton joined forces with Ramsay MacDonald to argue against the Parliamentary leaders, Clynes and Arthur Henderson, who sought to remain attached to the Coalition at least until peace terms were signed. MacDonald and Maxton argued for the resignation of all Labour Ministers at the point Parliament was dissolved. The MacDonald-Maxton amendment was carried by 12 votes to 4 at the National Executive, and by more than a million votes at a special party conference a week later.[4]

The 1918 election was to be the first in which all men over the age of 21 and all women over 30 enjoyed the right to vote, but the campaign and the eventual outcome were dominated by Lloyd George's exploitation of his role as a successful war leader. He negotiated a continuation of the war-time Coalition and invented a device which gave the election its name, the "coupon", a Prime Ministerial seal of approval dispatched to favoured Liberal or Conservative candidates in each constituency.

When the election was announced, there were millions who were not on the electoral register – half the homecoming soldiers were denied the vote, according to *The Times* – and because of this *Forward* called the contest "the most scandalous election in modern political history". The haste of the election meant also that there were whole areas of the country in which Labour's organisation was non-existent. Scotland, despite its reputation for war-time militancy, was little better.

In the last ten days before nominations closed, candidates had to be hustled into place in at least a dozen constituencies where Labour believed it had a chance of success. The elaborate plans that had been drawn up in Glasgow to raise finance, and helpers, even to form street committees in support of Labour candidates, had to be abandoned. There was time only to find candidates, and run the most basic of campaigns. Although Labour had planned to contest every seat in Glasgow, it failed to find candidates in three. More than 20 Scottish seats were uncontested by Labour. Red Flags had to be sold to raise vital cash, and campaigns in a number of constituencies went by default for lack of money.

Bridgeton, now the biggest ILP branch in Glasgow, was better prepared than most. Maxton had been selected as its Parliamentary candidate in 1917, and by March 1918 the Glasgow party had agreed to pay for his campaign. Reviewing the candidatures the *Scottish Cooperator* called Maxton "the most popular candidate in the entire Labour Movement".[5] Though selected himself, Maxton, as Chairman of the Scottish ILP and now also a member of the Labour Party's Scottish and National Executives, was to become involved in other, much more acrimonious selections. His old teaching friend, John Maclean, nominated by the British Socialist Party and in prison at the time of the selection, was a controversial choice as Labour candidate in the Gorbals. Labour's National Executive simply refused endorsement. James MacDougall, who had been in prison with Maxton, was another controversial candidate. He stood in the new Tradeston constituency, and he and Maclean campaigned on a slogan that voters should "not be misled by any attempts to reform capitalism". If elected, they would refuse to take up their seats at Westminster.

Though many prominent Labour leaders dissociated themselves from the Maclean candidature, Maxton supported it wholeheartedly. In a Scottish-wide ILP appeal for money he

90

wrote that there was a special reason why Labour supporters should give generously. The extra cash raised, he said, would be a gesture of support towards "our brave comrade" John Maclean and would help him secure election.

By polling day, Labour had 52 candidates in the field, but only 41 of these enjoyed the full endorsement of the Labour Party National Executive. In Glasgow, three candidates stood without endorsement. Not surprisingly, the ILP had secured most of the Glasgow nominations, fielding seven of the city's Labour candidates. As a consequence election manifestos there veered sharply to the left of the UK national programme which was a moderate one emphasising the need for reconstruction.

Manifestos abounded. Though nominally supporting the UK manifesto, Maxton and his ILP candidates made clear their support for two other, more left-wing, programmes. The Scottish Labour manifesto, to which Maxton had contributed, was a radical document which called for prohibition of alcohol, a Scottish Parliament, and the nationalisation of land. The programmes of the ILP federations in Glasgow and Scotland as a whole were even more extreme. Maxton's personal message to Bridgeton voters declared that "the Labour Movement is the organised attempt of the workers to raise themselves out of their position of inferiority and degradation", and more general ILP literature offered socialism as "the means to wrest political power from the present ruling class".

Campaigning in Scotland for the General Election of 1918 quickly degenerated into a vitriolic war of words between the right and the socialists. The Coalition Government's initial emphasis on promises of reconstruction ("homes fit for heroes") soon gave way to the parading of a monstrous vision of the socialist menace. That, and the narrow jingoism of the "Hang the Kaiser" persuasion, dominated later stages of the Coalition's campaign.

From the left, *Forward* recorded, midway through November, "the lines of the campaign are already apparent. Everybody who does not agree with the capitalists is already a Bolshevik."[6] So much did the Coalition tactics shift in the effort to defeat Labour that one Tory candidate issued two manifestos, the first promising new houses, and the second simply an attack on "the extreme Bolshevist views of those at present controlling the Labour Party".

Maxton's only serious opponent in Bridgeton was the sitting MP, Macallum Scott, a radical Liberal social reformer who would eventually, converted by Maxton's oratory, join the Labour Party. Another candidate, more acceptable to the Conservative establishment, had withdrawn to provide the Coalition with a straight fight against Maxton. Such arrangements were common and ceased only after Asquith, the Liberal leader, had openly criticised the Coalition. In Bridgeton, this disagreement brought late into the fight an independent Liberal who campaigned ineffectively and, with only 991 votes, lost her deposit.

In the last days of the campaign Maxton identified rent control and the need for new housing as major issues. Official estimates suggested that Scotland needed 125,000 new houses and the real figure was much more. Maxton claimed that a Coalition victory would lead to the abandonment of rent restriction, a 50% increase in rents, and "a rent war" between tenants and property owners. Leaflets to that effect were met by Conservative leaflets attacking Labour candidates such as Maxton on their war records and Communist leanings. "Blacklegs to the nation", they had "gone behind the backs of the fighting men" and were now accused of having sought to open negotiations with the enemy while war lasted and of proposing a Bolshevist state now that it had finished. "What Bolshevist revolution has done for Russia," one leaflet stated, "it would like to do for you. The millenium would be tickets for everything and officials to look after everything all the time."[7]

The election of December 1918 marked a turning point in British politics. Under the previous electoral system half the adult population had been denied the vote. With most adults now enfranchised, the voice of Labour was heard and 59 Labour MPs went to Westminster. From now on left and right would fight the issues out.

In Scotland, for the first time, the West of Scotland's Irish community swung decisively behind Labour, but that was not enough. Only seven of the new Labour MPs came from Scotland. The decisive breakthrough in the industrial areas was still to come.

For individual Labour leaders in Scotland, there were triumphs and disappointments. Neil Maclean won in Govan, but John Wheatley lost Shettleston by only 74 votes. Several mining constituencies in Hamilton, Fife and South Ayrshire, returned Labour MPs. In Bridgeton, Maxton achieved Labour's biggest vote yet, but with 8,000 he was still 3,000 votes short of victory.

10

Two New Jobs . . . and Marriage

Maxton's considered verdict on the 1918 election result was that it was "very satisfactory considering the wave of jingoism over the land". Though personally unsuccessful as a candidate, he was undismayed. His aims and commitment remained clear. "The Labour Movement had much to do in the industrial field and in the field of politics."[1]

Re-selection as candidate for Bridgeton was assured. In January 1919, the Glasgow ILP election committee had urged branches to take immediate steps to prepare for the next Parliamentary election and within a few months Maxton had secured the support of 16 Glasgow branches re-endorsing him as an ILP-sponsored candidate.

Another General Election was years away. "I'll have to tackle the question of employment seriously," he conceded to Sissie in a letter of 13 January. Having been sacked from his teaching job during the war, he could no longer return to his former profession. His political commitments were greater than ever. By now he was both a member of the National Executive Committee of the Labour Party and a member of its Scottish Advisory Committee. Time constraints alone debarred him from a conventional job.

The chance of paid employment compatible with existing commitments came when the Scottish Council of the ILP decided to increase its organisational staff. Maxton told Sissie, "If they decided to appoint someone I think I'll put in my application." He had some reservations. The job would be "objectionable from the point of view that I'd be away from Glasgow a good deal but it seems to offer the best opportunity of making a decent wage and saving some money".[2] The post was closely suited to his talent and experience. Meanwhile Sissie could carry on teaching "until we can get married which I hope will be very soon".

Maxton was appointed a temporary ILP organiser on £4 a week in January 1919.[3] By July his position was made more permanent and he was working with the Scottish Secretary, Willie Stewart, on a wage of £5 a week. However the party's finances remained precarious, and despite an increase in the affiliation fee from a farthing to a halfpenny per member, Maxton was often unable to draw his full weekly wage.[4]

A lesser election, the 1919 poll for seats on the new Glasgow Education Authority, offered Maxton a minor but useful opportunity. In March he decided to stand, with a view to serving alongside many of the members who had sacked him from his teaching job during the war.

These education elections were the first full test of post-war opinion. Reorganisation had abolished 900 city and parish school boards, replaced them by larger county and city authorities and increased central control. Labour disagreed with that and much else. The ILP manifesto demanded free school meals, free books and clothes, school baths, medical treatment for school children, decent teachers' salaries, democratic schools and an educational curriculum which would sponsor "citizenship".[5]

The elections were held in the cities on 4 April and in the counties a week later. Maxton was one of 21 candidates in Glasgow, and 185 in the country as a whole. Much organisational work went in to securing a Labour foothold in the new authorities. In Glasgow alone 24 meetings were held, 560 posters distributed, 44,000 election addresses and 15,000 handbills delivered.[6] For the candidates and for school board members, the party's Scottish Executive, of which Maxton was a member, organised an education conference.[7]

The mechanics of this election were more complicated than those of 1918. There was a system of proportional representation, which the ILP believed might suit Labour well. Local organisations distinguished between four categories of candidate: Labour nominees, like Maxton, those friendly to the party, those neutral and those hostile. Despite this, Labour hopes were high and much effort was expended in the campaign.

The results were disappointing. The poll was low and Labour did badly. *Forward* blamed "great indifference amongst electors normally Labour". But there was more to it than that. Catholic voters, urged by their clergy, to vote for their own distinctive candidates "polled splendidly and exhibited a magnificent organisation". The Labour vote, having been 31% in Glasgow in the General Election, dropped in the education election to only 10%.[8]

Of the 21 Labour candidates in Glasgow, only six won. Maxton did best of all, winning from the redistribution of second preference votes. *Forward* made sectarian calculations and concluded that the other Labour candidates who had won had depended on third or fourth redistribution Catholic votes. The Catholic Socialist notes in *Forward* recorded that "it is doubtful if in any constituency outside of Shettleston and Bridgeton a Labour member could have won without the Catholic vote and in almost every division the Catholics could have carried another candidate to victory had they preferred to do so instead of presenting the seat to Labour".[9]

Maxton himself believed there to be another reason. Writing later about his experiences on the Glasgow Education Authority, he said that one reason why Labour never succeeded in "making a serious impression" in education elections was the Scots belief that "the only people who were competent to undertake educational affairs were people like ministers, doctors, lawyers, ex-teachers or people who had university education".[10] It may have explained Maxton's success but also Labour's general failure.

Maxton was to be a controversial figure on the committee, at one stage offending the churches by supporting proposals to discontinue the use of the shorter catechism in the schools, and on another making the headlines by cross-examining the Secretary of State over his circular banning the education authorities from providing Poor Law children with school meals and school milk. But for the moment the lessons seemed clear, and emphasised the importance of Maxton's new job. As Herbert Highton, the Glasgow lecturer who had chaired the ILP election campaign, remarked, "the election has surely driven home the need for a constant propaganda among the people of the Labour Party on education, local government and civic politics, but everything depends on the rank and file who must be got to take an interest in their own affairs".

Previous Labour militants like Keir Hardie had failed to win any political office in Scotland, and had to move south to secure election: now Maxton had been voted into his first public office. Although his financial position was no better, his thoughts turned to marriage.

Maxton and Sissie had now been engaged for nearly three years. One reason for the length of their engagement was the Glasgow School Board bar on married women teachers. Maxton's financial position was so insecure that on only Maxton's income the couple could not have made ends meet. There were also difficulties in finding cheap enough accommodation. For much of the last year they had been looking out for a home. In February 1919 they had considered taking on two rooms and a kitchen that were to be vacated by their friend James Houston, but the yearly rent of £22.10s had discouraged them.

Meetings with Sissie were as irregular as ever. Typical letters to her from Maxton were apologies for not turning out at pre-arranged meeting places. "I intended to see you at four o'clock but couldn't manage," Maxton would write. "Will you meet me at 11 o'clock Saturday forenoon? Its too long to wait. PS Usual place."[11]

In the early months of 1919 the strain had become almost too much for Sissie, as Maxton's political activities caused arguments between her and her parents. The George Square Riots, and Maxton's support for the demonstrators, had brought matters to a head. When Sissie wrote of her "spirit being broken" by her parents' criticisms, Maxton responded to say that "I suppose it would be a personal attack on me. It seems to me that affairs in your household have got to a stage where three or four people are trying their hardest to make the life of one miserable because they are angry at 50,000 and can't get at them."[12]

The pattern of irregular meetings was frustrating to them both and once his full time position as ILP organiser was confirmed in the spring, the couple decided to be married. Despite his agnostic beliefs, Maxton succumbed to a church wedding, conducted by their friend Rev John McBain, on 24 July 1919 in the Episcopal Church of Scotland in Glasgow. In his marriage certificate Maxton described himself as "political organiser".[13] Lack of cash ruled out any honeymoon and it was only in the summer of 1920 that the couple managed to secure time away from Glasgow, holidaying on the Continent.

Like most newly-weds, they still had to find somewhere to live. Sissie believed that they encountered special difficulties because of Maxton's notorious left-wing militancy. House proprietors, agents and factors, when they learned their identity, invariably informed them that there was "nothing suitable".

The couple spent the first three months of their married life in cramped furnished rooms in Mount Florida. Conditions were poor and the new Mrs Maxton, who had rheumatic heart disease following an episode of rheumatic fever in childhood, was under considerable strain.

By the autumn of 1919 she had had enough. She set off house-hunting on her own and visited Glasgow Town Council's housing department only to be told by an official that there was a long waiting list of more deserving ex-servicemen. However, as she was leaving, the official dealing with her application casually asked, "Does your husband come from Perthshire by any chance?" Maxton had not and Mrs Maxton said so, but added that his father came from Perthshire. "That's a coincidence," replied the official. "I served my time as a mason with your husband's grandfather."

This happy chance resulted in the Maxtons being offered a new house in Garngad, an estate which Glasgow Corporation had built under the 1919 Housing Act. Garngad, like Bridgeton itself, was one of the poorer districts of Glasgow. The house allocated to the Maxtons was small, containing only three rooms, but it had a garden and it was their first proper home. Only gradually could they begin to afford the necessary furnishings and it was not until May 1920 that the Maxtons were able to afford the £48 required to purchase a full bedroom suite, but for the moment at least Maxton's personal life seemed secure.

11

"Bolshevism"

During 1919, the Conservative leader, Andrew Bonar Law, is said to have attended a Glasgow dinner party where speculation over socialism came to dominate the conversation. Bonar Law was asked what he thought Labour supporters really wanted. Looking round the dining room at the silver and crystal which adorned it, he replied, "Perhaps they just want a little of all this."[1]

Others in the Conservative establishment were less complacent. They feared that Scotland in general and Glasgow in particular had been infected by the "disease" of Bolshevism. The *Glasgow Herald* asked, "Are we to escape from this universal epidemic?"[2] The *Daily Record* diagnosed Bolshevism as the cause of industrial unrest and the *Glasgow Herald* claimed that the January strikes were "the first step towards this squalid terrorism".[3] People who held views like this asked themselves if moderate Labour leaders were the British Kerenskis who would prepare the way for a home-grown Lenin and a full-blooded revolution.

Maxton, the newly appointed Labour organiser, knew of these suspicions and the events which had given rise to them. He watched as the concept of direct action dominated the political stage and threatened to destroy the Parliamentary ambitions of the Labour Party and the ILP. To Maxton and his colleagues, it seemed that the new circumstances demanded a comprehensive review of their political theory and strategy.

Although Glasgow had been for years a home for a variety of political sects advocating the primacy of industrial action and syndicalism, the initiative had, in 1918, been with the legitimacy-minded Independent Labour Party. John Wheatley had spoken for Maxton and the rest of the ILP leadership when early in 1918 he had rejected syndicalism, revolution and direct action. In a series of *Forward* articles he examined some current criticisms of ILP policy and rejected both syndicalism and revolution. "The people of this country may have socialism when they consider it worth their vote."

> I fail to see how whether morally justified or not a popular revolt in present circumstances could be successful in Britain where political power is held by the capitalist ... a bloody revolution is far too slow whether viewed from the standpoint of democracy or expediency. I prefer the ILP policy of relying more upon brains than bullets.[4]

Wheatley castigated the apocalyptic left. Revolution was "the very wildest dream the propagation of which is to benefit capitalism by distracting the minds of our youth ... when the smoke of the revolution had cleared away, the debris facing us would not be that of the capitalist system but the socialist movement". Wheatley had a message for industrial activists too. Political action was more important. He had been "anxious not to minimise the value of industrial action", but his main concern was "to impress upon the workers of this country the tremendous importance of political power".

Electoral defeat created a new situation for political activists. *Forward* remarked early in 1919 that industrial action was "the longest way round and the roughest. They have the right to make their fight in the way that seems best ... having missed the parliamentary opportunity there is nothing else for it meantime than to fight industrially".[5]

Within days of the General Election, the miners, railmen and engineers had threatened strike action for wage increases and better working hours as a remedy for rising unemployment. In Scotland, disputes broke out in Dundee, Aberdeen and Glasgow, and in the mining areas. There was even disaffection amongst soldiers in Stirling. In Glasgow, shop stewards orchestrated demands first for a thirty-hour week and then for a stoppage to secure a forty-hour week. In support, the electricians had voted for a power black-out of Glasgow. Such was the unrest in the coal industry that intimidation and pressure from 30,000 miners prevented their Lanarkshire executive even meeting. By the end of January the shop stewards, the Glasgow Trades Council the Labour Party and the STUC had joined forces to demand a forty-hour week and to support that demand by strike action and demonstrations. The Glasgow strikes had begun on 28 January, and built up to a massive demonstration in George Square on the 31st. There was panic among the police, and local sheriffs read the Riot Act. David Kirkwood, Emanuel Shinwell, Willie Gallacher and other trades union leaders were arrested. The Government, all too aware of the parallel with recent events in Russia and, fearing revolutionary disorder, also panicked and sent troops and tanks to the Clyde.

Maxton was not present in George Square on 31 January 1919, although some accounts suggest he had been invited to be one of the platform speakers. He had been ill and confined to his home. He reported to Sissie that he was "getting fit again" but had only come into the centre of Glasgow because of a mix-up over a meeting in Cumnock where the ILP required a speaker. Maxton agreed to travel to Cumnock. "It may be just as well that I'm going out of town," he wrote to Sissie, "Campbell (Stephen) has just come in and told me there has been a baton charge at the Square and that Gallacher has been arrested."[6] Maxton went to Cumnock, returning later that evening to find Glasgow under military occupation.

The authorities had overreacted. In the Cabinet the Scottish Secretary, Munro, spoke of events similar to "a Bolshevist rising" and sent 2,000 special police constables to Glasgow, but the strikes although they were to last for two weeks more, were never revolutionary in their intentions. Most unions were simply pursuing their traditional industrial demands. There was little coordination among them, either locally or between them and their headquarters in London.

Maxton and the ILP threw themselves into the campaign to support the Glasgow strikers and to fight for the release of those imprisoned. Patrick Dollan edited the *Strike Bulletin*, whose circulation reached 20,000 at the peak of activity, and Maxton became a frequent visitor to the strike areas around Scotland, especially the mining areas.

When the Forty Hours strike was called off in the second week of February, there was little demoralisation, and no sense that the wave of militancy had passed. "We regarded the forty hours strike not as a revolution but as a beginning," recalled Harry McShane. "It was but the first rank and file agitation to be led by socialists after the war." John Maclean however drew nationalist conclusions, blaming London trades union officials for failing to support a militant Scottish movement: "We must emancipate ourselves from the dictatorship of the London juntas by building an organisation which will be under our control and function when we want it to function," he wrote, and by the early months of 1920 had decided to promote a policy for a Scottish Workers' Republic. But Maclean was more of a teacher and thinker then he ever was an organiser, or a revolutionary leader, and he drew little support for his position.

The Glasgow Forty Hours Strike was only one of the events in the industrial unrest of 1919. Miners, railwaymen and even soldiers and sailors awaiting demob were to threaten collective action to rectify their grievances. On May Day 1919 Maxton was one of 150,000 trades unionists marching in Glasgow. In September when the railmen went on strike, and the Government conceded many of their demands, the ILP gave support. In November the ILP called on the Glasgow Trades Council to mount a 24-hour strike against British intervention in Russia, and during 1919 and 1920 the ILP, other socialist organisations, and trades unionists came together in campaigns to defend the Soviet régime in Russia and to oppose the Government's Irish policy.

Amid this ferment, the Labour Movement carried on a furious debate about direct action: where it should be used, if at all, and to what extent it should be taken. For Maxton, Wheatley and the ILP the great problem was how to hold the centre of the stage, still advocating political action but, with no general election in sight, unable to mount any successful attack on the Government. In the presence of so much pressure for industrial and other direct action, a more sophisticated appreciation of the relationship between political and other action was required.

One school of thought, led by the Parliamentary leadership of Clynes and Thomas and supported by Scottish MPs such as William Adamson and William Graham, opposed direct action and sought to confine strike activity to purely industrial and conventional trades union objectives. Parliamentary action had not been encouraging. The first major contingent of Labour MPs were an embarrassment even to their own supporters. The Parliamentary Labour Party came in for much criticism at the 1919 Labour Conference and Maxton subscribed to it. He was later to complain that for the four years from 1918 too much of his time had been taken up in "apologising for its Members in the House".[7]

Commons attendances by the MPs were poor, and their performance, when present, if anything worse. Labour's Scottish Executive, on which Maxton still sat, joined in the chorus of complaints and the still precarious coalition of the young Labour Party was threatened by a split when a special meeting of the Glasgow ILP in August 1919 only narrowly rejected a demand for disaffiliation from the Labour Party.[8]

A second school, within the syndicalist tradition supported direct action as the only course for achieving a fundamental transformation of existing society. This divorce of industrial from Parliamentary and municipal politics ran counter to the traditions of the ILP, although its advocates came from a range of groups: the British Socialist Party, the Socialist Labour Party, the shop stewards' movements and the factions around John Maclean. Maxton favoured workers' control as part of the public ownership of industry, but, like Wheatley, he rejected a workers' state. Support for syndicalism rather than the Bolshevik idea of a vanguard party was the distinguishing feature of the infant British Communist movement. There were differences among syndicalists. Some argued for working within existing unions, some for extending the Triple Alliance of miners, railmen, and iron and steel workers and some for alternative workers' organisations to the existing trades unions. One tract, produced from the Clyde by J.R. Campbell and William Gallacher argued not simply for workers' committees in industry but also for social committees in communities.

The new feature of the 1919 debate was the emergence of a Third Way. It was a course embraced by *Forward*, the ILP, Wheatley, Maxton and trades unionists like Smillie, the President of the Miners' Union. The basis of the Third Way was to continue to stress the importance of Parliamentary action, to urge the Labour Party in Parliament to become more effective, and to emphasise the importance of propaganda and organisation as a means of developing a socialist consciousness. But the hinge of the strategy, and its novelty, was its support for direct action as a means of bringing the existing Government into line with its constitutional responsibilities to the rest of the country. Strikes and industrial pressure could be justified because the Government, elected in a rushed election, had to be pressured to respond to a hostile public opinion. Direct action was not an alternative to Parliament but a complement to it. As the militancy of 1919 and 1920 evaporated, the emphasis on industrial action could and did give way to a renewed emphasis on political organisation. This new flexibility of the approach allowed Labour and the ILP to hold the political centre in the Labour Movement as militancy first increased and then declined as the events of January 1919 showed it to be effective.

The first signs of the Third Way came in an unsigned article, "ILP" in *Forward*, which set out the arguments in favour of "a coming together . . . and agreed programme of action". Capitalism had been strengthened by the war, and though labour was restless, there was a danger that it would dissipate its energies in disconnected strikes. In the pre-war era, industrial and political democracy had been isolated from each other. The failures of trades union leaderships had nurtured the unofficial movement which had "developed the weapon of industrial action", so that the industrial movement could now claim "an independence of and equality with political democracy . . . The control of the workshop by labour is as important as control of Parliament by Labour." Yet the overriding commitment to Parliamentary democracy remained. "Socialism remains the guide . . . Under socialism the control of the workshop must be such as to give the worker a sense of liberty . . . The full doctrine of workshop control and industrial democracy can be stated only when the community of the workshop is set in the wider community."[9] The article offered support for industrial action to secure workers' control in industry, but only in the context of wider commitment to Parliamentary politics, and eventual public ownership of the country's institutions. The editor of *Forward*, Tom Johnston, later summed it up: direct action was "justifiable in a democracy where a minority prevents the majority from exercising its will" and the justification was that "it can compel constitutional action by a governemnt".[10]

By 1920 the whole emphasis would return to Parliamentary and council politics. But in 1919, in the face of widespread industrial activism, Maxton and others supported Johnston's view. He had been, he later said, an advocate of workers' control for years. That control should, as the Glasgow ILP had decided, take the form of management by workers of industries owned by the community. His aim was to unite the political and industrial wings of the Movement. As he concluded in judging an essay competition in July 1919 on the subject, "Can Industrial Action Bring the Socialist Commonwealth? If so how?", "The more reasonable course is a combination of industrial and political action."[11]

12

Splits in the ILP

By 1920 Scotland, with 20,000 members, was the ILP's biggest area. Maxton, as a full time party employee and a much sought-after speaker, was busier than ever. He resigned from the National Executive Committee of the Labour Party and the Scottish Advisory Committee so that he could concentrate on his propaganda work. He remained an active member of the Glasgow Education Authority. There was, however, time amid political commitments to pursue education and Maxton was soon taking classes in Law at Glasgow University. In the academic year from October 1920 he enrolled for a Law degree, taking classes in Political Economy and Forensic Medicine.[1]

A threat to Maxton's new and orderly existence arose when by-elections were called in North Edinburgh and South Edinburgh. Labour organisation in both constituencies was weak, and initially it looked as if one of the leaders of the British Socialist Party, William Paul, would appear as a Labour candidate in North Edinburgh. John Maclean too considered standing, evidently on the invitation of the left-wing local shop stewards' committee. Maxton also was invited and, but for the objections of the Bridgeton party, which was unwilling to release him for the fight, might have been willing to stand. By this time the Edinburgh Labour Party and the Scottish Executive had reviewed the position and, in view of the poor basic organisation, decided it was inadvisable to contest the seat. Nonetheless the local Labour Party fielded a moderate candidate who did not attract the support of the more militant shop stewards' committee. That body took it upon itself to issue its own pro-Soviet manifesto, and as the central organisation had predicted, Labour did badly, polling less than 4,000 votes.[2]

This futile by-election squabble was a side issue. The main questions for the Labour Party were those of political strategy and attitudes towards the Soviet Union. The latter question centred on the Third International, a recent pro-Soviet Lenin creation under direction from Moscow. Its predecessor, the Second International, dated from 1867 and embraced social democratic parties such as the British Labour Party and the ILP. Sections of the Communist International were now set up throughout Europe and parties joining the Comintern had to fulfil the stringent 21 conditions laid down by Lenin. These included accepting a Soviet system of government, a democratic centralist constitution for party life, and Russian domination of the International.

Again Maxton advocated a middle way. He rejected the Second International as too broad, and violently opposed the frankly Communist Third. A Maxton compromise popularised by the ILP as the "Two and a half International" could conceivably bring both sides together.

The Scottish ILP, however, adopted a more extreme position than that of its full-time organiser. The Scottish Conference in 1920 supported affiliation to the Third International and even discussed a clean break with Labour, a motion supporting the latter move receiving 53 votes of the 200 cast.

Patrick Dollan, now a leading Glasgow councillor, remained convinced that the ILP had not decided "to abandon political action in order to concentrate on the methods of Sovietism" but the decision to align with the Soviet International was one of some significance. A report to the Cabinet in 1920 on Revolutionary Organisations concluded that "the great mass of Labour is steadily shifting to the left. One sign is the increased membership of the ILP which in Scotland is becoming more extremist in its propaganda."[3]

Maxton had grave reservations about all this. He saw the decision as "a lazy means of escape from a serious problem". This was especially damaging when Labour was "on the threshold of a great national triumph". Britain in 1920 was not to be compared with Russia in 1917. In one of his strongest statements of the period, he warned suporters: "If we convey the impression to Lenin that the Labour and socialist movement is ready for revolution along Russian lines, we convey a lie."[4] With 158 delegates against this position and only 20 in favour, the conference vote was, for the moment at least, decisive.

There is little doubt that Maxton was a moderating influence in this furious division between pro-Communist and anti-Communist elements in the Scottish socialist movement. His speaking engagements up and down the country, in which he argued for Parliamentary socialism, were closely pursued by propagandists for the pro-Soviet element led by John Maclean. All this was a little confusing for those whose interest in political change was practical rather than theoretical. As John Macarthur, later to join the Communists, recalled of meetings in Fife:

> Each week we would be putting forward propaganda that had no relationship at all to what had been said the week before. We heard for example from the ILP James Maxton and Campbell Stephen from Glasgow and Stewart from Edinburgh. They would tell us that the only hope for the salvation of the working class was through Parliament. Then we had Willie Gallacher ... and one or two others ... who said that parliamentary action was dissipating the energy of the workers and what was required was industrial action by the organised working class along the lines of the shop stewards' movements.[5]

In an article in *Forward* in February 1920 Maxton made a plea for unity. Warring played into the hands of capitalists. He accepted that there must always be diversity of opinion between groups and individuals on the left, but "they must have some organisation that could collect all the different opinions and embrace the different sections". The provision of that organisation was the role of the Labour Party, in which all must share "a revolutionary outlook despite all the palliatives that come their way". All his experience had taught him that the ILP could be in the Labour Party "without losing anything".

He explained that his resignation from the Executive of the Labour Party and from the Scottish Advisory Committee had been on practical rather than ideological grounds. He had to withdraw from both to devote himself "to secure the working class for socialism". He had not, he stressed, left the Labour Party Executive because he thought it too tame but because he wanted "to help develop the socialist consciousness amongst the workers of Scotland". He advocated full working-class control of the workshops under workers' control – and had advocated this for five years. In Maxton's view there was "a revolutionary ferment going on in the minds of large numbers of workers". They needed the Labour Party and the Labour Party needed them because if the Labour Party was not inspired with a socialist conscience it would lose its way. For all concerned it was "the testing time".[6]

Wheatley took the same view as Maxton and wrote about it

in harsher terms in January 1920. He declared that democracy was the essence of public life and socialists had no right to impose socialism unless elected to do so. Election depended on organisation, and the practical demands of organisation must take precedence over propaganda. There was no place for revolution by industrial disruption. "The policy of industrial action only meant either peaceful starvation as a means of winning socialism or reliance on force. It assumed that people who did not want socialism would starve or die for it. If they did not want it there is no need to do either."[7] With such statements as these, the Scottish leadership of the ILP set its face against political campaigns of direct action and pressed increasingly for a commitment to winning power through the ballot box.

With the rest of the leadership Maxton stood aloof from the various movements designed to force the ILP out of the Labour Party and into association with the revolutionary groupings. All moves for unity on the left were to be unsuccessful. In March 1919 a conference of the ILP, BSP and SLP could not agree on a joint platform of action. In June 1919, when agreement was reached to support the Communist line and the dictatorship of the proletariat, the ILP was absent.

There was disagreement too on the proper use of the Labour Party and the Parliamentary process. The Socialist Labour Party opposed Labour and believed Parliament useful only for agitational purposes. When it rejected Labour affiliation its Executive decided to absent itself from future conferences for unity. But the BSP faction held out for joining the Labour Party and making use of Parliament.

There was another unity conference in January 1920 but little in the way of unity resulted. Moves to set up a pro-Soviet and revolutionary party were already in hand but when the Communist Party was formed in July 1920 it made little initial headway in Scotland.

Divisions on the extreme left remained, if anything, greater on the Clyde than in the country as a whole. Following the failure of the Scottish strikes in 1919 John Maclean, Maxton's former teaching colleague, reached the conclusion that Scotland should find salvation as an independent Communist republic. However, he remained outside the British Communist Party, and attempts in the summer of 1920 to form a Scottish Communist Party attracted only a few dissident ILP members and quickly foundered.

By this time the left generally was losing support, and more conventional leaders were reasserting themselves. A rents campaign following the end of rent restrictions imposed during the war allowed the ILP to regain the political initiative. Rent rises now being proposed led Maxton and others to direct their efforts towards stimulating a rents strike. The agitation was, in *Forward's* words, "not merely designed to save a few shillings ... but an indication of Labour's determination that an end must be put to the government policy of passing on the burden of the state to the poor and allowing the rich to escape".[8] It was to be "the initial step towards a great industrial struggle to resist any further attempts to reduce the cost of living".[9]

In May 1920, a Housing Association Conference organised by Scottish Labour decided by 940 votes to 8 on a campaign consisting of a 24-hour strike followed by a rent strike. ILP branches would organise Rent Strike Committees[10] and organise demonstrations in every district, and tenants would be asked to take out No-Rent cards.

A Parliamentary Labour Party committee opposed this, arguing instead for small and staged increases of 5% or 10%. The Scottish Labour Housing Association was critical, complaining of "evident lack of intelligent interest in the housing question displayed by the Parliamentary Labour Party".[11]

A special STUC Congress voted to take action to reduce the cost of living[12] and to support action on rents. John Wheatley issued a pamphlet stating that not a single family will be evicted, and that any attempt to arrest wages could "be answered immediately by a general strike". For the first time in history "the workers are united and success is certain".[13]

In August there was a one-day strike which closed the coalfields and took the trams from the streets of Glasgow. There were demonstrations in both Glasgow and Edinburgh with 100,000 and 10,000 supporters respectively. The sustained rent strike was less of a success. In Fife and in the poorer areas of Glasgow it quickly faltered and by September *Forward* was bravely trying to convince itself that "the rent strike is not dead". Districts like Maxton's Bridgeton had held the key to the success of the strike. "The battle – the great fight – will be in the poorest districts, Bridgeton, Dalmarnock and the Eastern Districts – Garngad, Camlachie, Hutchesontown and Kinning Park," wrote *Forward*.[14] Such brave hopes went unfulfilled, and there was little sign of a sustained response. Once more the emphasis went back to winning elections but even in traditional council politics Labour was losing ground.

The 1920 council results were disappointing. The rents issue still brought out support for Labour, but their identification with the Grundyish cause of prohibition did them much damage. Local plebiscites on whether or not districts should become dry were held on the same day as the election, and one of the reasons that Labour did badly was that "every public house virtually became a hostile committee room". Labour still had a long way to go.

13

Depression

Recession first hit Glasgow and Scotland during 1920 – and during the next few years unemployment continued its inexorable rise. Within a year industrial production had fallen by a quarter and unemployment had risen from 2% to 18%. In work, or out of work, trades unionists were badly hit as money wages also fell by a third over the next four years.

Glasgow depended on its shipyards and its engineering works. The shipbuilding workforce was halved in the years before 1925 and had fallen by 1932 to a tenth of what it had been in the war years. In most of the Clyde's shipyards and engineering works, as the Government reported in 1921, orders could not be secured "even with no margin of profit". Short time was "prevalent" for those in work. "Practically the whole industrial population at present employed are working short time," a Government report concluded, and there were wage cuts all round.

Within 30 miles of the centre of Glasgow were the coalmines of Lanarkshire, Ayrshire and Stirling. There were almost 100,000 mining trades unionists in Scotland in 1918: by 1926, the year of the General Strike, the figure had shrunk to 25,000.

Because of the post-war collapse of these basic industries, unemployment never fell below 10% for a whole period of 20 years and at times one in every three men was out of work. In the 1920s three workers in every five experienced at least one spell of unemployment and, in all, one-third of a million Scots were forced to emigrate.

Unemployment meant automatic poverty. Poor law benefits for the unemployed were never higher than half the average wage, and more normally only a third of average wages in the 1920s. Popular pressure brought some minor victories – the mining communities were given additional help during the 1921 and 1926 strikes – but a Scottish Office study of 1924 found that mothers and children were clinging to their slum communities as their only defence against destitution.

Faced with what they called a picture of "unrelieved blackness", Government officials prepared a secret report on the state of industry and politics in Scotland. A senior civil servant was commissioned to prepare an area-by-area and industry-by-industry survey of the extent of the industrial depression, and the political and social implications of it. Government Ministers spoke publicly of an early return to what they called "normal conditions": behind closed doors the political establishment concluded that the depression was neither temporary nor normal. They warned that "so far as industrial Scotland is concerned the position is one of almost unrelieved blackness ... almost all employers interviewed took a very pessimistic view of the future". The report's conclusions were that the "acute distress" would continue. In 1921 the central belt of Scotland was settling in for a long and bitter depression.

> The present condition of trade is almost uniformly bad and the prospects for the winter are little better. The relief available from private sources and co-operative societies for many workers has been considerable but is now largely exhausted. Distress is widespread and is especially marked throughout the steel and mining areas.[1]

The industrial population, the report recognised, was being pushed to its limits of endurance, and the civil servants warned of political militancy in Glasgow and the mining communities. "As resources diminish and distress becomes more acute these particular areas will have to be carefully watched. In them and principally in Fife, Lanarkshire and Glasgow there are very inflammable elements."

Unemployment, and its social consequences, was to dominate Labour politics for the next two decades. Its immediate impact was to transform an aggressive, class-conscious, militant socialist movement into defensive, rearguard campaigns designed only to protect communities from the worst effects of the dole and the slums.

By 1921 the less extreme views of Maxton, Wheatley and the magazine *Forward* once more enjoyed a majority in the Scottish Independent Labour Party. A syndicalist motion favouring workers' councils was decisively rejected. When attempts were made to amend workers' control for community control of industry in another proposal, Shinwell took up the fight. Railing against "camouflaged Soviet resolutions", he accepted that there were differences of opinion on many major issues, but power had to be won and established by constitutional means.

The conference completed the rout of the far left. A motion favouring the pro-Soviet Third International was lost by 93 votes to 57. *Forward* concluded that the debates raised the question "Is violence necessary to attainment of socialism? Is war, international or civil, the necessary midwife to a cooperative commonwealth?" It also concluded that the ILP's answer was "definitely and clearly no".[2] It was a view with which Maxton agreed wholeheartedly. Later in the year he reflected on the "huge amount of energy" that had been "wasted on fruitless divisions over the Internationals".

Maxton's wife was now expecting their first child, and although she found the people of Garngad "kind" to her, Maxton's frequent propaganda trips left her lonely.[3] Because of this and her ill health he had transferred in 1920 from his job as Scottish ILP organiser to that of Glasgow Organising Secretary, as the position offered more time at home. He was now working closely with Patrick Dollan, one of the main jobs being to prepare for the General Election now expected. Branches were urged to put their finances and membership in good fighting order, but just as the ILP settled to this task, the miners' strike raised once more the question of direct action.

The new unity that was being achieved came under immediate threat. The miners, deserted by the rest of the Triple Alliance, were forced into their industrial dispute with the Government by a policy of denationalisation and wage cutting. To Ramsay MacDonald it was "the nearest approach the country had had to a true and active class war".[4]

In the run up to the strike, *Forward* had urged the miners to concentrate on "getting Labour into power and fixing attention on nationalisation" but once the strike was declared Maxton and the rest of the leadership of the ILP threw themselves into the business of supporting the miners. The ILP's Glasgow Federation issued a statement that "we must prove to the miners by our deeds that we are with them in their stance for humanity", organised local support committees and local collections, and called more than a hundred meetings in support of the miners. Their premises and organisation were largely given over to the miners' cause, and as Organising Secretary Maxton immediately launched an appeal for £1,000, and had raised three-quarters of that sum within only a few weeks.

The miners returned defeated to work and by 1922 their union membership had been reduced by unemployment and various splits to only 66,000. The ILP drew its own conclusions. As *Forward* put it in an article, "The Lessons The Colliers Have Learned", they had failed to undertake the political work necessary for public support. Smillie had been right to say that they had been beaten as far back as the 1918 election. "The colliers are learning the unwisdom of leaving political power to the master class – learning it in sorrow and in anguish."[5] The moral was clear. The first responsibility was to secure the election of a Labour Government.

As the depression deepened, demoralisation and despair spread in Scotland, and the campaigning energies of the Labour Movement were dissipated and its momentum lost. The Scottish local election results of 1921 brought few successes, ILP membership fell by around 7,000 from its peak of 30,000 and Maxton concluded that the ILP, which had, he said, been damaged by internal splits up to 1921, was now falling back because "the heavy hand of unemployment has laid its weight upon the members". As Glasgow Organising Secretary Maxton set about repairing the damage. Good organisation might still prevail against unpromising circumstances, and later in the year, after the election committee recommended that no less than six or more than eight constituencies should be fought, convened a special conference on preparation for the election. As a result each branch was instructed to collect £200 to cover election expenses.

As the ILP organised, so did their opponents. With the Liberals divided and demoralised, the Conservatives mounted a strenuous and sophisticated campaign, building up in Scotland a propaganda machine simply to counter socialism. The Conservatives hired street orators to counter Labour's volunteers and a popular magazine, *People's Politics*, was produced to rival *Forward* and other Labour news sheets. For the young there was a Junior Imperialist League. Where Labour charged subscriptions to finance its campaigns, the Conservatives offered membership free or for a nominal fee. By such tactics the Conservative membership in Glasgow went from 1758 in 1919 to around 18,000 in 1922. They outnumbered ILP membership, even in Bridgeton, where Conservative membership was 1100 and ILP membership only 300.

All that and a newly streamlined local election organisation to counter the Labour advance amounted to one of the most successful political campaigns run by any party in modern times. It sought to emphasise the Conservative tradition of social reform, at the same time exposing socialism's links with Bolshevism and Russia. It did a great deal of harm to the ILP.

Under this pressure, Maxton, as the Glasgow organiser of the ILP, had to campaign harder than ever, but even as he threw himself into his propaganda work tragedy struck. His son James had been born on 16 May 1921 but within a few days had contracted a severe cold. Various complications set in and for weeks his life was at risk. In the family records, a notebook survives containing the doctor's instructions and the mother's notes on feeding the weak child milk, water and sugar at three-hourly, and sometimes hourly, intervals during both day and night. Gradually he recovered but for the next twelve months required to be tended night and day.

The mother, weakened by rheumatic heart disease following rheumatic fever in childhood, paid a terrible price for the twelve months of devoted care the child had needed. Only a few weeks after his complete recovery she became seriously ill. After a desperate two days' struggle for life she died on the last day of August in 1922. She had been, as *Forward* recorded in a moving obituary, a courageous wife and mother, and "her bright comradeship, her glowing simplicity of heart, the directness of her nature and her intense personal charm" would be sorely missed. She was, said *Forward*, "more proud of her man than any of us can ever be".[6]

Maxton was devastated. It was a tragedy from which he never recovered. Some of his friends recalled that he could not bring himself even to smile for many months. Nearly two years later, in a House of Commons debate on infant mortality, he recalled the events surrounding her early death. "I saw only one case and that made a mark on me I shall never lose. I saw a mother struggling with the last ounce of her energy to save an infant life and in saving it she lost her own."[7] The sense of loss and loneliness never left Maxton. Giving a toast at the silver wedding of his colleague, Rosslyn Mitchell, many years later, he was to confess, "if there are any people of whom I am genuinely envious – they are those who are happily married". His marriage, happy though it had been, was shattered after less than three years. For the next thirteen he and his young son struggled on alone.

One other Labour leader had lost his wife at a young age, Ramsay MacDonald. Grief, MacDonald wrote to Maxton, "lashes like a whip", "you must do your best in your own way to trudge through the valley without losing heart". But there was, he said, only one way to recovery: "Get back to work, work, work. It keeps you sane."[8]

Maxton's reply, a few days later, offered a glimpse of the pain he was suffering. He was, he confessed, "feeling rather limp but my mother is a wonderful woman and my friends have been very good". He told MacDonald:

> The party in Glasgow has relieved me from duty for a month ... Some of my friends have a scheme afoot to enable me to have a trip on the Continent. At the moment I don't feel I want to move from here for any purpose but I'll probably go because of their kind invitation and perhaps you could give me some ideas as to where and whom you think worth visiting in Europe just now.[9]

Maxton's brother John stood in briefly as ILP organiser and then joined him and his sister on a European journey. At the end of September Maxton revisited Munich, Strasbourg, Vienna and Prague. He looked for signs of poverty. "Can't tumble to it," he wrote home. "We are driven to the conclusion that the workers of the defeated countries have the advantage over those of the vanquishing."[10] The common people of Bavaria, he wrote, "were having a better time of it than the people of Bridgeton and Camlachie had at Glasgow Fair". But throughout the trip abroad Maxton's thoughts were for the welfare of his young son, Jim, whom he was "wearying to see".

14

Bridgeton for Socialism

The district of Bridgeton was a town within a city – a separate community with its own traditions, its own institutions, and even, some said, its own local language. In the nineteenth century it had been engulfed by Glasgow and transformed from a lace-making village into a centre of both engineering and textiles.

By the 1920s it was one of the poorest parts of Glasgow, a failing industrial community with derelict factories and scarcely any middle class. It consisted of drab tenement buildings punctuated by dance halls, theatres and shops of which it was said that only the florist and the undertaker looked prosperous. Its violence was famous. Two gangs, the Protestant and Unionist Billy Boys and the Catholic Norman Conquerors, who took their name from Norman Street, fought sporadically with each other and the City of Glasgow Police.

In the 1920s its three main centres were the Cross, where the unemployed congregated, the Employment Exchange, where they registered, and the Tuberculosis Dispensary. "Poverty and hardship are biting deep into the people," *Forward* recorded of it in 1921.[1] James MacDougall, Maxton's fellow prisoner of 1916, was later to recall: "Hundreds of woe-begone, dispirited, shabbily clad men hanging around different crosses, trying to preserve some interest in life by eager disputations as to which horse their tanner-double should be put on", and the "poor woman burdened with the impossible task of keeping a family on the dole or on parish relief, whom we see so often hurrying past the brightly lit windows of the bakers shops lest she should be tempted to look at the dainties far beyond the reach within."[2]

To this community James Maxton and the ILP sought to bring new hope. From a disused shop in Canning Street, the ILP organised canvassing, literature sales, social events and weekly Sunday night rallies at the Olympia Theatre. By 1922 the 300-strong branch was regarded by Glasgow's ILP establishment as "now the premier branch in the city of Glasgow both financially and organisationally".

From 1918 onwards Bridgeton was a seat which Labour had hoped to win, but when a General Election was called in November 1922, confidence had diminished considerably. Momentum generated by Labour's successes in the local elections of 1919 and 1920 was dissipated. Early in 1922, elections for the Education Authority had resulted in the loss of almost every seat held. Labour's programme for that election had been straightforward: "free books, and education, school baths, and trades union conditions for teachers". *Forward* had been optimistic. The elections presented "a unique opportunity of rejecting the savage cuts into the rights of our children". But sectarianism obtruded again. Protestants turned out in strength for the first time and, as *Forward* recorded, "the Catholics could not even return their own nominees much less pass on their later preferences to Labour as was the case in 1919".[3] Maxton was one of only a few Scottish candidates who survived.

Over the next six months, Labour's difficulties multiplied. When reporting to the Scottish Conference, the Labour Party's Scottish Executive had to admit that "economic conditions prevailing in industry are affecting the resources of our movement".[4] In Glasgow alone, 20,000 members had lapsed because of "the serious and protracted trade depression, with the huge inroads made by unemployed members upon union funds which will have an effect upon our fighting efficiency". "Destitution, hunger and unemployment," concluded Dollan, "are not aids to the Labour cause."

Maxton, as the Glasgow organiser, spearheaded Labour's attempt at a revival. (Dollan called him "general commandant".) A new campaign, advertised as "The Great Push", attempted to emphasise the importance of political involvement. From August 1922, a score of meetings were organised in Glasgow alone and the party considered it had broken new ground among women. Disappointment followed soon. In September, when the national campaign, "War on Capitalism", was instituted to advocate workers' control, the party had to concede that many of its branches had lapsed.

Maxton summed it all up in an article for *Forward*. The fightback had to be launched because the movement had been brought near to "breaking point" as a result of the retreats forced upon them on the industrial and political fronts since 1918. Unemployment had multiplied their propaganda problems.

Poverty stalks the land naked and unashamed and the morale of the working class has been lowered by the humiliation of their position and by grim want ... The fight has lacked the courage and vigour shown by men sure of victory and despair and hopelessness has taken the edge off the socialist sword. An apathetic half-hearted defensive must be turned into a vigorous and courageous offensive ... to achieve the spirit of the pioneers of thirty years ago.[5]

In October 1922, the Lloyd George Coalition was toppled and the new Conservative Prime Minister, Andrew Bonar Law, prepared to go to the country. The Labour position was serious. Money was tight. When the Glasgow Trades and Labour Council met local Labour constituency parties to discuss finance it could guarantee only fifty shillings to each candidate. As Pat Dollan was to recall, "we had little money in the bank, and only a skeletal organisation ... we borrowed most of the money for deposits and raised the election expenses by collections at meetings."[6]

Local elections too were unpromising. Just ten days before the General Election the Glasgow party recorded only three gains, to be set against two losses. Throughout the rest of the country performance was at best mixed.

In the General Election Maxton was, as Labour candidate in Bridgeton, one of 21 ILP candidates in the 40 Scottish seats in which Labour stood. As candidate, ILP Glasgow organiser and a member of both the Scottish and National Committees of the ILP, Maxton had to fight his own campaign while at the same time coordinating the efforts of others, all on a very tight budget.

For Scottish Conservatives and Liberals the election was a straight fight against socialism. Although in England the Conservatives had broken with the Lloyd George Liberals, Scottish anti-socialist forces could afford no such luxury. By prior arrangement the UK Conservative directive that there be no central pact with the Liberals did not extend to Scotland, and the aim was to ensure the biggest possible anti-Labour vote in each constituency by persuading at least one of the parties to stand down.

Even Andrew Bonar Law, the new Conservative Prime Minister, was concerned about the safety of his own seat in Glasgow. He too sought the maximum unity of anti-socialist parties. "I see no reason whatsoever," he told a Glasgow audience, "why in individual areas the people concerned with the two parties who have worked together up till now should not continue to work

118

together ... I should be very glad personally if something of this kind could be done in Glasgow."

So effective was the pact between the Conservatives and the National Liberals in Scotland that only in two seats, where local personalities clashed, did they fight each other. The *Scotsman* summed it up when it advocated that Liberals and Conservatives "cooperate without qualification or reservation." The alternative was that "revolutionary socialism may gain where reaction loses ... more and more the old issues recede into the background and revolutionary socialism emerges as the vital field of conflict."[7]

The Scottish left fought this united attack on a radical programme. As usual there were a few dissenters. Some MPs urged the party to make as few commitments as possible but at a stormy meeting of the Labour Party and its MPs on 7 October the pressure for a moderate approach was resisted. The final Scottish programme advocated nationalisation of land, coal, water, gas, electricity, rail, tramways and shipping. A capital levy would be imposed on "private fortunes over £5,000." The state had a duty to "provide work or adequate maintenance for every willing worker". Pensions were to be £1 for everyone over 60 and rents were to be set at levels tenants could afford.[8]

In his personal manifesto to the Bridgeton electorate Maxton offered "general support to the policy of the Labour Party", although he personally would "not rest satisfied" until there was "a new system of society". He wrote of his own work in Bridgeton "in rent disputes, in unemployment matters, in questions of workers' wages and the education of the children". Unemployment was the major issue, he said, with housing – and rent cuts – "next in importance". He favoured a capital levy to wipe out the war debt, industrial support for Ireland, and a Scottish Parliament, and more educational spending because "I know that every year many clever and capable boys and girls lose the opportunity of developing their talents to the fullest through the poverty of their parents."[9]

The subsequent campaigning was bitter. The newspapers called the election "the fight against socialism". Tory leaflets sought to identify the left with Russia and with Bolshevism. As the campaigns evolved the Tories identified as key issues Labour's proposals on capital levy, unemployed, and rents. Rents remained controlled under the 1920 Rent Act, but the Act permitted a 15% increase and an additional 25% where the landlord was responsible for repairs. This latter condition applied to much of Glasgow. A case under appeal during the election campaign questioned the legal basis of rent increases. The decision, said Tom Johnston, was "a gift from the gods".[10] Labour exploited the ruling to the full, warning that a Conservative victory would reverse the advantage given to tenants by the court decision.

When the election results were declared, Labour had won one in every three of the votes cast, taking 10 of Glasgow's 15 seats and returning 29 Labour MPs from Scotland. Labour, the Scottish party pronounced, is "now the predominant parliamentary party in Scotland".

Maxton had secured the largest vote in Glasgow. His agent recalled that "I never saw Jimmy worried about the result". Now amidst a flood of congratulatory letters – including one from the ILP National Secretary Francis Johnson – Maxton was on his way to Westminster. "How you will enjoy being an MP," Johnson wrote, "is quite another matter."[11]

What sort of Parliamentary representation could Maxton and the Clydesiders offer? Their views on the slums, the dole queues and the problems of poverty were well known but they had as yet no new programme to solve unemployment. Parliamentary experience was to force them further to the left. Perhaps the views of all of them were best summed up by Maxton when he wrote in 1922:

> We believe that an educated majority is the most active agency for the advancement towards the new order of socialism. The party are not advocates of force as a means to socialism. It believes that the constructive power of intelligence is greater than the destructive power of force. It is evolutionary rather than cataclysmic. It keeps an open mind and is not bound by iron dogma. The party does not predict the complete realisation of its programme tomorrow or next month or next year.[12]

Only later was he to argue a bolder course.

15

The Best Broadcasting Station in the World

A telegram awaited Maxton when he arrived in Westminster on the Monday after his election.

> Thousands of Glasgow children attending school suffering from hunger. Many absent because they have neither boots nor clothes. Only 1500 being fed. Probably 14,000 in need ... We demand immediate withdrawal of circular 51 so that children may be fed by Education Authority. If possible raise matter on King's Speech. Need is urgent.[1]

It had been sent by the Glasgow ILP on the basis of a statement made by Glasgow teachers who were members of the Educational Institute of Scotland, that "owing to the malnutrition of many scholars", they were "not able to carry on the work of education." Although the Glasgow Parish Council was to condemn these reports as exaggerated, the Tory newspaper the *Glasgow Herald* confirmed "a very disquieting state of affairs, substantiating the generalisation made by the Educational Institute Committee".[2]

Mobilising public support for measures to relieve poverty was to be Maxton's main task in his first year as a Member of Parliament. The previous Thursday, the day after the election results were announced, he had attended his last meeting of the Glasgow Education Authority on which he had now served for three years. When asked to refrain from political propaganda at the meeting, Maxton jested that the day of the need for propaganda was now past.

More serious business awaited him in the evening. A meeting of the Glasgow ILP Executive, which accepted his resignation as Organising Secretary, decided that Labour's victory owed little to what their opponents called the "stunt" appeals arising from the Rent Act decision. If there had been no Rent Act, Maxton reported, the party would have still been victorious. Anxious to maintain close links between the local party and the new MPs, they asked him to set up and then act as Secretary of the Glasgow Parliamentary Labour Group and ensure a liaison between Members of Parliament and the Trades and Labour Council and local town councillors.

The Clydeside Brigade travelled to Westminster as a group. With salaries of only £400 a year, and no travelling expenses paid, most travelled down sleeping on the seats and floors of third class compartments. In London, Wheatley was to book a hotel and Maxton, Stephen and Buchanan were to find a flat in Pimlico.

But their first decision was one of their most important: whom to support for the leadership of the Labour Party. MacDonald won it from Clynes by five votes, but the role of Maxton and the Clydeside Group in this election was controversial for long after.

Now that he had been returned to Parliament, MacDonald was an obvious candidate for the post of leader. Born in Lossiemouth, the illegitimate son of a farm servant, he was now, at the age of 56, Labour's most impressive national figure, a writer and polemicist, an imposing platform performer and an orator given to flights of rhetorical flourish about the socialist Utopia yet to be reached. His later speeches were almost devoid of any content ("We shall go on and on and on, and up and up and up. We shall increase productivity by this way and by that way and by the other way", or " The morning belongs to me but the day belongs to the world"). At one point he was to astonish the House of Commons with his observation that there was "no logic in the conduct of human affairs". Even in the early 1920s MacDonald's expositions of socialism tended towards the vacuous and platitudinous with much in the way of apology and handwringing regrets.

Yet in common with the Clydesiders was his Scots upbringing, his wartime pacifism and his long-standing ILP connections. In the post-war years he had deliberately sought to strengthen his links with the Scottish left by writing a regular column for *Forward*, but years of contact with the national leadership had already led Maxton and others to doubt whether MacDonald shared their passion for fighting the class war and their abhorrence of the status quo.

Was it then the Clydesiders who made MacDonald leader? The day after the result was made public, the *Glasgow Herald* reported that "the votes of the Scottish Group were cast practically solidly in favour of MacDonald".[3] Later Patrick Dollan was to recall that at the first meeting of the Parliamentary Labour Party, the Clydesiders had "united to elect Ramsay MacDonald as Leader", although "many of the Clydesiders regretted it afterwards when they learned MacDonald was more of an orator and philosopher than a leader and administrator".[4] Shinwell's account is different. Maxton, Wheatley and "all the others", he recalled, "voted for Clynes", although they had originally favoured Wheatley himself.

> My colleagues in Glasgow, Maxton and the others wanted Wheatley and indeed I remember Maxton saying to me at a meeting in the MacLellan Galleries in Glasgow when we discussed the matter. "Please", he said, "don't vote for MacDonald." I said, "I'm sorry Jim. I believe MacDonald's the best man."[5]

Although 18 of the Scottish MPs had travelled down to Westminster together, it would be a mistake to see the new Scottish, or Clydesider, members as a united, or cohesive, group. From the first, the Clyde Brigade had a central core – Maxton, Wheatley, Buchanan, Stephen and Kirkwood. At first they had the support of Tom Johnston. Invariably they could call on the Govan MP Neil McLean, who had been first elected in 1918. Though a former Chairman of the Glasgow Trades Council and a councillor in Glasgow, Shinwell was, however, "always a lone scout." Since their days on the council he and Wheatley had never been close and Shinwell always resented Wheatley who had passed him over when recommending Glasgow Bailies, one of the few honours that was to elude Shinwell in more than 80 years in politics. As Dollan said, "he and Wheatley could not in any case have ridden tandem in the same cycle championship. They were both individualists. Shinwell teamed in with the Clyde Brigade when it suited him."[6] Muir, Hardie and Stewart were the MacDonald stalwarts and distinct from the core ILP contingent. Many of the mining MPs, like the church elder James Brown from South Ayrshire, went their own way. Not all of them were members of the ILP. It was therefore unlikely that they would share the same enthusiasms or loyalties.

On their arrival in London, the ILP MPs met to discuss their Parliamentary tactics in advance of the first meeting of the Parliamentary Labour Party. Shinwell proposed MacDonald. Maxton had thought it was possible to replace Clynes with Wheatley, had been canvassing Wheatley's name even before the new MPs left Glasgow, and certainly suggested his name at the ILP Group meeting, whether he formally proposed him or not. The feeling of the Group was for MacDonald and if Wheatley was Maxton's first choice, MacDonald was almost certainly his second. Less than ten weeks earlier, when MacDonald had written to console Maxton on the death of his wife, Maxton had written back volunteering his view that MacDonald was "my chief".[7]

Even in these first few days Parliamentary pressures were being brought to bear on the new intake. Ramsay MacDonald was worried about opposition from the trades unions, and in particular the railmen's leader, Jimmy Thomas, and asked his close colleague Patrick Hastings, later Attorney General, and in particular his personal assistant, the Scot John Scanlon, to make approaches to the Scots group on his behalf. Scanlon, who had worked with Maxton on the Clyde during the war, was asked to sound out Maxton, who was considered to have influence on the Scots MPs. "My job was to see Mr Maxton and urge that every Scot turned up in time to vote," Scanlon recalled. "Mr Maxton refused to get excited. Probably his years on the Labour Executive had given him knowledge not vouchsafed to humble rank and filers like myself. He looked at me sorrowfully and said, 'Good God. Has he started that game already. You tell Patrick Hastings we are all voting for MacDonald but we are not playing at any games against Jimmy Thomas.' "[8]

There was no doubt as to the popularity in Glasgow of MacDonald's elevation. The Glasgow ILP telegrammed him assuring him of "undivided support" and the Scottish ILP through William Stewart sent their "congratulations. Glad and proud that the Labour Party have done the right thing at last." Prophetically, Arthur Henderson told Kirkwood it would only be a few years before "you Clyde men" were trying to get him out.

Maxton had sought to make his maiden speech immediately in the King's Speech debate in November. A large number of the Clydesiders had been called. But Maxton had not caught the Speaker's eye, despite what the *Glasgow Herald* political correspondent saw as a "carefully planned" campaign in Parliament by the Clydesiders. Wheatley and Stewart had spoken. So had Shinwell, already independent of the Clydesiders, Hardie, and Muir. But the common theme was unemployment and poverty.

Their speeches were much criticised in the press, the Clydesiders portrayed as an eccentricity in the House of Commons. But Maxton was to defend them in *Forward*. "No better socialist speeches have ever been delivered," he said, "than the maiden contributions of John Wheatley and William Stewart." But while the London press had not mentioned them at all, the Scottish press gave them only a limited coverage. "Already," he wrote, "we have experience of the press boycott."[9]

But Maxton was already making himself known. Within days of his arrival, he was dismissing his Tory opponents as "inept" and "vacuous", and doing so with a side swipe against his predecessors on the Labour benches. He could now, he wrote, assure Labour supporters in the country that "a much smaller part of the time of the party in the country will have to be taken up apologising for its members in the House." The size and quality of the new Labour representation would now ensure that "matters debated in the House shall be the real fundamental social issues." But, he concluded, the election of members of Parliament made it more imperative that there be more socialist orators in the country.

Maxton made his maiden speech on 8 December 1922. He had, he said, now "listened to the utterances of many eminent statesmen and I have observed the conclusions which have been come to and the one great conclusion I have come to as a result is that here, at the outset of a Parliamentary career, I am quite satisfied that I will never become one of the great statesmen. (A member, 'Thank God'.) Yes, I thank God most heartily."

He was to be no respecter of Parliamentary conventions. From the first he played the House as he might have played a half- *— rebel* hostile crowd in his stump-orator days, provoking interjections he could then handle on his own terms. At one point in his maiden speech, referring to a member on the other side of the House he called him by his name to cries of "Order, Order" and then corrected himself to "The Rt Hon Gentleman for North East Camberwell", adding "but it does not matter a damn." Corrected by the Speaker for his language, he apologised. Using this to his advantage he went on:

> We admit frankly that perhaps on the nicer points of good form we have different ideas from Hon members on the other side of the House. Our dialect is somewhat different also, and perhaps our mode of dressing is slightly different. But we think it is the very worst form, the very worst taste, that it shows very bad breeding, to kick a man who is in the gutter, or to withdraw a crust from a starving child. That is the Glasgow idea of conduct and breeding. Is it the idea of Rt Hon Gentlemen and Hon Gentlemen on the other side?

He was presenting himself as he was to do for the rest of the session as the spokesman for Bridgeton, Glasgow and Scotland in Westminster. Maxton's speech was given greater prominence in the national press than the earlier Clydeside contributions, not least because of the threat contained in his closing remarks:

> ... we will not go back to our people and tell them that they are to starve in peace and quietness. We will not do so. It would not be right. I am as great a constitutionalist as any member on that Front Bench or this Front Bench, but there is a point where constitutionalists have to give way before human necessity. I tell the working-class people of the West of Scotland that this House has nothing to give them. They will have to depend upon themselves and win through to security and comfort by their own efforts. I am quite certain that the working class of the West of Scotland will devise ways and means of making themselves felt in that direction.[10]

If the maiden speeches of the Clydesiders had been carefully orchestrated by John Wheatley, so too were the Parliamentary interventions of the next few months. Wheatley was to call Westminster "the best broadcasting station in the world, which could be used for socialist propaganda more effectively than any other agency". The Clydeside group spoke, as Dollan recalled, "irrespective of what the official Labour opposition might be doing and attracted the political limelight to themselves more than any other group during the twelve months duration of the Government".[11]

The Clydeside Parliamentary operations worked according to a plan. As Dollan recalled:

> We kept feeding them with questions from Glasgow. I sent to draft an average of 15 or so a week based on local grievances and those with other queries helped to make the Clyde Brigade formidable bombardiers at Question Time every day in Parliament. They were tireless hecklers and kept every Cabinet Minister in torment while they were in opposition.[12]

And they were well organised. Ramsay MacDonald had given them advice on where to position themselves in the House of Commons so that they were most likely to catch the Speaker's eye. He had also told them to sit in the same place on every occasion to become better known to the Speaker. The result was, as Kirkwood reported to his constituents, that "scarcely a day passed without speeches from the Scotsmen in the Labour Party ... the Speaker invariably selected the Scotsmen".[13]

As Patrick Dollan recorded, "the Clyde Brigade hammered away for almost a year at topics arising from poverty. They alleged that Scotland was the worst housed country in Europe. That its infantile mortality was the worst in any civilised country. They alleged shipbuilding and engineering industries had been ruined by German indemnities." In this Maxton went furthest. "Wheatley and the others made a general case," Dollan wrote, "but James Maxton and George Buchanan chanted the poverty theme of Bridgeton and Gorbals in preference to any other theme. They made Bridgeton and Gorbals more notorious than the Bowery in New York and Whitechapel in London. Correspondents came from America and London to study the so-called black spots of British civilisation. Maxton and Buchanan were quoted as frequently in the American press as they were in Clydeside journals."[14]

The *Glasgow Eastern Standard* devoted columns to reporting not just every speech but every question and intervention from Maxton, Wheatley and Campbell Stephen. As always Maxton seemed to go furthest. In a debate on housing building materials, when he complained that the majority of his constituents lived in one or two-apartment homes, he accused Glasgow landowners of being "a group of robbers." "That is why we came here," he said. "If we could have solved our problems in Glasgow we need never have left it. The local problems can only be tackled if you have sufficient power behind you."[15]

Parliamentary procedures also attracted his wrath. Aneurin Bevan was later to write of the awe that turned to anger at the conventions that dominated Parliament. Maxton was to express the same sentiments. "Round about Westminster, there hung nearly 800 years of hoary tradition. The rule driven into them from the day they arrived there was 'never mind about your political principles. Never mind about the suffering of the people you represent or your ideals, but for God's sake mind the etiquette of the place.' "[16] In these first few months his complaints were many. He was being "handicapped by regulations laid down in the House," he complained; and in the debate on the International Labour Conference he protested at "the shortness of time" for contributions as he denounced the morality of putting young children to work on the farms. Other Parliamentary conventions incurred his wrath also. Even as they had arrived at Westminster,

Maxton and his colleagues resisted embourgeoisement. Lady Astor, for one, had invited Labour Members to a house party to meet London society including the Prince of Wales. Maxton was livid. A round-robin sent by him to the Scottish Group of Labour MPs urged them to refuse to attend all-party social functions. It was unthinkable, said Maxton, to have Labour MPs "accepting salt from those you were bound to attack later on". It was said that only two Scots MPs refused to sign.[17]

Maxton concentrated almost exclusively on education, health and housing conditions in Glasgow and Scotland, although by this time Wheatley was expanding his specific case about rents and housing into a more general case for action on unemployment. Wheatley had already decided that the key to solving the unemployment problem was to expand the purchasing power of working people and he devoted a series of articles in his own newspaper, the *Glasgow Eastern Standard*, to developing this theme.

Wheatley was the general but he saw Maxton as the public leader. As Dollan recalled, "it was when the war against poverty was at its height that Wheatley became rhetorical for once he described Maxton at a meeting in the Gorbals as 'the saviour of the people', and called upon the multitude to follow him". But as Dollan stated, "some of us did not like that description of the Barrhead revolutionary as we thought it might give him a superman complex which we did not think desirable in the socialist movement".[18]

But while the Clydesiders settled down to life in Westminster, Scottish politics was becoming more militant, and the Clydesiders were pressed into more extreme responses to it. The 1923 STUC Conference was told by the Unemployed Workers' Movement that there should be a general strike to gain full maintenance for the unemployed. Although this proposal was referred to the Executive, Congress also passed a motion giving the General Council powers to negotiate with trades unions considering a general strike in any industry and to consider with other unions the possibilities for calling a national general strike.[19]

If anything, the Scottish Labour Party Conference moved further to the left. Patrick Dollan argued for the general rents strike if Parliamentary opposition to rent rises and evictions failed. He believed that the Government were in danger of provoking "a movement much more intense than that which gave rise to the Rent Strike of 1915". Ninety-four supported his proposals, with only four against. The Conference also agreed to hear a Communist spokesman from the Unemployed Workers' Movement who argued that Labour MPs "should fight the battle over jobs in the country rather than in Parliament". Although most delegates abstained the Conference agreed that the Unemployed Workers' Committee should be allowed to affiliate to constituency Labour Parties. Clearly the Conference had moved far towards supporting Communist affiliation to the Labour Party, something which Maxton supported, but Dollan opposed.[20]

Left-wing militancy increased the pressure on the Labour Party to take action on unemployment. Unemployed Committees were asking it to push for higher poor law allowances for the unemployed and suggesting an "all in" Labour Movement conference, and campaign, which would include the Communist Party. The Conference, which excluded the Communists, but had to allow four representatives of the Unemployed Workers' Committee to take part, urged a Government subsidy for parish councils and that parish councils pay the Board of Health minimum[21] It was popular pressure from the unemployed that was forcing the Government's hand and pressuring the Labour Party into action. It was in this atmosphere that Maxton raised the Parliamentary temperature.

16

"Murderers"

"The biggest rumpus Parliament had seen since the days of the Irish Parnellites." So Patrick Dollan described it, though as a Glaswegian and a socialist he might have been prone to exaggerate. Whatever its historical perspective, Maxton's suspension from the House on 27 June was the result not of impulse but of an act calculated to draw maximum attention to the grossly deprived Scottish social conditions the Clydesiders had come to Westminster to proclaim to the world.

On the night of his departure from Glasgow, after the election, Maxton had declared in the meeting at the Metropole Theatre his determination to bring Scottish social and economic conditions to the forefront of public consciousness. In his maiden speech he had explained both his commitment to that cause and his limited respect for restraining Parliamentary conventions. Around that time, in an article in *Forward*, he complained that the Westminster activities of the Clydesiders were receiving less than their fair share of newspaper publicity. A more dramatic approach, it seemed, might therefore be required.

As both Maxton and Wheatley had told the House, there had been few occasions on which such Scottish grievances could have been raised. Now, as he admitted to the House, his branding of the Tories as "murderers" was a charge "made quite deliberately, with no intention of being withdrawn but with a complete belief in its truth".

To most of the Clydeside contingent disruptive tactics were a routine part of political life. As Dollan recalled, "most of our MPs had learned obstructionist tactics when they were a minority in the Town Council and they applied the George Square strategy with success in Westminster".[1] In Westminster the issues they took up were slums, unemployment and the ever-worsening poverty on the Clyde, but the occasion selected by Maxton for his most dramatic effort was Circular 51, a directive from central government on the feeding of children by education authorities.

According to Maxton the circular deprived 10,000 schoolchildren of free meals. In the course of the debate on Scottish estimates he chose to attack Government economies in milk supplied under child welfare schemes and other cuts in the Health Service.

Circular 51 had been a source of grievance for nearly a year. Up until 1921 education authorities had used their powers under the 1908 Act to provide food, and in some cases clothing, to children in need. Now a ruling by the Scottish law officers had restricted the help they could give. Able-bodied, unemployed families, and all others on parish council relief, were now excluded from any help for "necessitous schoolchildren". Families with incomes below 37s 4d could receive help with meals and clothes if their breadwinner was in work. Families on only 30 shillings might, however, be denied help because their breadwinner was unemployed. As a result, all that an education authority could now do for the children of the unemployed was to offer meals for a standard charge of 2s 6d a week, deducted from the family's parish council relief. Few families could afford this and only 182 in Glasgow were being given school meals under this procedure. The overall effect of the ruling was to reduce the numbers of free school meals from 13,500 in 1921 to 1,500 more than a year later and a wide range of public opinion opposed the Government's measure.

In September 1921 the Conservative-controlled *Glasgow Herald* had written of "the most severe social conditions which the present generation of the community has ever suffered". The *Herald* returned to the theme in November 1922 after the Glasgow Educational Institute of Scotland had issued a statement saying that "owing to the malnutrition of many scholars", teachers were "not able to carry on the work of education".

The *Glasgow Herald* had conducted its own investigation. Some teachers were offering help at their own expense. Others were buying in food from restaurants. There were reports of general lethargy amongst pupils and even infants falling asleep. An eight-year-old Glasgow girl, suffering from an inflammation of the eye and suspected tuberculosis, was denied free school meals because her father, who was unemployed, received 38s 6d a week for his six children. A 13-year-old boy whose health was in a "delicate" condition and his sister of five who had no woollen underclothing for the winter months were also denied free meals. These facts, the *Herald* argued, "call for immediate consideration and it would seem for ameliorative measures of some description".[2]

As a former teacher and elected member of the Glasgow

Education Authority, Maxton had been closely involved in this campaign for action. The new Government decison went even further than that. Infants were to be denied free milk and children with infectious diseases were ordered to be kept at home rather than be put in hospital. It was upon these new restrictions that Maxton seized.

The Report of the Scottish Board of Health had only just been published. Policy, said the report, had been shaped "mainly by two factors – the need for economy and the distress among large sections of the population". It admitted that "the pull of these two factors in opposite directions has made the year a difficult one". A policy of rigorous economy had been pursued, and any developments that were "not urgently necessary" had veen vetoed. Expenditure cuts had been made where "restriction was possible without danger to the public health". The report concluded:

> The ban on development has meant more than appears on the surface for several of the health services – notably the school health service and maternity and child welfare – were practically new services that were only in the course of development when the need for economy arrested them.[3]

It was this report and the Government's Scottish Health estimates that the House was debating in committee as a supply day. Maxton began by citing the evidence of the Annual Report. It cost more than 58 shillings to maintain a family of four children in a poorhouse, but wages in Glasgow were as low as 32 shillings a week. 12,472 cases of tuberculosis had been noted in the last year. Fresh air and sunlight were important to the prevention of tuberculosis, as were good nutritious wholesome foods. Good housing was vital, but the report admitted 100,000 houses were required in Scotland. Previous speakers had urged that child welfare should be taken out of politics but the report was committed to "a policy of rigorous economy because we must save money". Yet the death rate, particularly the infant death rate, was much higher in Scotland than elsewhere.

Talking of the effect of poverty on child health, he referred to his wife and child:

> I only saw one case. I saw a mother struggling with the last ounce of energy to save an infant life and in saving it she lost her

own. I am not interested in the statistics of this. I am interested in the tens of thousands of fathers and mothers tonight watching over the cots of little babies wondering whether they are going to live or die. If I could strike the public conscience to see that this is absolutely wrong and unjustifiable in a Christian nation I should think I had rendered some service to my country.

A circular of March 1922, he said, had withdrawn milk from the list of entitlements to mothers and infants. The same circular instructed local authorities not to admit to hospital care babies suffering from whooping cough and measles.

In the interests of economy they condemned hundreds of children to death and I call it murder. I call the men who walked into the lobby in support of that policy murderers. They have blood on their hands – the blood of infants. It is a fearful thing for any man to have on his soul a cold, callous, deliberate crime in order to save money. We are prepared to destroy children in the great interests of dividends. We put children out in front of the fighting line.

But it was then that the storm broke. In succession, Maxton was asked to withdraw by Sir Frederick Banbury, the Tory Member for the City of London, by Ramsay MacDonald, by the Deputy Speaker and by the Financial Secretary to the Treasury, Joynson Hicks. When Sir Frederick Banbury asked him to give way and withdraw the accusation that Conservatives were "murderers", Maxton refused, suggesting that he was "one of the worst in the House" and when he again demanded that the word "murderer" be withdrawn, Maxton, amid calls from supporters of "It is true" and "He has proved it", asked him "to supply me with a word that described his action, other than that of murder".

The drama over deprivation, life and death was gradually reduced to a Commons procedural wrangle. The Deputy Speaker asked him to substitute "no better than a murderer" but Maxton stood his ground, saying that "I can never withdraw. I did it deliberately ... anything, any phrase that I could substitute to bring the idea before the House would be equally objectionable ... I do not mean to withdraw. I am prepared to stand the racket. I absolutely decline to withdraw. The whole business is a matter of historical knowledge."

From the Labour Front Bench, Ramsay MacDonald asked Maxton to withdraw his "direct personal charge", suggesting that distinction might be drawn between the motives behind the legislation, which were not "murder", and the effect of the legislation which may have been, and asked the Deputy Speaker to accept that "murder" was the result of the action taken.

John Wheatley then took up Maxton's case, arguing that the figures quoted proved that the starvation of children had caused murder. He too made a blunt charge.

> He said that was murder and the people who supported it were murderers. I repeat the statement and I will not withdraw. I say the Rt Hon Baronet the Member for the City of London sitting on that bench is one of the murderers.

In support of Wheatley, Duncan Graham, the Member for Hamilton, told the Deputy Speaker that he would "have to face the question of turning all of us out because we all hold the same opinions on this particular matter".

With unusual finesse, Joynson Hicks then asked Maxton to alter his accusation from a personal one of murder against Sir Frederick Banbury to a more general one against the Conservative Party. This only encouraged Wheatley to repeat his allegation and to assure the Tories that they would have to "bring back the lives of the Scottish infants" before he would withdraw.

Maxton and Wheatley were asked to withdraw but, as the minutes record, "refused to do so without force". The matter went to a vote and their expulsion was carried by 258 votes to 70.

No Labour Member voted for their suspension but many abstained. Tom Johnston reflected the state of mind of the Scots when he later wrote that "I would rather have died that evening than refrain from showing by every means in my power my sympathy and agreement with Maxton". Later in the debate, Campbell Stephen and George Buchanan, having made similar charges, were suspended too.

The Times recorded that MacDonald sat "white with anger at the folly of his own followers".[4] Walter Elliot, the Parliamentary Under Secretary of Health for Scotland, who had been at Glasgow University at the same time as Maxton, replied to the debate and referred to Maxton as a "most sincere man, most sympathetic and in many ways one of the finest characters in the House".

Whatever the ensuing Parliamentary civilities, the suspension of the four was the signal for a nationwide campaign to emphasise the squalor of conditions in Glasgow. From the starting point of child welfare, it broadened to include conditions in the slums generally and also the problem of unemployment.

A few Tories pressed for personal retribution on the four, suggesting their pay should be withdrawn. Maxton was unmoved, saying that it would simply have hardened their attitudes. They were after all the leaders of a movement in which the rank and file worked every day with the threat of their wages being withdrawn hanging over them.

Back in Scotland, John Maclean scorned what he termed these Parliamentary antics, claiming that Maxton "shouted murder because he knew that the ILP and pink Labour Party in general were losing ground in Scotland". The action had been "dramatic and extreme in order to retain their hold".[5] But the Clydesiders saw the cuts in children's provision as the signal for a national campaign against poverty. Speaking in the Glasgow City Halls, Maxton said that his protest was not simply against cuts in meals and milk but also against "the abandonment of housing reform, the sabotage of educational progress and the scuttling of all measures of social reform". He could not "submit quietly to any Parliament which considered the saving of money as of greater importance than the saving of life".[6]

There is some evidence that Maxton and Wheatley, initially at least, felt defensive about their suspensions and the public reaction of their constituents to them. They did not expect to be widely criticised. Maxton responded to hostile press reporting, writing in the *Glasgow Eastern Standard* to set the record straight. It was one of his "greatest regrets" that the Scottish press had "rushed in without having taken trouble to read our speeches". Previously he had "much greater respect for the Glasgow press than the London and English press".

Many were more concerned about the image of Glasgow than the dire social conditions there. Accused of selling Glasgow and Scotland short, Maxton pointed out that theirs was a reasoned case and that there were more rickety children in Glasgow than anywhere else. On his suspension he held that the Tories would regret voting for it, just as those who had voted for his dismissal as a teacher had subsequently recognised that they had made a mistake.

Going over the issues again, Maxton admitted that the causes of infant mortality were complex, but his basic charge still stuck. "A lot of factors go to cause infant mortality. I know that housing is a cause, that poverty is a cause, that the anxiety of mothers is a cause ... but child life can be saved and when the community withdraws that concerted child care, life is destroyed." That was why the policy was "murderous".

The whole argument sprang from his experience and observations as a teacher. He had come into the socialist movement because he was a teacher. "My whole soul revolted against the folly of a system which prescribes a school curriculum of physical education to a class of children such as I had seen in Calton in which 20 of the 60 pupils had twisted legs – children who were so maimed before they reached school age."[7] Maxton concluded that "I said what I said in the hope that the hearts of the people would be touched so that they may tackle this problem of the unnecessary loss of life."[8]

The Parliamentary outburst was, however, seen by the Labour leadership as a clear challenge to MacDonald's authority as party leader. One of MacDonald's confidantes, the Edinburgh MP William Graham, wrote to his brother that "MacDonald intends I think to deal firmly with them this time, although there was a considerable amount of provocation in Maxton's case. The others were merely advertisement men."[9] The newspapers had a field day, exploiting Labour's divisions to the full. The *Sunday Mail* had a cartoon of Ramsay MacDonald lecturing Maxton, Wheatley, Stephen and Kirkwood: "Revolutions, strikes and riots are all very well," MacDonald was portrayed as telling them. "But rudeness I will not tolerate."[10] The press built up the suspension into a major split in the Labour ranks. It was a "duel between MacDonald and the Reds", one paper reported. Another said that "sooner or later there will be a split in the Labour Party". The Scottish Whip Neil McLean had resigned, it was wrongly reported, because of the split. Such was the challenge to his position, the *Daily Telegraph* reported, that even Ramsay MacDonald was considering resigning.

At the beginning of July, while the four were suspended from the House, a special Parliamentary Party meeting was held at Caxton Hall to consider the matter. MacDonald made a fifteen-minute speech, urging better teamwork and pointing out that if the Labour Party damaged the Parliamentary machine while it was in opposition, it would pay for its folly when it came to power. As the *Daily Sketch* reported, MacDonald did not directly condemn the Clydesider MPs but said that their suspensions were "prejudicial rather than helpful" to the task of attaining a Labour majority.[11]

In the event, the formal decision of the Parliamentary Party was to condemn the "fearful infant mortality" and to urge the Government to re-establish child welfare work to at least its 1920 standards.

But the resolve of the Clydesiders hardened. They made their case the basis of a national campaign, with Maxton telling an ILP meeting in London that "compared with the lives of little children Parliamentary etiquette means nothing to me".[12] Wheatley rushed to his defence, saying that "at best Maxton was the greatest orator in Parliament".[13]

Maxton and his friends remained steadfastly against apologising. *New Leader*, 6 July 1923, contains an article signed by all four, explaining their case in full, and ending with the words, "We now want to know from whom apologies are due." In that article, "Infant Mortality: The Scottish Case", signed by Maxton, Wheatley, Stephen and Buchanan, the basis of their case was set out. Seventy thousand infants under a year had died in Britain, 11,600 of them in Scotland. Scotland's death rate was nine more for every thousand babies born. It was also "a death rate three times as high where workers live in Glasgow than in those wards where conditions were good". The Scottish death rate figures showed that in Scotland 2,760 infants had died who would have survived if the English figures had been achieved. During the war the Board of Health had prompted local authorities to be "generous" in their provision for infants when "there was a threatened shortage of human beings", but as they wrote, "In 1921 when the country had been glutted with foods and there was a surplus of workers, the Ministry of Health lost its enthusiasm. The cry changed from Save the Babies to Save the Money."[14]

Embarrassed by the glare of publicity that now surrounded the Clydesiders, MacDonald sought to ease the path of their return to Parliament. He consulted Baldwin, and then the Speaker and wrote to Maxton on 20 July saying "press as hard as I could I could not persuade him to have the suspension removed during this part of the session. He intends to move the resolution at the beginning of the autumn session and there stands the matter for the moment. I am still pressing him to take another view." A postscript after the typed letter added "while dictating this I have had another interview with the Speaker and have got him to move a little".[15]

The issue was whether the Clydesiders would apologise for their intemperate language, which Maxton and the others refused to do, and whether Parliament would follow the precedent of an Ulster Unionist MP who had been suspended for three weeks for referring to "the disgraceful trickery" of a Treasury Minister. In behind-the-scenes negotiations, MacDonald was to be successful, and by the end of July it had been agreed privately to readmit the suspended MPs.

By the subtle manipulation of events, the Clydesiders converted their re-entry to Parliament, which might have been an anti-climax, into a triumphal return. Wheatley had become aware that their suspension was to be withdrawn. They were having tea with ILP colleague Fenner Brockway in a London café when Wheatley came up with the idea of demanding readmission, so that their pressure would be seen to have been effective. This was exactly what happened.

Maxton wrote a well-publicised letter to the Speaker complaining about his bias against the Labour Party. He said that a Unionist MP, accused of a similar breach of Parliamentary procedure, had been readmitted after three weeks. The letter stated that Maxton and his colleagues would present themselves at Westminster on the following Monday asking to be readmitted. On Monday 30 July, after four weeks' suspension, they attempted to force their way into Parliament but were prevented by the police. On the Tuesday as they continued their demonstration an embarrassed Stanley Baldwin managed to secure an end to the ban. It all amounted to a highly effective publicity stunt.

In the House, Baldwin explained that the longest suspension of modern times had been that of the socialist Victor Grayson, who had been expelled for nine weeks. Half that time seemed "reasonable". Only Sir Frederick Banbury objected, saying that failure to apologise should mean recontinuation of suspension until the end of the session. The four were readmitted.

The manipulation of events made the Labour leadership even more furious. Earlier MacDonald had written to Maxton complaining about his "unfriendly" attitude and his refusal to meet with him in an effort to remove the suspension.[16] Now MacDonald wrote an angry letter to Maxton in which he complained that Maxton's letter to the Speaker, demanding his return, had been sent one day after arrangements for his reinstatement had been agreed. The result had been to make the Labour Front Bench look "as foolish and appear to be as weak as possible".

When Maxton replied defending his action, and emphasised there had been no intention to embarrass, MacDonald was unimpressed:

Statements are appearing which indicate that the Party here and myself have been lax in getting you back; that the only reason you were not back was that you would not apologise; that there is some great difference between men, either righteously indignant or moved by something that is quite unworthy of being described in these words, and those of us who are not suspended and who can conduct debates without a loss of temper.

MacDonald concluded

A limit has to be observed and I draw it at the point when I am convinced that individuality begins to express itself as a separate entity regardless of the obligations of comradeship and acting to all intents and purposes as an independent, self-satisfied centre of agitation. I cannot shut my eyes to what is going on.

The letters showed how much relationships between MacDonald and the Clydesiders had already deteriorated. He complained of a movement to undermine his leadership while saying to Maxton that he believed he was "the last man in the party to aid either knowingly or cunningly any such disruptive movement as I have described". But he issued a threat: "If this sort of thing goes on, I cannot remain quiet in the interests of the movement ... I can assure you I have no grievance against you I am only profoundly sorry that you give me so little chance of working with you and of enabling you to take the place here which you could quite easily occupy if you like."[17]

If this was an offer of a Front Bench job, Maxton was uninterested. Instead the Clydesiders claimed their outburst had brought Government action. They had wanted to make Scotland "a land in which it is safe to be born".[18] Their campaign had, they said, led to "more generous treatment". Child welfare was now being discussed in every town in Britain.[19] But it was only the first of many disagreements with Ramsay MacDonald. MacDonald disapproved of disruptive tactics in Labour's Parliamentary strategy. Even before the most publicised outburst, he had confided to his diary:

My difficulty is to interpret myself to three or four good fellows who have no sense of Parliamentary methods and who expect Front Benchers to live in a perpetual state of fighting exultation and be noisy. I go on exactly opposite lines.[20]

Maxton and his friends were "the three or four good fellows".

17

Taking the Slums into Parliament

"The British House of Commons now know there is such a place as Scotland," Maxton told an Edinburgh rally in November 1923.[1] But what had been achieved of that first session in Parliament? "Clydeside was at last put on the political map and it was not without some reason that it was sometimes described in the UK as the Moscow of Britain," Dollan wrote, "but the Clyde Brigade were evolutionary rather that revolutionary and, after they became known to other MPs, Westminster ceased to shiver with fear."[2]

Maxton and Wheatley worked as a team. Wheatley, according to Dollan, was "Director General of Westminster operations". Wheatley "planned most of the Clydeside attacks on the Government. He maintained that Clydeside was the most hunger stricken and slum-ridden area in Europe."

> Even Stanley Baldwin and Neville Chamberlain used to shudder when Gorbals was mentioned although if both had cared to walk arm in arm along Crown Street and Rutherglen Road nobody would have interfered with them except to ask them into a pub for a glass of beer.[3]

The Clydeside MPs had taken the slums and the dole queues into Westminster, and right to the doorstep of 10 Downing Street. For the remainder of the Parliamentary session Maxton concentrated on housing, health and education, while Wheatley broadened his attack to the problem of unemployment.

There was plenty to attack. One-quarter of a million Scots were on parish relief. Up to a million were in bad housing. 12,000 were emigrating from Scotland every month. Fifteen in every 1,000 died early. One hundred children in every 1,000 did not live out their first year, and one mother in 40 either died in childbirth or was invalided for life.[4]

William Bolitho, a journalist working for the *New Outlook* magazine, was one who visited Glasgow at this time. His book, emotively entitled *Cancer of Empire*, was designed to alert English public opinion to the fact of deprivation and the threat of revolution. Social deprivation had made Glasgow into "a boiler overheated with no safety valve". Its citizens endured a "misery which no passing calamity – war or earthquakes – could surpass". Conditions for the tenement dwellers of the cramped East End were worse "than any encampment of refugees, for they are starved of light, space and air".

Any sensible attempt to avoid overcrowding, and the health risks that imposed, would set the barest minimum standard of living space at 400 cubic feet. In New York, Bolitho wrote, the minimum standard was 600 cubic feet. In Glasgow, however, there were 600,000 who lived in poor accommodation and 300,000 who did not even enjoy that barest minimum of living space. Only the better off of the most skilled workers in the city could afford the price of the best working-class accommodation. A labourer who earned no more than 38 shillings a week could not afford the £40 or so rent demanded for the better housing in the city. Glasgow needed £60 million spent on its housing, and the political choice was either "subsidy or revolution . . . The Red Clyde will remain the focus of English politics until it has been cured or definitely appeased."[5]

In an article in the *Glasgow Eastern Standard*, "The Children Suffer", Maxton outlined his case for proper care and medical attention and used international parallels to show that Scotland could produce in a generation a race that could "remake the world". He argued his case for a new educational policy, calling for the raising of the school leaving age, and the lowering of class sizes, with the curriculum to emphasise "social and international service".[6]

The interests of the Clydesiders were not exclusively Scottish and during 1923 they further broadened their attacks on the Government. In January the Germans had defaulted on their war reparations and the French had occupied the Ruhr. Maxton's interest in the Ruhr reflected a concern widely held within the Labour Movement, and during the Easter of 1923 Maxton, Wheatley, Stephen and Kirkwood joined a deputation of MPs who visited the French-occupied Ruhr. They had repeatedly expressed the view that the punitive terms of the Versailles Peace Treaty with Germany harmed both international trade and the prospects of peace. Maxton returned from his visit to complain that the occupation was "a French capitalist move" and in a pamphlet the

141

Clydesiders called for the internationalisation of the Ruhr and for the profits from the coal industry there to be used to pay off the German war debt.

On the prompting of the socialist writer and lecturer R.H. Tawney, Susan Lawrence, an ILP Executive member, wrote to Maxton in June urging him to lead a campaign for justice for the German workers. Writing to him about the dangers of "a complete breakdown of society" in Germany, she called on Maxton to help secure changes in the German reparation terms and to ensure German membership of the United Nations.[7] Once again the Clydeside MPs spoke out in favour of a new departure in foreign policy, but could gain neither the support of MacDonald nor the backing of the Scottish or British ILP.

More importantly, John Wheatley was now beginning to outline a plan to tackle unemployment. Wheatley struck on the argument that the manipulation of purchasing power was the key to economic growth. It would pay the Government, he argued, to provide rent-free houses to raise demand in the economy. A lost producer, on the dole, was also a lost consumer in an economy which depended on its own purchasing power.

Maxton took up the case, claiming unemployment could be reduced with speed. By its emphasis on exports and its policy of waiting for the world economy to improve, the Government, he claimed, had started "the wrong way round". The issue was not supply, the state of industry, but demand, the state of the consumer. More clothes, better houses, better furnishing and fittings would create work. The dole should be doubled and "shopkeepers would know the difference in a week".[8]

According to the Clydesiders, the debate now raging within Government circles between free trade and protection was a diversion from that central issue. Talk of there being free trade and the suggestions of Government-sponsored protection in import tariffs were simply "lies". Free trade no longer existed because the trusts and cartels dominated the markets. Planned control of trade, rather than protectionism, was the answer.[9]

Such policy intitiatives, which followed from their campaign over children's health, brought further conflict with MacDonald who wrote to Clifford Allen of the ILP in September, saying, "I am just a little concerned about some of the things some of our people are saying. A recent speech by Maxton in Glasgow is really terrible ... it is fearful nonsense. And Maxton is such a good fellow."[10] Tension between MacDonald and Maxton was obvious when, in October, to MacDonald's chagrin, Maxton received a warm ovation at the 1923 Labour Party Conference even before he spoke. His "murderers" speech and subsequent poverty campaign had made him a national party hero, but even as Maxton moved towards the rostrum a jealous MacDonald sought to restrain him from speaking. "His path was barred by Mr MacDonald," John Scanlon, an onlooker, recalled. "Remembering his dignity, Mr MacDonald could not forcibly push him back and so he contented himself by jabbing his elbows into Mr Maxton's ribs just as one schoolboy would jab another in the hope that the jab would escape the eye of the school teacher."[11] MacDonald could not, however, complain when Maxton made a plea for loyalty to the leadership and for party unity.

But how far had the Clydesiders already gone in formulating an alternative to the policies the Labour leadership now pursued? Patrick Dollan believed that the setting of a new socialist agenda began with the MPs' international policy on German war debts, and their support for "no indemnities, no reparations and no territorial annexations". In his unpublished autobiography Dollan wrote:

> Everybody can now see it was a wise tactic but most politicians and electors thought it was a daft exercise in 1922. It was then that Wheatley elaborated the economic formula of "hunger in the midst of plenty" and every time he got his chance expounded the theory in and out of Parliament that Clydeside was suffering from overproduction and underconsumption.[12]

One of the first results of the election victories of 1922 had been a flood of new Labour and ILP members in Scotland. The number of Scottish ILP branches increased from 150 to 200 during the year, with Glasgow recording a threefold increase in its membership. In Glasgow, a series of Sunday evening cinema and theatre meetings were called in which the new MPs spoke to enthusiastic crowds. As Dollan recorded, "these were attended by record audiences who contributed liberally to the funds so that we ended the campaign with a large surplus which was banked and came in handy for the general election which followed ten months later".[13]

Propagandist classes were organised. Maxton had warned of the need for more street corner agitation. He had written in *Forward* that "in recent years new propagandists have not developed so spontaneously as at an earlier stage in the movement's history", and had offered two to three nights in January to run a speakers' course.[14]

Scottish Labour organisation had been little improved since the doubts over its effectiveness had been expressed in 1922. Some seats which had not been contested in 1922 – more than 30 – were assessed for the first time. But while progress was made, Labour's Scottish Executive had to concede that "some of these local Labour Parties were not very active at election times".[15] In fact of 66 parties only 15 were affiliated to the 1923 Scottish Labour Conference.

The propaganda work, which Maxton had urged be stepped up, had continued throughout 1923. May Day celebrations in Scotland had been "disappointing in many places. Processions are no longer attractive and meetings such as we had in Glasgow have lost their appeal."[16] But the Scottish Party received a boost from the controversies surrounding the suspensions of the Clydesiders. Maxton and the other Clydeside MPs set summer aside for successful, and enthusiastically received, campaigning in what they called "the backward areas". During the summer months, he records, he "had travelled Scotland from north to south". In Stornoway for example a branch of 70 members was formed after Maxton visited the area.[17] *Forward* argued after the visit that "most if not all of the Highland constituenceies can be won".[18]

In the event Labour fielded only five additional candidates in Scotland in 1923 – a lower proportion of candidatures than in England or Wales. Maxton was to spend only £113 in securing his election in Bridgeton, paying out only £1 for every £4 spent by Labour in the average Scottish constituency.

By the autumn of 1923 it became clear that another election could not be far away. The issue Baldwin selected was his Government's conversion to the policies of protection. Labour saw the conflict between protection and free trade as spurious, arguing the real issue was whether capitalism could survive and, if not, how socialism could replace it. As Maxton pointed out, "The Labour Party would not fight on free trade against protection but on socialism against both of them. They would fight the Government on their record on the condition of Scotland today under capitalism."[19]

The Conservatives had made a reassessment of their position after the election. One tactical lesson was that seats had been lost "due to the moderate vote being divided between two or three candidates". But there were four more general reasons for the decline in votes all round: unemployment, reduced wages, the existing housing conditions and "the confident expectations raised by the Labour Party among the working-class tenants that if they

The Clyde Group: Kirkwood, Buchanan, Stephen, Maxton, Mrs Maxton and John McGovern. (Photo courtesy of Scottish Daily Record.)

Maxton with a group of well-wishers.
(Photo courtesy of Scottish Daily Record.)

Sissie Maxton, his first wife.

Maxton and his second wife, Madeleine Glasier.

Maxton, his son Jim and Campbell Stephen, Largs, summer 1928. Jim was then seven.
(*Photo from Maxton Collection, Mitchell Library, Glasgow.*)

Maxton at ILP summer school.
(*Photo from Maxton Collection, Mitchell Library, Glasgow.*)

James Maxton MA: Maxton graduates from Glasgow University, summer 1909.
(Photo from Maxton Collection, Mitchell Library, Glasgow.)

Maxton and son boating on the Thames
(Photo from Maxton Collection, Mitchell Library, Glasgow.)

voted Labour they would get back a sum equivalent to a year's rent of their houses". Conservatives wanted to believe that it was "this hope and expectation of an immediate pecuniary benefit" and "not a sudden and wholesale conversion to the abstract doctrine of socialism" that had driven electors into Labour's hands.[20] The conclusion was that Conservatives needed "a sound progressive policy as far removed from reaction as it is from revolution".[21]

Because of previous widespread discontent about housing and rents, the Scottish Unionists were pressured into demanding special subsidies for Scottish housing. The flat rate subsidy proposed in the Housing Minister Neville Chamberlain's Bill was to be £6 per house. The Scottish Office pressed for separate assessments. Although this was widely supported it was not accepted and the Scottish Minister Walter Elliot was to express the views of many when he told the House of Commons of his disappointment that Scotland did not receive special treatment.

When Parliament was dissolved in 1923, Scottish Labour Members, Dollan recalled, "were delighted and believed they would return to Westminster in increased numbers".[22] The decision to go to the country caused disarray among their opponents who opposed an early election as "most detrimental to the party interests in Scotland".[23] Although Baldwin believed protection would unite the Conservatives, his Scottish Secretary, Viscount Novar, argued for a referendum instead, warning from his Scottish assessment that the election might result "in handing over the fortunes of the country to the socialist party".[24]

Conservatives and Liberals were divided in 1923. Asquith believed he could reunite the Liberals on free trade, and the Conservatives believed they could reunite the country over protection. It was perhaps remarkable that any basis for anti-socialist cooperation existed. In Scotland, however, protection was less of an issue than socialism. In the majority of the industrial seats, a Liberal or a Conservative stood aside to ensure a straight fight between either and a socialist. It was to little avail. Labour won 34 of the 48 seats it contested, 16 in straight fights, and 18 where the Liberal and Conservative opposition was split.

Throughout Britain Labour gained 50 new Parliamentary seats ensuring, in all, a Labour Parliamentary Party of 192, to the Conservatives 258 and the Liberals 151. In Scotland, Labour's 34 seats were won with 36% of the vote, making Labour the most popular of the three parties in Scotland. The anti-socialist *Scotsman* remarked that "the advance of socialism in our midst is the most unpleasant feature of the situation. Formerly its strength lay mainly in Glasgow and the Clyde and the industrial parts of Lanarkshire but it has now spread its tentacles considerably in Eastern Scotland, particularly in the mining areas bordering on the farms."[25]

In Bridgeton Maxton secured a 9,634 majority over Conservative and Liberal opponents. Glasgow was "solidly united behind Labour". The debate now began on whether the party should attempt to form a Government. But even as Labour celebrated, Maxton was in mourning after suffering yet another personal tragedy. During the general election campaign, his mother had suddenly collapsed and died. Since her husband's death 20 years before she had single-handedly brought up a family of five and had joined in their political crusades even to the extent of taking out membership of the ILP and, at the age of sixty, serving as an ILP representative on Neilston Parish Council. For the last 14 months she had taken on the additional responsibility of bringing up Maxton's young son at the family home in Barrhead. Her death was, Maxton wrote, "a sickening blow coming just as it did when I was beginning to adapt myself in some degree to the loss of my wife". Among the letters of condolence that arrived was one from Ramsay MacDonald. Scarcely disguising his sense of loss, Maxton replied saying that "my mother was so active, keen and alert that I'm afraid all of us in the family group forgot she was getting old and allowed her to comport herself as if she was of our own generation".[26]

18

Government but not Power

In January 1924 the young Welshman, Emrys Hughes, travelled north to take over from Tom Johnston and his colleague, the new Lanarkshire MP Tom Dickson, as the editor of *Forward* newspaper. His salary of 5 pounds 10 shillings a week was agreed at a meeting between him and Johnston in the 6th floor of a tenement office building in Howard Street behind St Enoch Square, where *Forward* now had its offices. A few minutes walk from the *Forward* offices, at Cranston's tearoom in Renfield Street, the leading men of the Glasgow ILP were meeting for one of their regular working lunches.

It was the weekend before Parliament reassembled following the 1923 election and the Glasgow MPs, with friends and advisers including the solicitor Rosslyn Mitchell and the Orpheus Choir conductor Hugh Roberton, were discussing the prospects of a Labour Government. In the new House of Commons the Conservatives were the largest party but in any Commons confidence vote they were almost certain to be defeated by the combined votes of Labour and the Liberals. Most now felt it inevitable that a Labour Government would soon be installed and the Clydeside socialists were discussing their Parliamentary tactics. Joking amongst themselves they even made up their own Cabinet to loud laughter as they gave the most unlikely persons the least likely jobs.

"In January 1924 optimism was the keynote," Emrys Hughes recalled. "They sat at a round table and with each new arrival the circle grew wider and the table receded until they sat with their plates and cups of tea in their hands or on their knees interested only in the conversation and argument. James Maxton was there with his long black hair down to his shoulders and over his forehead and looking very grim and sinister until his face lit up with his charming smile and one realised that his outward appearance of being the stern revolutionary was merely

147

a pose. Next to him sat John Wheatley bland, inscrutable behind a pair of glasses. He did not say a lot but when he spoke they listened to him.

"George Buchanan, the most youthful of them, red haired and headstrong, a patternmaker from the shipyards, had the most to say. He had not so much faith in MacDonald ... If the Labour Government wasn't going to do this and that and the other thing they would hear from him. What the people in the Gorbals ... wanted was not some superman Prime Minister but someone who would give them work and, if not, better unemployment pay. David Kirkwood the engineer from Clydebank was more favourably disposed to MacDonald. 'George, Geordie,' he said rolling every 'r', 'Gi'e the man a chance' ..."[1]

Since the formation of the Labour Representation Committee in 1900, the great dream of the left in Britain had been a Labour Government. When that dream approached realisation in the early 1920s, just about every senior Labour leader – MacDonald, Snowden, the ILP Chairman Clifford Allen – had committed themselves to nothing less than majority Government. For socialists to hold office at the mercy of any other party would be to betray that dream. Maxton agreed with what they said but would not entirely trust them to resist temptation. In a speech to the ILP Summer School in 1923 he warned of the dangers of coalition. "There are elements in the Labour Party that would be prepared to form a coalition with some other party or fragment of a party," he said. "We are not going to be put into power by buying off that opposition that ought not to be bought off but clubbed out of existence. Everyone has to be prepared to have the habits of his life and the conditions of his life altered fundamentally."

But neither the Clydesiders nor the Parliamentary Party were consulted as Ramsay MacDonald isolated himself in Lossiemouth and prepared to take office, even without the necessary Parliamentary majority. The decision to form a minority Labour Government had been approved by MacDonald and four senior colleagues before Christmas. It was a decision that the Tory leader Stanley Baldwin wanted, and had urged an intermediary, Lord Haldane, to press on MacDonald, and it was a decision also endorsed by Asquith and the Liberals, all of whom believed that a minority Labour Government would pose little threat to the establishment.[2]

When MacDonald accepted power under conditions that made him a prisoner of his Parliamentary opponents, the Clydesiders and the Labour Party were philosophically unequipped to deal with the problem. MacDonald resisted a number of options open to him as the first Labour Prime Minister. Liberals had expected him to request a form of pact or agreement on a Parliamentary programme. This did not happen, yet Labour's choices were not as limited as they may seem now. Labour might have entered office, introduced a bold socialist programme, and then faced defeat in the Commons and a fresh election. A series of commissions might have been set up while Labour acted to alleviate the distress of the unemployed, or Labour could have rejected office outright. Even one of the new Prime Minister's most loyal supporters, Patrick Dollan, was to argue later that taking office was "the biggest mistake of MacDonald's career".[3]

Maxton's initial response to the 1923 election results was one of jubilation, because, as in 1922, the Clydesiders had been pessimistic of their electoral chances. Maxton immediately declared that at the next election 150 more seats would swing to Labour, and that on the basis of the results, and further organisation, only six Parliamentary seats were outside Labour's grasp. Maxton believed the Liberals would combine with the Conservatives in a Coalition Government, and told an ILP audience in December 1923 that "the proper thing to do was for the statesmen to form a Liberal-Tory coalition. Let them call themselves the Centre or Moderate Party . . . and prove that private enterprise was the right method of managing the industrial and commercial affairs of the country. Let them take one, two or three years to demonstrate that fact."[4]

Wheatley took a stronger line. Although they were urged "to recognise points of agreement between Labour and Liberals . . . the real issue was between capitalism and socialism". It was not for Labour "to compromise with their principles". To ally with the Liberals would be "the greatest betrayal in political history".[5]

In public and in private, neither Wheatley nor Maxton would tolerate the prospect of Coalition Government. However, while their public statements seemed to reject office under any circumstances, privately their opposition was less than vehement. When, on 29 December, Maxton wrote to MacDonald, he appeared to be offering loyal support. Maxton was writing in response to MacDonald's condolences about the death of his mother:

It would have been a great satisfaction to your mother had she been alive today to see our movement and your place in it. I'm glad you hold that place. I think it will be for the good of our

149

country and of the world and you can count on me if not for slavish subservience or uncritical obedience, certainly for unflinching loyalty in all essentials.

With best wishes for the season and the future,

James Maxton[6]

In his private letter to MacDonald, Wheatley was even more enthusiastic about the prospect of government. Writing on 23 December, he appeared to be in no doubt that all Labour MPs should support a Labour Government and that Glasgow MPs should have a prominent role in such an administration.

'Fine' just describes the Glasgow results and in my opinion this city has won a place in your team whoever you may choose to fill the place. Whatever the fate of your first administration your name will occupy a prominent and lasting place in British history. My hearty congratulations.[7]

Although Maxton's public statements remained critical of minority government, they were modified somewhat as 1924 opened. When Maxton and Wheatley spoke together at a New Year rally at the Metropole, they offered MacDonald some encouragement. The political situation, Wheatley said, was "pregnant with possibilities". He was "not at all afraid of the consequences of the Labour Party going into power". The party could not destroy the movement "even if it made the greatest blunder". Maxton was now impressed by the responsibility of Labour's position in the House of Commons. The press, he said, were predicting a Clyde breakaway "in a month", but, he asked, "what possible ground in the history of Labour MPs on the Clyde could lead anyone to think they were out to cause dissensions and splits in the Labour Movement"?[8]

The more constructive position now put by Maxton and Wheatley was not simply because the Clydesiders were bowing to the inevitable – the Labour Party National Executive had already decided that it would be fatal for Labour to decline office and so allow the Liberals to take power – but also because they now hoped that a minority Government, in power even for a few days, might pave the way for a permanent majority Government, At the Cranston's tearoom conversations in the first days of January there was, as Emrys Hughes recalled, a sense of hope. "Many of them believed that once the country had a Labour Government and it showed the people what it could do there would never be another kind of Government again," he later wrote. "The ILP had a new up-to-date programme called Socialism in Our Time. Many of them round the table at Cranston's thought that this was going to be an accomplished fact."

Stanley Baldwin tendered his resignation as Prime Minsiter to the King on 22 January 1924. Shortly afterwards, following a meeting of the Privy Council, at which Ramsay MacDonald was sworn in as a member, the King asked MacDonald to form a Government. The country now waited for MacDonald to announce the names of the first ever Labour Cabinet.

In press speculation Maxton was mentioned as a possible Minister. In his unpublished autobiography Dollan recalled that "it was rumoured that Maxton had been offered the Parliamentary Under Secretaryship at the Ministry of Education which offer he declined on the advice of Wheatley who wanted him in the Cabinet".[9] Dollan's story does not bear close examination. When, in December, MacDonald was first contemplating a list of possible Ministers, he had written round to a number of MPs including Wheatley. The miners' President, Robert Smillie, was, for example, asked to indicate whether he wished to be considered for office but while pledging MacDonald he would "give loyal support as a true and loving comrade", he wrote back that, on health grounds, he "did not want and would not accept office".[10] No approach was made to Maxton about office, even though MacDonald had in that same week written to him expressing his condolences about Maxton's mother's death. Far from Maxton being considered for or contemplating Government office, it seems clear that he was suspicious even of Wheatley seeking it and may even have advised his friend against this.

It was indeed difficult enough to persuade MacDonald to accept Wheatley into the Cabinet. Wheatley had momentarily been on Labour's Front Bench in April 1923 when he had moved Labour amendments to Neville Chamberlain's Housing Bill. In December, when MacDonald wrote asking "if you would be prepared to consider coming into the team", Wheatley expressed keen and immediate interest in a reply that bordered on the deferential.

It was noble of you to think favourably of me after all the trouble I gave you last session. I have given careful consideration to your

151

offer to include me in the list of possibles and decided to place my services at your disposal.[11]

Wheatley's enthusiasm and unexpected deference might have merited a better outcome. In January Wheatley was offered only the Under Secretaryship of Health in charge of housing, but held out for the headship of the department and Cabinet rank. MacDonald yielded when his first choice for Secretary of State, Arthur Greenwood, stood down "in order to smooth things".[12] In fact MacDonald thought that this concession to the Clyde – together with the appointment of James Stewart and John Muir as Under Secretaries – went far enough, remarking in his diary, "Wheatley finally fixed. Necessary to bring Clyde in – will he play straight? Anxious for office."[13]

Dollan was later to accuse MacDonald of excluding Maxton and other Clydesiders for being over sensitive to "the fear of the Anglo-Saxons against too many Scots in the Cabinet". Wheatley's promotion was MacDonald's gesture of appeasement to "the Clyde", but MacDonald felt that any further Clydeside representation would put at risk the responsible and respectable public image he sought for his new administration. Most of all MacDonald feared a repetition in Government of the "murderers" scenes that had, in his view, clouded the previous year of opposition.

Not only Dollan but other Clydesiders believed this was the case, including Neil McLean, whose anger surfaced in an acrimonious correspondence with MacDonald and with the Labour Chief Whip, Ben Spoor. McLean was passed over for a ministerial post and offered only a job as a Government Whip. "If I have neither capacity nor ability to merit promotion I would be doing the party a disservice if I accepted the offer," he sarcastically told Ben Spoor, but the real reason for his exclusion and the exclusion of other Clydesiders was more political. He had, he said, been omitted because of "the attitude I adopted during the suspension of the four members". This had been his "unpardonable sin". Wheatley, he argued, was in only to secure "the placation of the Clyde".[14]

MacDonald's new administration was announced in stages during the final days of January and the early days of February. There was no place for Maxton and none for Tom Johnston. Former Liberals, such as Lord Haldane, featured prominently and two ostensibly non-party political appointments, Lord Chelmsford at the Admiralty and Lord McMillan as Scottish Solicitor General, let to considerable anger within the Labour Party. Maxton had expected the Glasgow Labour lawyer Rosslyn Mitchell to be made Solicitor General and he saw in the appointment of McMillan unfair pressure brought to bear by the Faculty of Advocates.

When Maxton returned to Glasgow in February, much of the hope and excitement of January 1924 had already given way to dismay at MacDonald's conduct of affairs, and especially his exclusion of almost all the Clydesiders from office. "There was deep disappointment at Cranston's," Emrys Hughes was later to recall. "When Tom Johnston and Maxton returned from London they were obviously disgruntled. I thought it too personal a matter to discuss with Johnston but I remember Maxton telling me. 'I'm not angry about it but Johnston is. If Mac had only sent for us and said, "Boys I think it's best to keep you out for tactical reasons", we would not have minded. But they are talking as if he's not put us in because we haven't got the brains.' "[11]

It was almost certainly Wheatley's decision to join the Government that tempered any initial criticism of it from Maxton. By February he was promising positive support. The Cabinet was "a good sound one". Speaking at the City Hall he explained the fears of a Clydeside split were "misguided". The Government would have "nothing but loyal and faithful support as long as it was going forward". If it turned back he hoped "the men from the Clyde would rise up and protest".

Maxton's public statements became even more enthusiastic in support of the new administration. He was impressed by the responsibility of his position, he told an audience at the Glasgow Metropole. The Cabinet was man for man twice as good as any previous administration. MacDonald could rely on the Clydeside MPs that they would not cause a split.[15]

The *Glasgow Eastern Standard* Political Correspondent, probably briefed by Wheatley, explained that although many of the Eastenders did not understand the attitude of Maxton and Stephen, "not only are they standing four square in defence of the Government but they are enthusiastic about its work and capacity". Their role in the Commons was to be "spurs to socialism".

The Labour Party in Scotland was even more enthusiastic. The Party's Scottish Chairman spoke of how "the accession to office of Ramsay MacDonald and the first Labour Government was welcomed by the entire Labour Movement ... the leader is a man who in the past has had the courage of his convictions".[16] The March conference of the Scottish Council pledged itself, "in every possible way to ensure the success of the present and the first Labour Government", and an extensive national campaign of support was organised in rallies and meetings round Scotland. At the Scottish conference Agnes Dollan would say of the decision to take office that it had been "justified by the Government record of the first few months", a comment in stark contrast to the later conclusions of her husband.

The results did not justify the enthusiasm. The first meeting of the Cabinet agreed to drop one of Labour's central proposals, that of the capital levy, from their legislative programme. Sidney Webb, hardly the most radical of the new Cabinet, had "come away feeling that the Cabinet would err on the side of respectability, too many outsiders, too many peers ... JRM oddly enough does not like the element and chooses as his immediate associates not the workmen but the lawyer".[17]

With the exception of a bold housing programme promoted by John Wheatley, the Labour Government of 1924 was hardly a success, judged by anyone's standards. There were some minor advances. The existence of Russia was recognised, and diplomatic channels were opened. This pleased Maxton and the ILP, especially when negotiations for a trade treaty were opened. Steps were also taken by MacDonald to renegotiate German war reparations although the changes were limited and much criticised. Disarmament talks were begun and eventually led to the Geneva Protocol. In part of course the Government benefited from an improved international atmosphere, but MacDonald was following the lines laid down by the Labour Party since 1918. Where disagreement arose was on how far MacDonald should go, for example, on a sanctions clause in the Geneva Protocol, the scaling down of reparations to cover only devastated areas, and the extent of the efforts towards disarmament.

In other areas Labour was to prove a disappointment. The Empire remained as it was with no real attempts at colonial liberation. J.H. Thomas, the Secretary in charge, spoke of how "the Labour Party were proud and jealous of, and were prepared to maintain, the Empire". In all economic matters the new Government did little. Despite growing scepticism of free trade economics, little was said or done to ensure bilateral or multilateral attempts at economic revival. On economic questions as a whole – the Budget strategy and the relief of unemployment – Labour's measures were completely inadequate.

A committee of the ILP chaired by Smillie was set up to smooth over differences. Maxton was one of the 12 MPs who sat with three Ministers in efforts to resolve differences. Maxton's initial criticisms were minor, but, by April, Maxton had voted against the Government on three occasions. His first rebellion came over the offer of £3.5m trade credits to a private firm in Sudan, when he told the Commons that he was "one of the simple people who believed that the advent of a Labour Government would bring fundamental differences. I did believe that and I am still very much wanting to believe it."

Maxton voted against the Second Reading of the Trade Facilities Bill, when he urged for the first time in the House a planned approach to trade. Trade credits were needed for the working people of the country before they were required for foreign traders.

> I believe that my friends on the Front Bench came into power not to tinker with the economic laws ... If you issued a credit of £2 for each working-class family in Britain today, the trade of Great Britain would be £40m better on Saturday. That would go into the hands of shopkeepers and rent collectors and it would help them if they would open their heads and voted money not to the Sudan, or to Cairo, but to their own British people. I don't see how the Labour Government can defend this Bill.

Later he voted, against Government advice, for the abolition of the death penalty in the armed forces, and against the Government's Army Estimates because of their decision to order new cruisers. His fear was, he told the Commons, that "the new British Government is as anxious to maintain and extend the policy of British imperialism and conquest as any of its predecessors".

But Maxton defended his voting record on these occasions when he spoke in a House of Commons debate on 7 April: "We did so when they had the enthusiastic support of Hon members opposite and below the Gangway."

As yet Maxton would not seek to bring his Government down. Indeed when the Dawes settlement on German reparations was agreed, Maxton urged the ILP not to make its opposition to it public, to avoid embarrassing the Government. He even defended the Government for their refusal to consider a capital levy. He had accepted there could be no capital levy in the Budget, he told a Barrhead audience. It was lower food taxes, not the capital levy, that he would fight for.

But Maxton's support was always made conditional. By now he was becoming involved in a number of Parliamentary incidents that were to be embarrassing to the Government. In a late night debate over evictions in Woolwich, the Tory Leo Amery and

George Buchanan had had a verbal, and then a physical, scrape. Unparliamentary insults like 'swine' and 'guttersnipe' had been exchanged. Maxton had rushed over to Amery and had appeared to take a swipe at him. There were apologies the next day. In an article for the *Glasgow Eastern Standard* entitled "Should an MP fight?" Maxton conceded his mistake but did not rule out any form of protest in order to ensure advanced socialist measures.[18]

The Maxton faction was not alone in advocating a bolder course. The 1924 Conference of the STUC had demanded national ownership, credit control, an eight-hour day, pensions after 55, amongst other radical proposals. Alongside the Scottish Executive Committee of the Labour Party, a joint union-party committee was formed to urge "speedy action from the Government".[19]

But part of the move leftwards came from the infiltration of Communists into the Labour Party. Communists could not be individual members, but it appeared that they could be trade union delegates to party conference. In 1924, the Scottish Labour Party Chairman estimated that of the 150 delegates "not less than 20 communists" were registered.[20] While the 1923 Scottish Conference had approved the affiliation of the Communist-led National Unemployed Workers' Movement, the Executive had successfully resisted its implementation. In 1924, while this proposal was thwarted, the party moved straight to the acceptance of Communist membership. The Conference urged the National Executive of the Labour Party to again consider the application of the Communist Party for membership and urged that the question was one for negotiation.

Maxton had always favoured Communist affiliation to the Labour Party, although he disagreed with Communist aims and policies. Nowhere was the split between the Maxton faction and the leadership more visibly highlighted than in the 1924 Kelvingrove by-election, the one Scottish by-election of the 1924 Labour Government and a serious defeat for Labour. The "Labour" candidate was Aitken Ferguson, the 1923 General Election candidate and a member of the Communist Party. When the by-election was announced, both Patrick Dollan and Rosslyn Mitchell were mentioned as possible alternatives but Pat Dollan stood down ostensibly "in the interests of the unity of the party". The real explanation was that under no circumstances would the local party accept an alternative. The Glasgow Trades and Labour Council, to whom Kelvingrove was responsible, accepted the choice of Ferguson. But the National Executive refused endorsement. Ferguson described himself as "a Labour Party candidate fighting for the full Labour programme" who would accept the majority decisions of the party while endeavouring to win increased support for his own point of view.[21] Tom Johnston felt he had given satisfactory assurances of working with the Labour Party in Parliament, and so did Maxton, but Ferguson's campaign scarcely made this clear.

The Conservative candidate was Dr Walter Elliot, a student contemporary of Maxton's, who had transferred to Kelvingrove after losing his Lanarkshire seat in the 1923 General Election. He was credited by the *Daily Express* with being "the man who like Horatius at the bridge met single-handed and repulsed the first onslaught of the Clydemen in Parliament". Writing to Lady Astor from what he called "in partibus Bolshevorum", he spoke of "the Clydeside Bolshies". There was, he said, "not a single defender of the Labour Government in that campaign. Mr Ferguson attacked it."

By spring of 1924 Maxton was making clear what he considered to be, above all else, his role while a Labour Government was in office. There never was a time in the history of the working class, he said, when it was more necessary for the working class to be organised, determined and audacious. He wanted to see emblazoned in their banner not the word "tranquillity" but the word "discontent". Don't be peaceful, he concluded, not even for the sake of a Labour Government. Generally, Maxton was mapping out his self-assumed role as the spokesman in Parliament for socialists in the country, and the agitator in the country for socialism in Parliament. He saw himself as the keeper of the conscience of the Labour Movement with a duty to keep working-class spirits alive and defend the principles upon which the Labour Movement was founded.

He backed this view up in Parliament in a speech which consolidated his position as the most articulate leader of the left. Amid industrial unrest and the accusation by the Tories that strikes were "Communist inspired", Maxton defended the right to strike as in the national interest. There was trouble too over what Maxton alleged to be famine in the Highlands and then over threatened evictions on the Clyde. In his position as Housing Minister, Wheatley was attempting to introduce legislation that would guarantee security of tenancy, but Labour did not have the Parliamentary majority to ensure the passage of the legislation. Maxton urged Labour to take their case to the country if their rent restrictions Bill was not accepted by Parliament. As usual he went further than his colleagues, threatening to "take the battle to the streets" if he did not receive satisfactory assurances that unemployed people would escape eviction. As he explained in the Commons debate, he was not a pacifist, but prepared to use force "for his own purposes – the class struggle": "I warn our Front Bench that unless they secure the homes of the people of Glasgow I will show force in the streets of Glasgow defending them." He was looking for "a definite pitched battle between the working class and the employing class".

Wheatley failed to secure the passage of his Bill to halt evictions. When the Bill was rejected, Maxton immediately urged MacDonald to hold an election on the issue.

Incidents such as these convinced Maxton that the Labour Government could do little without a majority and that continued office was proving an embarrassment to the movement as a whole. Maxton was speaking for many of the left when in August at the ILP Summer School he passed his verdict on the Government's performance.

> He did not think that the Labour Government would take office as a minority Government to do little things in administration which they could do little better than the Liberals or Tories. They were returned to Parliament to make fundamental changes ... if there was a movement in which there had been fools, twisters and crooks, it has been our movement ... we in Parliament have to keep the pressure up on the Cabinet to keep them as common men.

Privately Maxton was even more critical of the Labour leadership, and especially of MacDonald. In July he was asked to speculate what was likely to happen in the future. "Ramsay will become leader of the Conservative Party," Beatrice Webb records him as saying, "And he will be in for twenty years."[22]

19

Conscience of the Party

If Ramsay MacDonald represented Labour in Government, Maxton represented Labour in Opposition, as the conscience of the left and the man by whom uncomfortable issues could not be forgotten. One such issue was Scottish Home Rule.

From the beginning Labour in Scotland had been committed to the creation of a Scottish Parliament. Standing at Mid-Lanark in the 1888 by-election, Keir Hardie had promised he would fight to establish a legislature in Scotland. The commitment remained and became even more precise in the 1918 Scottish manifesto. In that manifesto, signed by James Maxton on behalf of the ILP, three distinctive Scottish policies had been singled out for priority – land nationalisation, prohibition and Home Rule for Scotland. In 1919 the Scottish Executive of the Labour Party had, with the unanimous approval of the Party Conference, threatened industrial as well as political action in a "determined effort to secure Home Rule for Scotland in the first session of Parliament". The devolution campaign, they said, should be "taken out of the hand of place-hunting lawyers and vote-catching politicians by the political and industrial efforts of the Labour Party in Scotland". The commitment fell short of complete independence, but Labour believed Scotland was a nation and nations needed Parliaments.[1]

In both the 1922 and 1923 elections, almost every Scottish Labour candidate had personally pledged support for a devolution bill for Scotland. In 1922 the national Labour Party had also issued a statement promising "statutory legislatures for Scotland, Wales and England as well as Ireland as part of the larger plan of constitutional reform which will transform the British Empire into a Britannic Federation of Commonwealths and British self-governing communities".

As the Clydesiders had made their triumphal descent on Westminster, John Wheatley had told newspaper reporters that "in Scotland there is no subject which aroused enthusiasm as much as the subject of Scottish Home Rule",[2] and during 1923 Maxton, with nine other Labour MPs, had addressed a Home Rule rally in Glasgow, and told them that his experience at Westminster "had converted him absolutely to the necessity of making a strenuous effort to keep their own Parliament in Scotland".[3]

For some years Maxton had been a dedicated devolutionist. In 1918 he was a founding member of the Scottish Home Rule Association, an all-party pressure group which sought to publicise the demand for a Scottish Parliament. Alongside the miners' leader, Robert Smillie, he joined the Association's national committee and had pressed their case for Labour Party support. Only when the Labour Party, in January 1919, advised party members to work through the party's own channels – and not an all-party campaign – did he withdraw.[4]

His experiences as a Member of Parliament in Westminster strengthened his commitment to a Scottish Parliament. After a year in London he addressed his former colleagues in the Scottish Socialist Teachers Society in November 1923, and told them "it was a humiliating experience to sit in the House of Commons, one of a majority returned to the House of Commons to push on a policy of fundamental social change for the benefit of the Scottish people and to find the Scottish majority steadily voted down by the votes of the English members pledged to a policy of social stagnation. It was now over two hundred years since the Union of Parliaments and although one was perpetually told of the blessings conferred on Scotland by the Union, it was difficult to find many blessings except the somewhat doubtful one of fighting England's wars."[5]

In the 1923 election, Maxton and the majority of Scottish Labour candidates again signed a round robin from the Scottish Home Rule Association declaring themselves in favour of Home Rule. In January 1924, 14 of them, including Maxton, signed a Parliamentary motion regretting the omission of Home Rule proposals from the King's Speech. They repeated their commitment to "a Parliament for Scotland and giving to that country a measure of Home Rule". The stage was set for George Buchanan's Home Rule Bill of May 1924. Maxton was one of its sponsors. It was modelled on devolution in Northern Ireland and proposed a system of Federal Home Rule for Britain. Scottish MPs would remain at Westminster until Home Rule all round was achieved. All Scottish backbench MPs backed the Bill and it was supported by the Scottish Secretary William Adamson and by the Prime Minister.

In a display of extra-Parliamentary support for the Bill,

a nationwide publicity campaign was launched by the Scottish Home Rule Association which reached a climax with a rally in St Andrew's Hall, Glasgow, at which Maxton appeared to come out in favour of independence. A cartoon in *Punch* had portrayed Ramsay MacDonald as a London railway booking clerk and Wheatley, Maxton and the rest of the Clyde Group purchasing "single" tickets from London to Glasgow. Now Maxton told the rally that he did not want to return to London again – "not to Parliament. He might go to the International, or to hear the Orpheus Choir, or something worthwhile, but never for the sake of legislating for the British Empire."

In a memorable speech he asked for "no greater job in life than to make English-ridden, capitalist-ridden, landowner-ridden Scotland into the Scottish Socialist Commonwealth", and in doing that he thought he would be rendering a very great service to the people of England, Wales and Europe and to the cause of internationalism generally. He for one was convinced that a Scottish Parliament could achieve more in five years than a British House of Commons could deliver in 25 or 30 years.

He would not approach the question "in the spirit of national exclusiveness", for they were "brothers of all other nations", but he urged:

> Give us our Parliament in Scotland. Set it up next year. We will start with no traditions. We will start with ideals. We will start with purpose, with courage. We will start with the aim and object that there will be 134 men and women, pledged to 134 Scottish constituencies, to spend their whole energy, their whole brain power, their whole courage, and their whole soul, in making Scotland into a country in which we can take people from all the nations of the earth and say: This is our land, this is our Scotland, these are our people, these are our men, our works, our women and children: can you beat it?[6]

Maxton was later to say that he regretted only his use of the words "English-ridden", for he had no quarrel with the English people.

In no sense were Maxton and his Clydeside colleagues advocates of complete separation. Theirs was "not a narrow nationalistic creed", explained Wheatley's *Glasgow Eastern Standard*, but a demand for "decentralised organisation". To the Clydesiders, "the exploited factory worker in Bridgeton had much more in common with the sweated seamstress in Whitechapel and the agonised toiler in the Ruhr than the self-satisfied, vulgarly spoken plutocrat of Kelvinside".

When Parliament debated the Bill, the Scottish Secretary William Adamson told the House that the "government gives the general principle of the Bill their approval . . . what they suggest they are prepared to do is appoint a committee to examine the whole question and report to the House". But although the Bill enjoyed some Liberal support, Conservative MPs were hostile, and talked the Bill out. The Clydesiders were furious, believing they had an agreement with the Speaker that Buchanan would be allowed to move the closure on the debate and so keep the Bill alive. Their anger boiled over into a Parliamentary disturbance and the House of Commons had to be adjourned.[7]

Under pressure from the Scots MPs Ministers attempted to rescue the Bill's proposals. Clynes, the Lord Privy Seal, was asked to draw up terms of reference for a committee of enquiry, but the Cabinet could neither agree on a Royal Commission, which would exclude MPs, nor on a Commons Select Committee, on which the Opposition parties would demand a majority. To his Scots Labour colleagues Ramsay MacDonald had to confess that while he favoured devolution he could not take any immediate action to secure its implemenation.

This was the nearest Home Rulers were to come to achieving a measure of Scottish self-government, despite Labour's continued support, and the Clydesiders' insistent pressures throughout the 1920s, and it was the nearest Scottish pressure groups came to presenting a united front on the Home Rule issue. By the time the Rev James Barr introduced a new Home Rule Bill in 1926 (he proposed dominion status for Scotland, and excluded Scots MPs from Westminster), there were acute divisions within the Home Rule forces. The majority favoured devolution but by now the demand for separation was being mooted by more extreme nationalists, who, in 1928, formed a separate National Party. "When the Scottish nationalists came to us, who were the supporters of International Socialism," Maxton later explained, "and told us that if we were to secure their support we would have to place nationalism in front of international socialism in our programme and in our activities, I declined to do it."[8]

In July 1924, when the Labour Government's days were numbered, there appeared in a Communist newspaper, the *Worker's Weekly*, two articles written by John Ross Campbell advising British soldiers not to oppose workers during industrial strikes and calling upon members of the armed forces to go forward in a common attack upon capitalism. A number of copies of the paper had found their way into Aldershot barracks and the Government decided to take action and prosecute John Campbell under the Incitement to Mutiny Act.

On 30 July, Campbell was arrested, charged, then released on bail. Maxton was immediately informed by his friend John Scanlon, assistant to Sir Patrick Hastings, the Attorney General, of the arrest, and quickly understood the risks to a Labour Government in proceeding with a prosecution. Only a few years earlier Labour had campaigned against the prosecution of Tom Mann and a fellow socialist on a similar charge. For the moment, however, Maxton chose to do nothing to minimise the damage. According to Scanlon, "he sarcastically asked if wrecking the Government would be a tragedy and then said quite definitely that the sooner they were out the better, as every day they were in led us further from socialism".[9]

A week later, after news leaked out, the Attorney General publicly accepted responsibility for endorsing the prosecution, and Maxton and others asked whether Ministers were aware that Labour MPs shared the views of the author. After his embarrassment in the Commons, the Attorney General immediately instigated further enquiries and called Maxton in to consult him on Campbell's background. Maxton told Hastings that Campbell was not the editor of *Worker's Weekly*, but said he knew Campbell well. He was a man who had fought the war from beginning to end and had been decorated for exceptional gallantry after being wounded in both feet. It was this conversation with Maxton that convinced Hastings that a prosecution would be counter-productive. Hastings sent for the Director of Public Prosecutions, and his assistant, Sir Guy Stevenson, arrived to confirm Maxton's information. They discovered too that Campbell had agreed to a letter of apology for his outburst. When Ramsay MacDonald appeared, he took the same view as Hastings. The prosecution, said the Prime Minister, had been "ill-advised from the beginning".

When the Cabinet met that evening they confirmed that the Attorney General was right to drop proceedings and resolved that no public prosecution of a political character should be undertaken without the prior sanction of the Cabinet. The Cabinet had acted properly: the problem was that the events offered perfect political fodder for the Liberals and Conservatives to attack the Labour Government over using the law to assist their political friends, and when, during the summer recess, MacDonald volunteered the information that the Cabinet had been involved in dropping the prosecution, Churchill was only one of many Opposition politicians who drew political advantage from arguing, "it is only one step from twisting the law in favour of their political friends to twisting it for the persecution of their political opponents".

Maxton could legitimately claim credit when charges were dropped, but almost certainly he had made a political mistake in claiming that credit publicly. "I know better than anyone else in Great Britain that no undue pressure was brought to bear on the Attorney General," he later said, "as I was the one person who saw the Attorney General on the matter . . . I would have been doing a blackguardly thing if knowing something to the man's credit I had kept my mouth shut."

Parliament resumed for the autumn session with the Liberals demanding an enquiry into the incident, and the Tories committed to a vote of censure. MacDonald, however, was more furious with the public statements of Maxton and other Labour backbenchers than he was with the combined assault of the Liberals and Conservatives. Shinwell was called in to see MacDonald at Downing Street.

> I went over and found him in the drawing room on the first floor, pacing up and down, obviously much disturbed. I asked what was the matter, only to discover that he was more furious about the criticism by some of his ILP colleagues, Maxton, Lansbury and others, than he was about the Liberal Party suggestion. I can recall saying to him, "Pay no attention; all they are doing is repeating their election speeches. They have to in order to retain the support of their constituencies." This, however, I admit, had little effect. Then the telephone rang and Ben Scurr, the Chief Whip, came on the telephone and informed MacDonald that the Liberal Party had decided to press their amendment. "That settles it," said MacDonald, "I shall have no more of it. I shall resign."[10]

Labour was overwhelmingly defeated in the Commons votes which followed. MacDonald tendered his resignation and Parliament was dissolved on 9 October 1924. In the election campaign which followed, Maxton adopted a more moderate line. His own address to the Bridgeton electorate tempered his criticisms of the leadership. The Government had been, he said, "wise and prudent" to stop the Campbell case, "having made a mistake in starting a prosecution". A majority was needed to begin the "big changes" in society, especially in the control of the banks and the land. But Labour had proved itself "fit to govern" and although the results may have been "small", they were "very great compared with the five years previously".[11]

But manifestos mattered little in the controversies that were to surround the campaign. The Labour leadership had taken a conscious decision to concentrate their campaigning on the reputation of MacDonald and on the successes of the Russian Treaty. Promises were few and far between. Mining reorganisation but not nationalisation was proposed. There was no mention of the capital levy. The campaign which started badly was to end disastrously in accusation and counter-accusation about the significance of what was to be called "the Zinoviev letter".

The letter, which was printed in the *Daily Mail*, purported to be from Zinoviev, the President of Comintern, to the Communist Party of Great Britain. The letter called for increased pressure on the Labour Government to satisfy the trade agreement with Russia. It commanded British Communists to intensify their propaganda, especially in the army and navy, to bring about the downfall of capitalism. The letter was later proved to be a fraud, but MacDonald made the mistake of assuming it to be genuine and wrote a strong protest to the Soviet Government. The Tories had a field day. It was to be a self-inflicted wound – as bad as if MacDonald had written the letter to himself. The Labour Government was in the pockets of the Soviets, Tories claimed. MacDonald, they claimed, had known of the letter and had sought to supress it.

Tories and Liberals fought Labour candidates, but few Tories and Liberals fought each other. As MacDonald remarked, the wolf had once again lain down with the lamb. In all but two exceptions in Scotland, Conservatives and Liberals fielded only one candidate against Labour. But alliances of convenience need not have been made. "We were swept away on the tide of the Zinoviev letter," one Scottish candidate remarked. The Conservatives triumphed, with an overall majority of 210 seats. Labour had increased its total vote by almost one million but had lost 40 seats, two of them in Glasgow. Bridgeton remained secure but in line with the national trends Maxton saw his majority reduced, to 6,217.

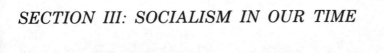

SECTION III: SOCIALISM IN OUR TIME

20

New Alliances

"We were like the Children of Israel," said Maxton of the experience of Government in 1924. "After journeying 40 years in the wilderness, we sent out spies to view the promised land, and they returned and told us it was truly a promised land flowing with milk and honey, but filled with fierce giants." The short-lived Labour Government had no more been able to make capitalism work than any other. Disillusionment with Government made electoral defeat for Maxton almost a relief. Socialists in politics could do nothing unless "they had a mandate to carry out a socialist policy into full operation". Without that mandate their place was not on the Government benches but in Opposition and free to campaign for the indispensable socialist majority.

At the first meeting of the PLP in December, Maxton was the 1924 Government's fiercest critic. In defeat MacDonald's leadership seemed at risk from both left and right. From the right, Snowden pressed Henderson to stand against MacDonald. MacDonald himself probably considered the most dangerous challenger to be Wheatley, from the left. Most of all the ex-Prime Minister feared an alliance between the left and his moderate opponents. He had grown impatient with the left, confiding to his diary that "some members do no work but do much talking and wish to turn floor of House into a sort of national street corner soapbox". This is believed to be a reference to Maxton. A further analysis in his diary concluded that "the difficulties of our party are within more than without and though I write 'the left wing' the inspiration really comes from those who were disappointed that I did not put them in the Ministry".[1]

Wheatley refused to stand, perhaps feeling he would gain more in a later contest. Beatrice Webb's diary recorded that he "did not mean to be too previous", but MacDonald was right in thinking that "the left wing were out for my blood and had not the sense to restrain itself".

In the event, Maxton proposed Lansbury to lead the left-wing challenge but Lansbury withdrew. An enquiry into the Zinoviev affair proved an opportunity to attempt to delay the vote on the leadership. This would have allowed for further manoeuvres aiming at a left-wing challenge but that delaying tactic too was defeated, and the leadership election became simply a vote of confidence in MacDonald.

Only five votes were cast against him including Maxton's. MacDonald, who had "expected more", was greatly relieved.

Maxton's view of leadership was that the leader himself did not matter very much. He was more concerned with the content of the socialist agenda than with who led the movement. To Maxton the difference between the socialist movement and others was that socialism had not been a movement of leaders. It was not built from the top downwards but was a movement of the working class. While others criticised MacDonald, Maxton criticised the direction now being taken by the party.

Maxton defended MacDonald over the Zinoviev letter, urging the ILP Conference to remit for further consideration by the Executive rather than vote on MacDonald's handling of the affair. But if he would not indulge in further personal attacks, he would not allow uncritical acclaim for MacDonald's record. At the 1925 Scottish Labour Party Conference MacDonald was being praised rather than blamed when Maxton chose to intervene. William Shaw, the Party Chairman, had already praised "the value and amount of legislative work accomplished" in 1924. But it was when Maxton's colleague and friend Patrick Dollan rushed to the defence of MacDonald that Maxton stirred.

Party support for the manifesto on which MacDonald had fought the election, said Dollan, had been "absolutely unanimous". The entire party had taken the view that the Campbell incident and the Russian treaty should "be the issue fought upon", and MacDonald had been "asked to do the work that a dozen men should not do, for instance his tour round Great Britain". One million extra votes had been won in 1924, hardly "a disaster". Having elected MacDonald leader, we ought "either to sack him or support him. No other man was available in our movement who could take his place."

Maxton immediately asked for speaking rights and launched into a public attack on one of his closest colleagues. He was, he said, "astonished at Councillor Dollan in taking up the position that the leader of the party should be regarded as above criticism". Although Dollan intervened to deny this was his view, Maxton carried on, "it was a very bad frame of mind that assumed there is only one person in the party who can lead it. He held that it was not a good thing to prevent the differences. Differences had their merit."[2]

Two central issues were to divide Maxton from the official Labour leadership in the months that followed: whether Communists should be allowed membership of the Party, and whether compensation should be paid in the event of nationalisation. Maxton, a "confiscationist", opposed paying compensation to mine owners and landowners if and when industries were nationalised, and argued against the ILP Executive's proposals for compensation when they came before the ILP conference at Gloucester in April.

Maxton was also one of the few Labour leaders who supported Communist affiliation to the Labour Party. When the Scottish ILP held a full debate on the issue in January 1925, Dollan and Maxton were the principal adversaries, Dollan speaking for the majority when he called the Communists "a disruptive influence". Labour had "only made headway in the ILP during the past two years because they had made it clear there was a difference between them and the Communist Party".[3]

Maxton questioned why "there was no proposal to expel Communists from the trade union branches but they were not to have faith in them in the political field". He claimed the Labour Party had always been "a federation of organisations". If "the slow moving machinery of Parliament" was "to act with speed", they needed "a widespread revolt among the people, determined courage and readiness to sacrifice everything". The Communists would help Labour in that direction. Only if Communists would be excluded from the world, would there be something to be said for the proposal. At the end of the debate, Dollan's arguments prevailed by 127 votes to 86.

Within the Parliamentary Labour Party both Maxton and Wheatley were on the ascendant. Maxton was appointed to the Committee of Inquiry set up by the Labour Party to investigate the circumstances surrounding the Zinoviev letter mystery. He and Wheatley were also elected to Labour's Parliamentary committee alongside Lansbury and Kirkwood. Coming fifth in the ballot, Maxton looked as if he was ensured Cabinet office in any future Labour Government.

It was propaganda for socialism, not the prospect of government office, that was Maxton's principal concern in the early months of 1925. Maxton and his colleagues toured the North, visiting Caithness and Wick where their arrival was such an event that Maxton spoke of the "menagerie coming to town". People had turned out as if "to see some kind of wild beast".[4] Kirkwood and Stephen joined him in a visit to the Western Isles, where overflowing meetings were held in all parts of the islands. There was much enthusiasm. Maxton was asked by one islander to provide them with an ILP candidate for the next election. He replied, "We will send you no candidate . . . choose one of your own men and we will adopt him."[5] The visit was to prepare the ground for a Labour victory in the seat ten years later.

Already Maxton's health was beginning to break down. On the way back from Kyle of Lochalsh he became unwell and suffered acutely from pain in the chest. He refused to summon a doctor but accepted treatment in the form of brandy and a mustard poultice from Kirkwood and Stephen. Whether because of this or despite it, the pain settled and he was able to continue his journey to Glasgow.

In April he was back in the centre of controversy. For a time the Glasgow ILP had been campaigning against the growth of Fascism in Glasgow. They had claimed that a raid on the Communist offices had been Fascist inspired, as had an attempt to kidnap Harry Pollitt, the Communist leader. At the ILP's Gloucester Conference in April Maxton had been approached by a man claiming to be an ILP sympathiser who had invited him to visit a farm in Gloucester for a discussion on ILP land policy. Outside, according to the account, were 20 men with black ties manning a large motor vehicle. The intention, said the *Glasgow Eastern Standard*, had been to kidnap Maxton and they had detailed evidence to that effect.[6]

In the months immediately following the collapse of the Labour Government, Maxton and his colleagues turned to discussing Labour's strategy and politics. These discussions centred on the Lansbury's Socialist Club, and later the Communist inspired left wing movement built around the newspaper, *Sunday Worker*

The Socialist Club had been founded early in 1925 when Lansbury, the left-wing MP for Poplar, started the newspaper, *Lansbury's Weekly*, and brought together both MPs and trades union leaders outside Parliament. The Club's programme concentrated on the tactics of Labour in government and advocated the abolition of the House of Lords, and of five-year Parliaments, and the use of special emergency powers to extend the first truly socialist House of Commons. Thus there would be "no more ins and outs" of the kind just experienced. Some of its prescriptions now read strangely – "no fraternisation with the enemy and no wearing of court dress ... no secret diplomacy and no dictatorship by the PM". Even the Labour Party would have to change. A Labour Cabinet would be elected by and accountable to the Parliamentary Labour Party.

Although Maxton respected Lansbury's idealism and fighting qualities, the Club had picked up too much in the way of tiny ideological baggage. Perhaps they knew what to do about court dress but they had, as yet, no clear ideas about what to do about unemployment. Even *Lansbury's Weekly* conceded in May 1925 "the left wing does not know where it stands ... Can we not work out a common programme of action?" Only later in December did the Lansbury group get down to a serious list of practical objectives, including immediate remedies for unemployment such as raising the school leaving age, public works by local authorities, the extension of electrification and promotion of industrial settlement schemes. The aim was to take one million out of an already "overstocked labour market". This programme was a precursor of the Mosley memorandum for reconstruction of 1930. According to their friend John Scanlon, neither Maxton nor Wheatley was "widely enthusiastic over its contents".[7] Most of the MPs were to support MacDonald's administration in 1929, and they did little to develop an effective programme to counter the economic and social problems of the 1920s.

Maxton preferred to concentrate his energies on the narrow and predominantly Scottish group of ILP MPs. Lansbury in return resented the exclusiveness of the Scottish contingent. One Scottish ILP member, Arthur Woodburn, recalls how Lansbury explained "how hurt he sometimes felt when the Scottish MPs banded together to fight for socialism all by themselves and excluded English comrades who were as energetic, as able and as willing as themselves".[8]

The rights of Communist Party members within the British Labour Party was a running debate throughout the 1920s. Advice from outside came as early as 1919 when Lenin had advised British Communists to apply for membership of the Labour Party. "Members of the Labour Party support the Labour Party like a noose supports a hanged man." "Offer," he said, "the Labour Party the right hand of friendship while leaving the left hand free for the knockout blow."

Maxton did not share that view. Long experience on the Clyde had taught him to be suspicious of Communists. He rejected Bolshevism and favoured neither democratic centralism as a philosophy nor full-blooded Soviets as an instrument for managing a socialist society. Most of all he believed that socialism in Britain did not need to be achieved by violence.

On the other hand Maxton took a pluralistic view of the Labour Party, regarding it as a federation of socialists, a broad church, not a band of the Exclusive Brethren – and therefore saw a role for individual Communists inside it. There were after all no more than a few thousand Communists in Britain and although their views had a right to be heard they would be swamped within the much larger Labour Party. He argued this position throughout 1925 despite the early defeat in the January Scottish ILP Conference. For Maxton, tolerance was the issue. A movement which could tolerate Fabianism, he argued, could tolerate Communism.

The debate within the Labour Party went on. MacDonald was determined to exclude Communist membership in any form. Maxton and others argued that individual trade union members who were also Communists should still be eligible for membership.

The same position was argued by the Communist Party via its newspaper, the *Sunday Worker*, and the Left Wing Movement, a tactical amalgam of Communists and non-Communists, a group professedly "for anyone who is on the side of the workers in the class struggle and is prepared to stay on their side to the bitter end". With all the other major left-wing figures – Wheatley, who frequently wrote for it, Kirkwood, Ben Tillett, Tom Mann, the Communist MP Saklatava and the miners' secretary Arthur Cook – Maxton was a *Sunday Worker* shareholder.

He attended a number of meetings, most importantly a *Sunday Worker* rally in May which launched a united left-wing campaign to end any ban on Communist membership of the Labour Party. A few weeks later Maxton suffered an important political setback when the ILP delegation to the Labour Party Conference voted 13 to 10 in favour of the exclusion. Despite this, he went on to sign the *Sunday Worker* appeal to the Conference to bring the Communists in.

In supporting Communist affiliation, and in flirting even peripherally with the new left-wing groupings, Maxton was articulating an as yet unspecified dissatisfaction with the direction the party was taking. The October Labour Party Conference of 1925 simply confirmed these misgivings. Communists were banned from individual membership of the party, and the rules prohibiting their entry tightened up. Maxton could not endorse the majority view, and in a speech on the weekend after the Conference in St Andrew's Hall in Glasgow he explained that he "did not believe in the use of force to crush reason and by shutting the Communists out of the Labour Party they did not kill Communist ideas in the country". He would "rather have men of differing ideas alongside him where he could argue, persuade and reason than shut them out because he knew perfectly well that their ideas would continue".

Maxton's own constituency party in Bridgeton supported him, one of a handful of parties in Britain who refused to operate the ban. The Bridgeton Labour Party claimed that their Communist members were "enthusiastic and valuable" and that they had "more in common with the constructive Communist than with some non-Communist elements within the wide limits of the Labour Party as constituted".[9]

With Labour in Glasgow divided over the Communist ban, the growing rift between MacDonald and the Maxton group deepened, particularly after a small crisis concerning the reselection of MacDonald's old friend, the municipal councillor George Kerr. Kerr blamed Communist infiltration for his failure to be reselected as a Labour Party candidate for the Town Council and gained MacDonald's support for standing for the same seat under the ILP banner.

Maxton was in fact sympathetic to Kerr but his general support for Communist inclusion brought him under suspicion. In the end MacDonald blamed Maxton for Kerr's discomfiture and the loss of a Town Council seat. It could be argued that MacDonald, leader of the party, its hero in 1922, and the first Labour Prime Minister, should not have become involved in matters of reselection in the municipal ward of Springburn. He did and he lost, and that momentous issue proved to be a breaking point with Maxton. One of MacDonald's letters at the time splutters, "the matter will have to be fought out. Glasgow is becoming the laughing stock and at the same time the fear of our movement. If Maxton continues his present policy I shall come definitely out against him. We cannot allow the good results of Liverpool to be frittered away by people who put up no fight there and who prefer to continue to do mischief from the platform when our backs are turned." So began the trial of strength between MacDonald and the Clydeside group that was to dominate Labour politics for the next four years.

21

Moving Left

During his 24 years as an MP, Maxton published few books or pamphlets outlining his socialist faith. Most of his energies were spent doing what he did best, addressing crowded meetings up and down the country. When he wrote the result was most likely to be a newspaper article for *New Leader* or one of the other socialist weeklies. Only rarely did he attempt to write anything longer, but in 1925 he produced a 16-page socialist manifesto, published by the ILP as *Twenty Points for Socialism*. The message was that socialism alone could guarantee the maximum production of wealth and ensure its proper distribution.

In his charge against capitalism he drew evocative illustrations of the extremes of poverty and inequality, which ranged from the slums of Glasgow to child slavery in Shanghai. His proposals for socialist advance included policies for public ownership of the banks, land, food supply and the distributive industries, and the mines.

The pamphlet demonstrated his evolving philosophy. Capitalism was not only immoral but inefficient. Wasteful of resources, slow to innovate, lurching from phases of overproduction to phases of underproducing, it actually prevented the generation of wealth. During the war state ownership had proved itself far more capable of allocating resources and making proper use of them.

The capital levy was still an important element in any advance towards socialism. Stressing that the levy would be imposed on the top fraction of wealth, Maxton gave details of recent research which showed that only 36,000 people owned a third of Britain's wealth and that less than 2% of the population owned two-thirds of it.

The Living Wage proposals of the ILP were not yet in final form but in 1925 Maxton had already identified the low purchasing power of working people as the main problem. By denying itself markets at home, capitalism required militarism and arms spending to survive. "Only armaments can guarantee its operations," he wrote. "Capitalism makes the dreadnought and it makes the slum."

1925 marked the beginning of the Clydesiders' systematic efforts to formulate an alternative strategy for socialism. Perhaps predictably, Wheatley had already been active, running from 1923 onwards in his own newpaper, the *Glasgow Eastern Standard*, a series of articles.

Quite early on, both Wheatley and Maxton had come to the conclusion that free trade and socialism were incompatible and that Labour must support a programme of protectionism and planned trading based on socialist ideas. Their new economic policy relied on achieving an increase in purchasing power and drew on work already prepared in the ILP Living Wage Committee recently constituted by ILP Chairman, Clifford Allen. Now Wheatley went further, arguing that they should reject free trade in favour of a socialist block within the British Empire. He had noted that five Labour Governments had been elected in the Dominions, which, with a Labour Government in Britain, could "form the basis of a block against world capitalism. We would try to induce Soviet Russia to join this grouping. We would oppose such a pact based on mutual working-class assistance to the military pact of the capitalist states."[1]

Both knew that, at home, a miners' strike was not far off. In May 1925 the Prime Minister, Stanley Baldwin, had conceded a year-long subsidy to delay a confrontation over wages with the miners' union but it was simply a postponement of an industrial fight, which, for Wheatley, would be "the greatest struggle in our history". The mines were "the first trench of the industrial battlefield". If the miners were defeated, "I can see no hope of a successful rally". Ten million trades unionists were required, he said, to force the Government to sustain the miners' wages and to solve unemployment by increasing the purchasing power of working people. Wheatley's intervention in trade union affairs angered traditional union leaders. When Ernest Bevin of the Transport Union took exception to his call for militancy, Wheatley replied that industrial peace also required industrial strength at the negotiating table.[2]

Maxton was determined that the concept of the "British Road to Socialism" was developed. Speaking at the ILP Summer School in Dunoon, he spoke of socialism "as a home grown article and not an import from foreign lands". Owen was "the first wild man from the Clyde". Marx had been "influenced by British thought and worked out his theories in relation to British conditions".

At the ILP Summer School, Maxton set himself at a distance not only from MacDonald but also from the Communist Party.

177

His thinking was developing towards a strategy which linked the industrial and political wings of the movement. He was not opposed to Liberals and upper-class members joining Labour, although "they must be prepared to tread the hard road" in what he considered was a class party. He was convinced that the working class could beat the capitalist class by the use of its organised power. The working class could bring capitalism to its knees and "the strike weapon was the most moral weapon that could be used" to this end.[3] Elsewhere that summer he talked of a "great constructive plan for an ILP educational policy" and proclaimed that "the Inevitability of Gradualism is not a fact.... Parliamentary majority means nothing unless it has a mandate springing from the spirit which creates revolution." He criticised the use of the term "evolution". Evolution was a quite meaningless political term suggesting processes during which men waited while forces external to themselves worked changes. The changes which were needed were "well within the hands of men and women".

In the autumn of 1925 Maxton's health broke down once more. He was ordered to rest and cancelled a number of engagements in October and November. With David Kirkwood he went on a cruise to Northern Africa in search of rest and sunshine. On his return he was compelled to deny that he had included a gambling session in Monte Carlo in his itinerary. He was active again early in 1926, addressing a number of demonstrations, but his health relapsed again. Ellen Wilkinson had an explanation. Maxton drank too much tea.[4]

Accession to power within the ILP, growing disenchantment with official policy, and new links on the left worked together to produce a change in the Clydesiders' Parliamentary tactics. Although Maxton was still a member of the Parliamentary Committee alongside Wheatley and Lansbury, the rift with MacDonald was now irrevocable and pressure was being brought to bear for a more independent approach in Westminster.

The radical Wedgewood, in a letter to Brockway, wrote:

> The question really is: will the ILP members help us to fight the Government on everything? The Labour Front Bench is anxious to get through business ... a sham fight ... in order to get days to discuss our questions. Lansbury and I and others are determined to fight whatever the Front Bench may arrange. If by good luck you have a majority at the meeting for a live left wing, do back us up. The danger is drifting into the Tory Party.[5]

Lansbury and Wedgewood proposed that groups of 30 be organised to hold up Government business "save such as may be considered by the party as tending to reduce unemployment". This proposal was vetoed by a PLP subcommittee to inquire into the best way of improving the opportunities for participation by backbenchers. By this time Maxton was absent from the House through illness, and it was Buchanan who took the public eye claiming that although he rejected any split, a new "ginger group" was required in Parliament.[6]

While ILP proposals were being made to change the Parliamentary Labour Party, the ILP Parliamentary Group itself began a series of discussions on the future of the ILP Group. Maxton had been nominated by the Group to lead this discussion but because of his illness the debates had to take place in his absence. One ILP member, John Scurr, was worried that there seemed to be no difference between the activites of the ILP in Parliament and the Labour Party as a whole and deplored the fact that there was "no relationship between the resolutions at the National Administrative Council on political issues and the policy of the Group in the House of Commons".

The ILP Parliamentary Group set up a Committee under Stephen's chairmanship to consider what the Group might do. The committee proposed that they seize all available opportunities to express the ILP position in the House of Commons, and at a meeting of the Parliamentary Group in February 1926, attended by 38 ILP MPs, it was agreed that there had to be closer liaison between the ILP in Parliament and the ILP in the country. One other decision was taken by the ILP MPs, which would strengthen Maxton's position. The full Group, it was decided, need meet only occasionally and the Executive would be entrusted with day-to-day decision making. While Maxton could not guarantee to control the full Group of ILP MPs he was the dominant voice in the Executive.[7]

In 1925 Maxton was still a member of the Labour Shadow Cabinet alongside Wheatley, Kirkwood and Lansbury, but the rift with MacDonald was widening daily as the ILP adopted a more independent stance. Maxton resigned from the Parliamentary Committee, and refused to respond to Henderson's call that he should stand for election. Lansbury, Wheatley and Kirkwood, who had originally planned to stand down, were persuaded to stand again. MacDonald organised a right-wing slate to engineer their defeat. Maxton was unperturbed. As he explained, "I do not think the position in the House of Commons is satisfactory for those who have a revolutionary point of view."

The ILP Parliamentary Group now announced the reorganisation of its operations designed to create the effective Opposition that they believed was required. In March 1926 the Parliamentary Group was reorganised, as Strachey put it, "to watch for all opportunities to bring forward socialist proposals and to state the socialist case in the House of Commons". Tactics would include socialist amendments to the King's Address, socialist motions, ten-minute bills, and amendments to other bills. Informed by the ILP Group of their proposed new line, MacDonald was typically furious. He complained of "a rival and concurrent authority" which would "not endear the members to their other colleagues in the House of Commons". Maxton was undismayed. As he had explained to a rally in Glasgow, on his return from illness, at the end of January 1926, "the duty of the left wing of the Labour Party will be to aim for the establishment of socialism within a reasonable time, and even suppose this clashes with ordinary Parliamentary procedure, the liberation of the workers is of much more consideration than the ancient Parliamentary institutions".

22

Splits and Succession

In 1925 the Chairman of the ILP was Clifford Allen, a bourgeois
socialist converted at Cambridge University who had risen on
the left as Chairman of the No Conscription Fellowship during
the First World War. Like Maxton he had been imprisoned for
anti-war activities and his health, like Maxton's, had suffered.
In 1921 Allen had become Treasurer of the ILP, joining Maxton
on the party's National Administrative Council, and he had been
instrumental in relaunching the *Labour Leader* as the *New Leader*
which with sales of 47,000 a week soon eclipsed the *Spectator*
and the *New Statesman*.

Allen became Chairman in 1924 with support which included
that of Maxton. The two had worked closely together for some
years. At one point, in 1919, Maxton, as Glasgow organiser, had
tried to persuade Allen to stand for the party in the Gorbals
constituency, only Allen's health preventing this.

In his three years as Treasurer, Allen had set out both to
raise money and to instil new organisational enthusiasm into
the ILP which he saw as the intellectual powerhouse of the
Labour Movement. He established a series of working parties to
produce policy development reports such as that on the Living
Wage. Another committee was set up to develop a strategy, later
published as *Socialism in Our Time*.

Conflict between Maxton and Allen was inevitable after Labour's
drift in Government in 1924. Allen had supported Ramsay
MacDonald and the two men had met regularly at Downing Street
where Allen had hoped to influence MacDonald's premiership.
After Allen's brilliant Chairman's address at the 1924 ILP
Conference, Maxton moved the vote of thanks in glowing terms.
He also voiced a reservation which was to assume considerable
significance. "The address counselled too much patience."

After an earlier brush in 1923 on the question of British policy
towards the Ruhr – then still occupied in the aftermath of the

war – Maxton and Allen confronted each other in 1925 on the much more important issue of land nationalisation.

Allen and the majority of the ILP accepted a specialist committee's view that compensation should be paid for nationalised land. Maxton, a member of the committee, publicly opposed this. His position was mocked by Hugh Dalton who pointed out that he had been present at only two of the committee's 24 meetings and therefore brought a "fresh mind on the matter". Maxton was ridiculed as well as defeated.

In the months that followed disagreements between Maxton and Allen multiplied.

In September 1925, the ILP National Council discussed the future of their magazine *Socialist Review*. Clifford Allen tried to persuade the National Administrative Council of the party to invite MacDonald to resume the editorship. After a long and exhausting discussion he was forced to drop the suggestion. Instead, it was agreed that MacDonald should be asked to write the monthly editorial notes, and that Allen should become editor himself.

The final split occurred over the issue of land nationalisation, and in particular over compensation. Maxton was the ILP representative at the Standing Orders Committee at the Labour Party's October Conference and used his position to incorporate the ILP resolution on land into a composite resolution for the Conference. The new composite included a clause precluding compensation for expropriated property owners. By doing this Maxton committed the ILP to a view it had rejected at a recent annual conference: a view, however, that he himself held passionately. Allen was just as passionately opposed to it.

Conflict over compensation and confiscation is as old as the Labour Party itself. In many ways it illustrates the difference between the reformer and the revolutionary, and with hindsight it is clear that confiscation other than in the circumstances of a revolution was not a tenable policy. Democratic socialists distinguish between taxation policies aimed at redistributing wealth from rich to poor, and economic policies to take control over land and industry. Maxton's views pre-dated the formulation of this position and had been developed at a time when the distinction between reform and revolution was not sharply drawn. Nobody knew how the socialist transition was to be carried out. Opposition could be expected of an undemocratic nature and for Maxton confiscation of land or industry was simply the logical extension of the capital levy on personal wealth.

Maxton argued from first principles, and in this matter paid little attention to questions of tactics and strategy. If wealth and the titles of ownership had been unjustly acquired in the first place, the community was right to appropriate them without paying compensation. When the state intervened, it was not violating the rights of wealth holders, but righting the wrongs that they and their predecessors had inflicted on the rest of the community. His argument drew its greatest strength from Scotland where one hundred individuals owned half the land and he was much influenced by Tom Johnston's famous argument for land nationalisation in *Our Noble Families*, written in 1909. Maxton's views had been set out only a few months later in an unpublished and uncompleted pamphlet, *Is Lloyd George a Socialist?*. Landowners and capitalists had, he wrote, "no claim to a share of the wealth produced. The prosperity of many of the wealthy families was founded on robbery, swindling or vice and historical records bear out this contention."

Maxton's views were well known. He had expressed them as recently as the ILP Conference in April and at an ILP Summer School, in Essex, in August 1925. His views were no different, he said, from the policy pursued by the present Conservative Government which had "raided" the unemployment and health insurance funds and had deprived pension contributors of the full value of their pension entitlements. The capitalist system was, he said, "based on theft". Compensation was "a recent outbreak in socialist theory" and Labour support for it was part of a "huckster spirit which would destroy the soul of socialism". It was a form of "commercial socialism" which was prepared to accept "the capitalist view of barter".

Strongly as he held these views, Maxton was prepared to accept a compromise initially suggested by Ramsay MacDonald but supported also by many Scottish socialists including Patrick Dollan. The advice of MacDonald was, Maxton said, to "treat each problem as it arose and in keeping with the circumstances of the time". He believed that the mines should be taken over without compensation but "if the majority of the nation did not support that opinion he as a democrat would be obliged to accept that decision without protest".[1]

Dollan was to propose such a compromise to the ILP's National Council. It supported the MacDonald position of treating every case on its merits. Maxton, who had been chosen as the ILP speaker on both land and workers' control, may have felt that this compromise allowed him the latitude he had used at the Standing Orders Committee meeting. He may also have felt that his appointment as the ILP speaker in the land debates amounted to an endorsement of his personal views, but there was no doubt as to the damage done to the unity of the ILP.

At the ILP National Council meeting that followed there was, according to Fenner Brockway, "a thundery atmosphere. Allen sat at the head of the hotel-room table with a bottle of thick pink medicine in front of him." Maxton's action on the composite resolution was endorsed – Dollan's switch of vote to Maxton was crucial – and Allen was defeated. He "dramatically resigned the chairmanship and, with white face and lips tight shut, walked out".[2]

Allen, explaining to MacDonald his resignation on grounds of ill health, said that his physical weariness was due to months of "unintelligent bickering" which had come to a head in "the series of disgusting events" concerned with the Liverpool Conference and the *Socialist Review*. He was more frank with Maxton. "Your political actions at Liverpool were perhaps the most decisive factor in making me do what I did."[3] He refused, he wrote to another friend later, to be "a cypher chairman", and he could not face "the bickering and unhappiness of the NAC any more".[4]

Maxton, Allen wrote, was guilty of "political irresponsibility, which fell not far short of political untrustworthiness. You of all men I have trusted even when I have fought your opinions." He was "alarmed at the standard of political morality involved". By deserting declared policy on compensation "the future of the party was destroyed".[5]

Allen believed that the ILP and all he worked for was at risk. He criticised Maxton for "the failure of the ILP group in the House of Commons" and in letters to MacDonald he wondered whether the party could survive in any form. He told MacDonald that he found it "useless going on with these people, unless a new group of loyal and reasonably intelligent colleagues can be found".[6]

Allen was not alone in his criticism. Brailsford, then editor of the *New Leader*, wrote to him saying that "your irritation with Maxton and the Glasgow gang extended more or less to everyone on the left".[7] Brailsford was later to resign his editorship of *New Leader*, claiming he had been pushed out by the Maxton group.

MacDonald was now convinced that the new domination by Clydeside would bring the ILP to the point of disaster. Clearly referring to Maxton he complained of "a petty small-mindedness on personal matters and a cheap melodramatic appetite on propaganda". The question, MacDonald said, was "ought we to try and save the party?":

If the ILP would preach the positive doctrines of socialism and give out positive views on social service then it would be of the utmost value. But if it is only going to run on the Wheatley and Maxton line of pose and drama, thinking of effect and not of truth, of heroism and not of wisdom, it has no useful purpose to serve.

The leadership now being offered by the Maxton group was "one of the greatest calamities that can overtake us as it leaves us without real socialist propaganda".[8]

But there was no doubt who was in control now – the Clyde Group. Fred Jowett was interim Chairman only until the Annual Conference of Easter 1926 when Maxton took over. Although Allen was to be invited by the Council to give an address to the 1926 Conference, he refused even to turn up. The 1926 Whitley Bay Conference of the ILP was to make, as one ILP activist put it, "the complete victory of the policy for which Maxton stood". Maxton was elected Chairman with 500 votes more than his nearest rival. What was he going to do with his leadership?

23

Chairman Maxton

"One of the great men of his time, in direct line of succession from Keir Hardie," wrote Tom Johnston. "A natural successor to Keir Hardie in socialist leadership," said Dollan. In April 1926, when Maxton succeeded to the chairmanship of the ILP, he was 40 years old. His unique quality, Dollan explained, was that "his faith is of the kind which the scriptures inform us will remove mountains". Maxton was "convinced that socialist society could be achieved within two decades and his activities are directed accordingly". For him, "socialism is more religious than economic . . . he is the type who could not enjoy if others are without". Dollan said that he reminded him of the holy and angry eloquence of the apostle James.[1]

What sort of Chairman did he plan to be? He was not a writer, he told the *New Leader*. Speech was his normal medium of expression. He was a democrat and a devolver, who wanted power dispersed throughout the ILP, and he did not intend "to exercise a personal influence". He had been told he was "an extremist" and "would not argue the point", but he wanted the ILP to steer clear of feuds and dissension and to act as "a unifying agency". This was his "Easter vow" for 1926.[2]

For all his talk of devolving power, Maxton had a clear view of the direction in which he wanted his party to go. In his first Chairman's address, he spoke of a Labour Party now absorbed in its Parliamentary responsibilities with "a tendency to lose sight of the ultimate ideal. The ILP's duty is to keep the ultimate ideal clearly before the working-class movement of the country. Political success for the Labour Party is a certainty, but political success is itself a poor end unless, behind the Parliamentary majority, there is a determined revolutionary Socialist opinion. It will be part of my duty to try to make as far-reaching as possible this feeling which I believe is the feeling of the party."

From the first, Maxton as Chairman was forced to defend the

ILP's very right to existence. It was attacked from both left and right. Trotsky had ridiculed the Clydesiders as "only a left variety of the same fundamentally Fabian type", and from the right MacDonald was still fuming both over the confiscation issue and "some oratory" at the ILP Scottish Conference in Edinburgh which he blamed for the loss of two by-elections.[3]

Undismayed by these attacks Maxton proposed the nationalisation of the Bank of England in the first of a series of Bills the new ILP leadership put before the House of Commons. He defended the role of the ILP. "There has been a disposition in certain quarters to regard the Independent Labour Party as having served its day as a pioneer vitalising force in the working-class movement, and the suggestion has been made that if it is to have a continued life its functions should be subordinated to the work of the Labour Party. No one who attended the recent conference at Whitley Bay could have felt that the Independent Labour Party has any such intention, but that it intends to continue as a body propagating revolutionary socialist ideas which have still to gain acceptance by a big majority of the people."

In line with his new departure in policy, Maxton and his colleagues set in hand a reorganisation of the ILP to make it a proper vehicle for new tasks. Middle-class experts, hired by Clifford Allen, disappeared from the ILP staff. Salaries of officials were cut to bring them in line with workers' wages. The *New Leader* was to become a paper more suited to the factory floor. Noel Brailsford, a brilliant editor whom Beatrice Webb considered to be the real author of *Socialism in Our Time*, was replaced by Fenner Brockway after Kirkwood criticised his salary as "luxury seized from the bread of my workers". To save more money, the party's headquarters were moved from their expensive buildings in Westminster to less imposing accommodation at Finsbury Park. Under Maxton's chairmanship the ILP, Brockway recalls, was "transformed overnight".[4]

It was a high risk strategy. Snowden was soon to resign from membership, Allen's financial contributions ceased, and MacDonald was now openly hostile."The resources in money and brains of the ILP will dry up," Beatrice Webb predicted in her diary of April 1926. "Most of the larger subscriptions and the greatest interest have come from genuine admirers or persons wishing to ingratiate with MacDonald."[5]

One event which adorned the ILP calendar survived, and indeed prospered, in the Maxton years: the regular summer schools that were organised at Lady Warwick's Easton Lodge in

Norfolk. Lady Warwick had been the mistress of Edward VII but now announced herself to be a socialist. National figures, such as H.G. Wells and Bernard Shaw, were regular lecturers at the schools. At other ILP occasions, international statesmen such as the future German Chancellor Willi Brandt came into contact with the ILP, but the dominant figure at the schools, as lecturer, organiser and entertainer, was Maxton himself. Here, as at conference social occasions, the non-drinking, egalitarian Scot thrived as the master of ceremonies. "Maxton was a supreme entertainer," wrote Brockway, "he would have made a fortune on the stage."[6] Whether singing or dancing, Maxton enthralled his audience, as Dollan recalled.

> Maxton was the compere . . . he was irresistible. He could dance as well as sing and I cannot think of anybody who could make an audience laugh as easily as the ex-Sunday school teacher.
> He was the star artist at all the conference socials in England and Scotland and at the Glasgow functions. His pet turn was the "Pirate King" sung in costume. He wore a coloured bandeau, pirate fashion on his head, and a leather belt round his waist with holders for imitation knives and pistols. The audience always joined in the chorus which had to be repeated ad infinitum. Another ditty he liked was "Darkie's Sunday School" which he had learned at the University and adapted to suit political themes. He would write verses about all the leaders of the Party.[7]

Such was his success as an actor and comic that Maxton once told Brockway he had been offered a leading part in the London stage production of a Galsworthy play.

By now, in the spring of 1926, the whole political attention of the country was concentrated on industrial unrest in the mines. The year's subsidy was due to run out in May, and negotiations were likely to break down over a settlement of the grievances. A General Strike seemed inevitable.

Although now physically exhausted, Maxton returned to his constituency at the end of April. Ignoring all medical advice he took part in a demonstration on Sunday, 2 May, at Glasgow Green. Together Maxton and Wheatley again attacked MacDonald and some of the trade union leaders, calling upon all trade unionists to support the miners but warning them not to take part in riots. It was said Maxton, "a strike against the constitution".

Then Maxton returned to London. Shortly after midnight on

3 May it was officially announced from Downing Street that negotiations had broken down. The General Strike had begun. The miners' slogan, voiced through their leader, Arthur Cook, was "Not a penny off the pay; not a minute on the day", and in a manifesto that was immediately issued by Maxton and the ILP support was offered for "the living wage" demanded by the miners. The ILP was "unreservedly placed" at the miners' disposal, and Brockway was seconded from the party to edit the official Trades Union journal.

Nine days later the General Strike was called off, and the miners struggled on alone. Maxton and Wheatley were furious at the turn of events. Prominent labour leaders, wrote Wheatley, were "whining and grovelling" with the result that "the Labour Movement was deserted in its hour of trial by those in whom it placed the greatest trust". He warned that "now that trade unionism has been mortgaged to its enemies a new form of organisation may be necessary".[8] Maxton agreed. The General Strike, he said, was merely the "end of the first round . . . they were entering the most strenuous and bitter struggle the world had ever seen in which the ILP was bound to play a big part".

Maxton authorised a levy on ILP members, which had raised £50,000 by November, and the ILP became what William Stewart, their Scottish organiser, called the miners' "auxiliary force". Branch rooms and "the entire propaganda organisation" were placed at the miners' disposal. So many ILP branches were rooted in mining communities that in June 1926 Dollan persuaded the National Administrative Council to ask for the resignation of those ILP members who had not responded to their unions' call in the General Strike.[9]

Maxton had once more set off from London to Glasgow. A friend had agreed to drive him and Wheatley by motor car so that they could address meetings on the way. During the journey Maxton again became ill and had to leave the motor car and lie on the road-side before recovering.

Still ignoring the pleas of his friends to rest, he attended a social function organised by his supporters in Bridgeton where he was presented with a portrait of Keir Hardie. But George Buchanan's brother, a doctor, who was at the social, saw how ill Maxton now was, and walking home with Campbell Stephen said that it was time something was done about Maxton's health. Both went to Maxton's home the next day and Maxton was persuaded to go to the Royal Infirmary in Glasgow for an X-ray. He was suffering from a duodenal ulcer at present in grave exacerbation.

The crisis in Maxton's health was not unexpected. During the early months of 1926 he had been complaining of stomach trouble and of his inability to eat certain foods. His diet of cigarettes and tea hardly helped, and his friends had become so alarmed about his health that they persuaded him to go with Kirkwood on holiday to Morocco and France. No improvement resulted. For most of the time Maxton sipped hot milk and refused the choicest delicacies. Even the waiters were alarmed by his haggard appearance.

When he returned he had thrown himself into propaganda work in an attempt to forget his illness and for weeks he travelled the country addressing meetings. He had even tried a diet recommended by Tom Johnston. It consisted of raisins, nuts, cheese, a small portion of fish and other light food – but no meat. For two weeks he kept strictly to it but felt worse as a result and returned to his normal diet of meat, eggs, toast, tea and cigarettes.

When Maxton went into hospital in May he was so weak that doctors doubted whether any operation could be performed for his presumed duodenal perforation. His temperature gradually fell and he recovered sufficiently for surgery to be carried out. For two days afterwards there were fears for his life but the following day the crisis passed and from then on he improved steadily.

In hospital he received many letters and enquiries about his health. Churchill sent him a present of books, MacDonald wrote him a friendly letter, Lloyd George telephoned the hospital, and the entire Liberal Group of MPs hoped he would soon "return to the House where your transparent sincerity, powerful intrepidity in attack, always sweetened by a smile, and, above all, your great human sympathy have endeared you to all men".[10] There followed another month in hospital – and three months of recuperation. A number of aristocratic country mansions were offered for convalescence but Maxton decided to spend several weeks with his five-year-old son on a small island on Loch Lomond.

It took many months for Maxton to recover. In August he appeared in public to attend the funeral of David Kirkwood's son and later a church garden fête in his constituency. He remained on Loch Lomond for two months, the rural solitude broken only by a visit from 30 members of the Bridgeton ILP. Maxton borrowed a motor yacht which he piloted to show them round the Loch Lomond islands.[11]

By the end of October, the *New Leader* announced his return to work. Maxton felt better than he had done for years, and had not only gained substantially in weight but was "berry brown" from his island holiday.

Divisions on the Scottish left were reflected even in the manner in which he was welcomed back to political life. The Scottish Divisional Council of the ILP had arranged a welcome-back reception for Maxton in Glasgow without consulting the Glasgow Federation. In the eyes of the Glasgow Federation this constituted political propaganda and should not have been undertaken without its consent. "Drastic action" was threatened. Happily Maxton remained unaware of this at the time.

Maxton's illness, his operation and his convalescence had prevented him taking any significant part in the events surrounding the General Strike and the subsequent miners' strike. On his recovery he returned to his chairman's duties and began to write a regular weekly column in the *New Leader* which was to continue almost until his death. One of the first was written from home and entitled "The Miners and the Future of Socialism". The General Strike, he said, had been "an enlightenment to the latent power of the working class". A defeat for the miners now would bring "only a temporary truce until Labour rallied its forces for another trial of strength". It would depress wages, increase unemployment and prolong stagnation. Socialists should be demanding more than simply a return to work on previous terms and conditions. "Whether defeat or victory, it seems to me that the Living Wage policy of the ILP must be accepted by the Labour Movement as of first importance in immediate Labour policy."[12]

For Maxton the industrial struggle was only part of the political struggle. Maxton has often been accused of what one writer, Middlemass, has called "a fundamental misreading of history", because he said that the General Strike, and the miners' action, were the opening shots in a new wave of industrial militancy. Certainly Maxton did call the General Strike a notable precedent and at the 1927 ILP Conference said that the miners had "left behind in the hearts of all sections of the working-class movement a bitterness and resentment which will yet find expression in a stronger and more definite form". But throughout, Maxton was more struck by the passivity and apathy of working people and it was this that motivated him, and Wheatley, to campaign yet more effectively for a fundamental change in Labour's policy on unemployment.

24

Socialism in Our Time

Throughout the 1920s Maxton had been at work evolving his main contribution to socialist thinking. This was "the middle way", a radical critique of British capitalism, fully socialist in inspiration, but based on a plan for the immediate amelioration of social conditions as the first step towards socialist change. In his first article of 1927, in the *New Leader*, entitled "MacDonaldism, Communism, and the ILP", Maxton decisively rejected Communism, and the official view of the Labour leadership, elaborating instead what he now defined for the first time as "the third alternative".

> There is a third alternative presented to the working class, neither a long period of misery under capitalism, nor a great economic and social collapse. The third alternative aims at securing political power by the ordinary political machine, aims at developing industrial power by strengthening of the trades unions and at increasing economic power by strengthening the cooperative movement. It aims at coordinating and convincing their movements as they have never been combined before. It tries to get their mass enthusiasm behind the united government and to give it life by making the living income for all the prime object of every human being.
>
> With such a force and such an aim we believe it possible to make the necessary changes through an elected national assembly and to suppress by ordinary legal power backed up by labour organisation any attempt at revolt, to avoid long continued strife of the working class and to reach a decent stable foundation quicker than by any other methods.[1]

The starting point of The Third Alternative, what the *New Leader* now called "the middle way", was an immediate living income for all, the first and irrevocable step in a long-term programme to take control of industry and the financial institutions. To

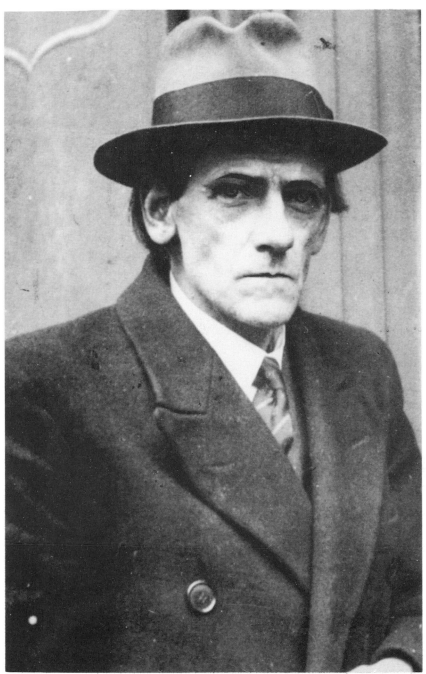

James Maxton
(Photo courtesy of Scottish Daily Record.)

Maxton, Jennie Lee and Mr Tang Li, a delegate from China, at an ILP summer school. (Photo from Maxton Collection, Mitchell Library, Glasgow.)

Scots ILP leaders at a social occasion in Glasgow in 1935: Maxton seated centre, George Buchanan behind him, Campbell Stephen, standing, third from left, William Stewart, the veteran secretary of the ILP seated, extreme left.

Maxton, with hand on chest, addressing a large crowd in 1934.

VOTE FOR MAXTON
AND SAVE THE CHILDREN.

Maxton : the photograph used for his 1945 election address.

Strachey, Maxton was "feeling his way towards a new conception of Parliamentary government".

The Third Alternative was based on the ILP policy of *Socialism in Our Time* and the specific and detailed proposals of their Living Wage Committee. Any study of the politics of the 'twenties is incomplete without understanding that Maxton, Wheatley and the ILP leadership felt they had discovered and evolved a solution to the problem of mass unemployment and its consequences, mass poverty. *Socialism in Our Time* was the distinctive policy of the ILP, and Maxton later explained to the ILP Conference of 1930, "I was asked to use my chairmanship to spread the ideas of socialism in our time by propaganda, to urge its acceptance through the whole Labour Movement and to get it accepted by the nation. That is the task which I have honestly and sincerely tried to fulfil."[2]

In no sense were Maxton and Wheatley adventurists or impossibilists. They had developed a clear conception of an alternative economic policy and a political strategy to go with it before they fought their battles with the official Labour leadership in the late 'twenties. A new urgency arose from the disappointments of the brief period in Government in 1924.

Even before MacDonald became Prime Minister, the Clydesiders had come to two conclusions. The first was that the main reason for unemployment was the lack of demand within the British economy and that only increased working-class purchasing power could remedy this. The second was that neither free trade, supported by the Labour establishment nor the protectionist policies advocated by Stanley Baldwin had anything to offer. Instead Government must plan and control imports and exports in the national interest.

The ILP was seen as the think-tank of the Labour Movement and its Living Wage Committee had done much work on the nation's economic problems. Maxton and Wheatley drew from this and from the documents the Living Wage Committee produced. Their final report was produced in two stages, in 1925 and 1926, Maxton being involved in both as a committee member.

The novelty of the final report, published in September 1926, was its identification of the low demand for goods as "among the potent causes of the widespread unemployment". Low wages diminished domestic purchasing power. "We produce less wealth than our technical resources would enable us to create because the mass of wage earners lack 'effective demand', " the report concluded. "The owning class has misused the advantage of its position." The final report proposed to increase purchasing power by redistributing wealth and laid great stress on fiscal policy. A major family allowance scheme financed from taxation would expand working-class purchasing power as would a minimum wage in all industries.

Nationalisation was supported as a vehicle for the control and direction of the economy, especially in the mining industry and in the financial sector. In depressed industries such as textiles and shipbuilding an Industrial Commission was proposed to enforce "living wages" with the right to impose industrial mergers and amalgamations to achieve these.

Inflationary pressures were, the committee accepted, inevitable as real wages rose, but in conditions of slump the banks should expand credit and reduce interest rates, even at the risk and expense of inflation. Some price rises would be restrained by the bulk purchase of raw materials. To achieve control of credit, the Bank of England was to be brought under public ownership. Additional controls would govern imports and exports.

The proposals were drawn from many contributors and intellectual traditions. Keynes had seen the need to increase demand in the economy but was still concerned by the prospect of inflation. Hobson, whose great contribution to economic thought was the theory of "underconsumption", had demonstrated that economies stagnated when workers could not afford to buy the goods they produced. Though he was not an ILP member, he had agreed to sit on the Living Wage Committee. He did not however agree with all the proposals of the group and "found some disposition to utilise the minimum wage in a way that semed to me dangerous". The young socialist economist Hugh Dalton had argued the importance of distributing wealth and income. Oswald Mosley and an ILP colleague advocated the nationalisation of the banks and the expansion of national credit in order to increase demand.

John Wheatley, described by the then socialist Mosley as a British Lenin, was a major contributor to many of the new ideas. The ex-miner, ex-publican and shopkeeper and now publisher from Lanarkshire had no economic training and indeed no higher education, but had done more than anyone to guide Maxton's political and economic thinking. Many of his ideas were tentative, such as his schemes for a socialist trading bloc consisting of Britain, its colonies and Russia, an idea less extraordinary then than now. The main theme of his programme was the expansion of home demand by improving the purchasing power of British workers. "When you smash the purchasing power of your home market, you destroy the nation," he wrote.[3] It was "not that foreigners were too poor to buy from us but that we were too poor to buy from the foreigners".[4] The first step to socialism was not nationalisation but "national regulation of income and prices" to ensure higher demand. We had to "begin our socialism by socialising the product of labour and raising purchasing power of workers before the nationalisation of the means of production".[5]

Political strategy followed the economic arguments and therefore reduced the role of public ownership in the short term to that necessary for the expansion of demand. 40 years would be required for the complete socialisation of key industries, he wrote, and 40 years of poverty would be intolerable.[6] The only way to get socialism going and minimise mass deprivation was to end the competitive system of fixing wages, incomes and prices. Socialisation of the means of production could proceed more effectively and more successfully once purchasing power was raised. In this way the country could enter socialism "through an era of prosperity".[7] The alternative was a long period of poverty and hardship.

In 1926 and 1927 it was clear that Wheatley and Maxton had begun to outline a wholly new socialist economic policy. For example in January 1927 Wheatley was to contribute an article to the *Glasgow Eastern Standard*, summarising his views and headlined, "The Socialist Policy Explained". The first priority was to raise standards of living.[8] To do this, National Income should be "under national control". The exchange of goods should be in the hands of the nation.[9] Public ownership should take second place to a policy for controlling prices, incomes and wealth.

The "main object and first consideration", even before nationalisation, he concluded, was to raise purchasing power. "It is the income that matters" if property is to be controlled,[10] and he explained in his Budget submission that if by taxing wealth everyone was promised an income of £40 a week, the national income could be raised and the abolition of poverty begun. In a debate with Clynes in December 1926, Wheatley had argued that "you might nationalise any number of industries in this country and be as far away from socialism as before. It is the national control of wealth, it is the collective control of its distribution, that differentiates fundamentally between individualism and socialism."[11]

Socialism in Our Time united many of these themes in a coherent economic and social policy for the Labour Movement. As yet little was understood of the "multiplier", that one family's spending multiplied the amount of activity within the economy, and this prevented economists of the time reaching Keynesian conclusions. But the rightness of the proto-Keynesian solutions as the answer to 'twenties unemployment is now beyond dispute. It was clear to the ILP that high unemployment was caused by low demand, and that demand could be best increased by a system of family allowances and living wages for all.

In its original and later forms *Socialism in Our Time* included provision for a national health service, non-contributory pensions, the nationalisation of key industries and the reorganisation of banking. But at its core lay three policies: state control of credit and money; the payment of family allowances; and the guarantee of a realistic living wage through the establishment in each industry of a commission to stipulate wage rates. It was a socialist way of spending out of slump.

From 1926 onwards Maxton's whole energies were directed towards winning support for the "Socialism in Our Time" programme. He had first to win over his own party. In 1929 when he addressed the London ILP Federation, he spoke of what had to be done.

> Three years ago in spite of "Socialism in Our Time" ILP members were still wedded to the enthusiasm and loyalty of yesterday. It was necessary to bring them to a realisation of the distinctiveness of our policy . . . the gradualists were now in a minority.

Through 1927, and 1928, there were to be major disagreements over precise elements of the programme – and especially over the form in which the "living wage" was to be implemented. In the Living Wage Committee's proposal, the living wage was not to be imposed by law, but an industrial commission could indirectly intervene to stipulate such a wage. Later, under Maxton's influence, the living wage policy was strengthened. It would be compulsory for each industry to implement it within two years.

In 1928, the Scottish ILP conference decided that the essence of "Socialism in Our Time" should be a minimum wage. For Wheatley and Maxton this was merely a plan to control the incomes of the poorest, and was no more than an extension of the trades boards system. Maxton argued that his living wage proposals went further than simply a minimum wage. The incorporation of the minimum wage proposal in "Socialism in Our Time" meant that what had been for Maxton a revolutionary programme to make the payment of wages a basis for nationalising industries and redistributing income and wealth had become little more than an extension of the trades board system. Maxton explained the difference between his programme and wage control.

> I admit that the old method of approaching the living wage problem would be correctly described as patching up capitalism. The old method looks at a particular industry and lays down such a minimum as the industry can afford. Our approach is fundamentally different. We see that the miners, cotton workers and railwaymen are serving the nation and it is the first duty of the nation to insist that they shall be paid a living wage for their services. If their particular industry cannot afford a living wage, the nation certainly can.

In the 1929 plan, industry was required to pay the living income within two years or be taken into public ownership. By 1931, the time limit was one year. In later versions, greater emphasis was placed on Government intervention – including the controversial proposal to reject compensation when industries were taken over. A National Investment Board was to be responsible for the control of credit. The key industries – coal, transport and banking – would be nationalised; Government control would be introduced over the bulk purchase of imports and exports; other industries which failed to pay the living wage would be taken into public ownership; and greater controls would be exercised over credit and prices, with increases in taxation.

Although as an individual ILP MP and as a committee member Maxton had contributed to the production of "Socialism in Our Time", his greatest contribution was his effort to popularise it. As Chairman of the ILP he stood at the centre of a movement which, at various times, embraced most of Britain's leading radical economists, including Hobson, Keynes, G.D.H. Cole, the young Frank Wise, and Hugh Dalton. Maxton saw his job as translating the new economic and social programme into a political campaign which would win both the support of the Labour Movement and that of the country.

The "middle way", as embodied in the "Socialism in Our Time" documents, sought to tackle the economic and social problems of Britain in the 1920s in a way that took account of the realities of British political traditions. Without revolution, it offered reconstruction and redistribution. It tackled unemployment and poverty by methods which, had they been applied, might well have been effective. All this was to be achieved by rejecting both the pathetically subservient and hence ineffective gradualism of MacDonald and the Communist alternative of social improvement by civil catastrophe. Maxton and Wheatley had always believed that social change could be achieved with speed, within the Parliamentary tradition and without violence. Now they had a detailed manifesto which if implemented would do exactly that. Maxton was that manifesto's principal propagandist, and for the next three years he sought to win over the whole Labour Movement to support "Socialism in Our Time".

25

The Rebel Spirit

Maxton's illness had taken him from the political arena for six months. At the beginning he had been desperately sick with complications of a duodenal ulcer which are rarely seen nowadays. Surgery ("some weird and wonderful work to my inside") had saved him at the price of further risk. His convalescence had been long and slow.

The Crusoe-like sojourn on a Loch Lomond island had restored his health. His good humour had remained intact throughout. There had been great interest in his illness from hundreds of friends and supporters, and he joked about capitalising on this by exhibiting the surgical landscapes of his abdomen, at "a shilling a time to cover household expenses".

He returned to his life's work with zest, and in response to the impossible number of requests for appearances and speeches he ventured into a new medium, making a black disc recording of a short speech about the socialist task. Though he knew that thousands flocked to hear him, the sound of his own voice on that record displeased him. Over the frying-pan noises of the technology of the day, it rings out, clear and fairly high-pitched, his accent neutrally Scottish rather than Glaswegian, that of an educated lowlander who has worked to develop a clear and carrying diction.

Maxton was now 41. He had been only four years in Parliament during which he had experienced both the exhilaration of socialist election victories and the disappointment of a Labour Government's failure. He was now fully in control of the Independent Labour Party, its Chairman and its dominating force, and he had a prospectus which had been the product of years of debate and discussion. If in 1922 he had come to Parliament to speak for the slum-ridden tenants of Bridgeton, he had now, in 1926, charged himself with a far bigger mission as the spokesman for an alternative brand of socialism. Ignoring warnings about further risks to his health, he saw it as his duty to propagate his message the length and breadth of the country.

His first speaking engagement was in Derbyshire where he and Kirkwood planned to address meetings of miners at Clowne and Staveney near Chesterfield. Maxton spoke at Clowne but both were banned from the later meeting at Staveney under the terms of the Emergency Powers Act passed to maintain order for the duration of the miners' strike. Kirkwood was arrested. Maxton mused that "the first day in seven months he had attempted to address any meeting other than one or two social gatherings in Glasgow last weekend", the weight of the law fell upon him. As a member of the House of Commons, Maxton insisted that he was "not an irresponsible street corner agitator", and if he could be prevented from speaking in the country at a time of national crisis then "the Parliamentary system was at an end".[1]

Kirkwood was charged with disaffection under the Act and when his case came before Derbyshire Police Court on Monday, Maxton was there to support him, as were Neil McLean, Tom Johnston and Campbell Stephen. Kirkwood asked for time to prepare his defences and it was granted. A few days later he was fined £25. During the first court hearings Maxton had interjected to accuse the prosecuting counsel of offering "impertinent advice" and the magistrate had ordered his removal from the court. To prevent an incident Maxton volunteered to leave. At the station Maxton used the event to swipe at the moderation of the Labour leaders. There were, he said, "a great many statesmanlike people in the Labour Party who went around the country watering the rebel spirit. The Clyde men did not believe in that. Everywhere they saw the outbreak of the rebel spirit, they said 'Thank God'."[2]

There were divisions in the Labour Party over foreign affairs too. War was threatened in the Far East over Manchuria. Maxton defended Labour's commitment to the Chinese people when they were threatened by Japan. The Baldwin Government were acting like "hooligans" in refusing to support China's right to self-determination and the Labour leadership was backtracking over previous commitments. He proposed an emergency motion accordingly at the ILP's National Conference in April. Yet again Maxton and Wheatley had set themselves up in opposition to MacDonald.

The ILP's strong internationalist traditions were nurtured by the contacts they made with foreign socialists who attended their summer schools and lecture courses. In the early 'twenties Maxton was one of a majority in the ILP who had sought to keep alive the unity of anti-war socialists in what was called the "Two and a Half" or "Vienna" International. That gathering had despaired of both the pro-war factions in the Second International and the pro-Soviet Third International which was dominated by Moscow. When the "Two and a half" in its turn failed, the ILP attempted to bring all international socialists together in one new International, and then reconciled themselves to the Second International after it was reconstituted at Hamburg in 1923.

One weakness of the Second International was the omission of colonial countries who were fighting for self-determination and in February 1929 Fenner Brockway, who was also on the Executive of the Second International, became Chairman of a new League Against Imperialism, a conference which represented nationalist organisations from colonial dependencies and working-class parties from Europe. When the new organisation was opposed by the Second International because of its known links with Moscow, Brockway resigned and Maxton took over as Chairman.

The Maxton chairmanship of the League was brief but full of incident. When he travelled to the Cologne conference of the League almost two years later in February 1929, he was detained at Ostend, told he could not proceed further and was able to reach the conference only after angry exchanges with the British Foreign Office. On his way back, he was again detained, this time at Dover, where his luggage was searched. Maxton and Wheatley raised the incident in the House of Commons, Maxton complaining that he and his colleagues had been treated like "international crooks and dope smugglers". Replying, the Foreign Secretary, Austen Chamberlain, gave them little comfort. Chamberlain admitted he had been considering a restriction on the issue of passports "in certain cases". Clearly Maxton was one of these cases.[3]

Maxton's chairmanship ended abruptly six months later, just after the 1929 election. In a speech to a further conference at Frankfurt, he had spoken out against the "imperialist policy" of the new Labour Government. The Moscow-dominated group, then in control of the League, ordered him to republish his speech in the New Leader. Angry, as always, at any hint of improper pressures, Maxton refused, and was unceremoniously expelled from the League. Maxton heard of the decision when he was on holiday in Largs. Undismayed, he said he was "more interested at the moment in the solution of a mystery story than half a dozen expulsions from the League Against Imperialism".[4]

In 1927, however, over their support for the League, Maxton and his colleagues had set themselves up in opposition to MacDonald.

Local events brought open conflict nearer. The Liberal MP for Leith, Captain Wedgewood Benn, had defected to Labour and resigned his seat, in the expectation of the Labour candidacy in the subsequent by-election. Instead the Leith Labour Party chose a left-winger, Bob Wilson. His loyalty to the Labour Party was in doubt, but under the pressure of Arthur Woodburn, now a Scottish party organiser, he agreed to be bound by the party line.

In the heat of the by-election Wilson had come out for "confiscation" which may have lost him the seat. Woodburn certainly thought so and the Scottish Executive complained that Wilson had single-handedly sparked off a Liberal revival. Wilson was called to account on the issue by the Scottish Executive of the party. For good measure Maxton was too, after the appearance of an article by John Wheatley which emphasised his friend's views on the matter of confiscation. "Labour electors are not afraid of his policy," Wheatley wrote. "The people who denounce it are opposed to social ownership on any terms."[5]

A third divergence between Maxton and MacDonald concerned the annual election of the Labour Party Treasurer. At that time MacDonald himself was Treasurer, having been nominated by the ILP in previous years. In July 1926 the National Council of the ILP had passed a resolution stating that all ILP nominees were expected to support ILP policy. When Dollan had pointed out the decision was unconstitutional it had been ruled out of order and rescinded.[6] But matters came to a head when the National Council refused to renominate MacDonald for the 1927 Treasurer's election.

Nine Scottish Labour MPs signed a Round Robin letter opposing this action. Others who signed included Pat Dollan's wife, Agnes, and three former MPs. They protested at the way MacDonald had been treated by Maxton and his colleagues on the Executive. Although the ILP Conference ratified Maxton's views, by 211 votes to 118, Wheatley claiming MacDonald still enjoyed their respect and loyalty, the press highlighted yet another division in Labour's ranks. The tension was heightened by Maxton's Chairman's address, which contained sharp criticism of the 1924 Labour Government's record and called for 100,000 new members to support "Socialism in Our Time".

As Maxton continued to invite criticism for his swipes at the party leadership, and was becoming more isolated in Labour and ILP circles even in Scotland, John Wheatley was considering leaving politics altogether.

After four years on the Labour Front Bench Wheatley made a speech attacking official Labour policy on the Poor Law and regained the freedom of the back benches. There were other more personal reasons for Wheatley's withdrawal. In a private letter of July to Ramsay MacDonald he confided that he was considering leaving politics altogether. A minor consideration was anxiety over his health. The more important reason was a complicated law suit which threatened to bankrupt him. Wheatley had taken exception to remarks made by a Conservative opponent about propriety in his business life and had, perhaps inadvisably, sued for damages. Now, as a result of legal technicalities, he faced the prospect of losing. As he told MacDonald, he had "carefully refrained from revealing what is passing through my mind to anyone outside the family", but

> I have three strong reasons for retiring temporarily from politics. It is not fair to have the party bear my burden.
> The litigation will cost me several thousand pounds. Contrary to popular assertion, I am not rich and must retrieve this sum. To do so my undivided attention to business is essential.
> I had a dangerous attack of blood pressure during the 1924 election and have been medically warned on three occasions. I am very well now but a strenuous campaign will do damage.[7]

While, in that summer of 1927, Wheatley pondered his future, Maxton continued to act independently of the Labour leadership. Independence went as far as being suspended from the House of Commons.

On 23 July the House of Commons was giving a third reading to the Trades Disputes Bill, which outlawed any future General Strike and attempted to break the connexion between the Labour Party and the trade union movement by compelling workers to "contract in" to pay the political levy. Maxton had been incensed by the speech of the Attorney General, who had sought to argue that the Bill was based on principles of natural justice. First Maxton ridiculed the Government's case, calling the Attorney General "a sort of Moses who was descended from Mount Sinai and presented us with principles which are presumably to take the place of the much more ancient Ten Commandments". Then Maxton attacked the integrity of the Attorney General directly, accusing him of "prostituting" his legal knowledge to weaken the bargaining power of working people.

He has used his skill to deny them the right to struggle for something better. I say that this is political blackguardism, that this is political treachery and I say that the Rt Hon Attorney General is a blackguard and a liar.

Refusing to withdraw the word "liar", Maxton was once more suspended from the House.[8]

As previously, he was philosophical about his suspension. To his Bridgeton constituents, who knew about irony, he described the offence against Commons procedures as "a frightful crime". The Trades Disputes Bill mattered because it encouraged trades unionists to stop paying the political levy to Labour and its real purpose was "to deny them the right to struggle constitutionally to get out of their poverty", part of a Government strategy "to disarm the trade union movement prior to the next election".

Relations between Maxton's ILP and the Labour Party were now so bad that at the Labour Party Conference a resolution was tabled calling for the abolition of the ILP. Maxton said he had "no reason to believe that any of the Labour Party leaders support this idea".[9] Instead he called on the Labour Party to abolish capitalism. Their aim must be, he said, "to penetrate the heart of the citadels of capitalism controlling the country's nerve centres". He wanted a "clear majority on socialist issues undiluted to meet timid people here or prejudiced people there or interested people in some other place".[10]

Parliament had resumed for only a few days when Maxton was suspended yet again. On 23 November, during the committee stages of the Unemployment Insurance Bill, the Tory committee chairman, Mr John Hope, had prevented George Buchanan from introducing new amendments. Buchanan had wanted to force Ministers to enquire into the finances of the Unemployment Insurance Fund every year, but his real objective was to press the Government to consider the plight of the unemployed who depended on insurance benefits. Maxton queried the Committee Chairman's ruling and called his behaviour "damned unfair". When he was asked to withdraw these words he refused, claiming that the Chairman had been "both offensive to myself and degrading to the dignity of this House". Despite efforts by Ramsay MacDonald to intervene on his behalf, Maxton was suspended from the House by 262 votes to 131.

But the incident was once again transformed into a Parliamentary drama as one by one ILP colleagues also courted suspension. George Buchanan called Hope's behaviour "contemptible", and was ordered out. He was followed by Dick Wallhead, who found the Chairman's ruling "a damned disgrace", and then by Neil McLean who accused the Chairman of bias. As a new Parliamentary storm raged around him, Maxton told the waiting press that he had "no regrets and no intention of apologising". He had, he said, never been in trouble "except when he believed that the circumstances were grossly unfair and prejudicial to his case". Because it was "my second offence within a year" he was suspended until after Christmas.

On MacDonald's personal recommendation, the Parliamentary Labour Party had voted against Maxton's suspension but a few days later MacDonald wrote him a stinging private rebuke:

> I decided to put in the official Whips to tell against your suspension last week but I want to be perfectly candid with you in saying that had I known the language you used which occasioned your suspension I should not have done so. I wish to make a very strong protest against that language. Several members have spoken to me about it and I can assure you it gave great offence to the vast majority of your colleagues. Its effect is to drag us down to public house level. I was informed that Hope had shown his usual insulting hand and that I shall not tolerate, but cursing and swearing in public, in the House of Commons, to crowded galleries, and in front of representatives of the newspapers, is one of the great disservices that any man can do to our party.
> I am very sorry to have to write this, but the case demands it.[12]

But for Maxton Parliamentary theatricals were only part of a broader campaign highlighting the needs of the poor and canvassing support for the "Socialism in Our Time" policy. In a typical speech in Glasgow, just before his second suspension, he outlined the details of his programme. All along he had "been dissatisfied" with both Communists and Gradualists. Violent revolution in Russia had brought "tremendous suffering" which should be avoided. He wanted fundamental socialist change "without bringing one additional scrap of suffering to any human being". Nevertheless it was "better to have a few months of turning up than centuries of degradation". Yet he had to concede he was disappointed after "unsuccessful industrial action".

Nationalisation was now taking second place in the programme which Maxton was putting forward. His most immediate priorities were the five shilling (25p) family allowance, a £4 a week minimum wage backed by state subsidies and increased pensions, paid for by a two shilling (10p) in the pound surtax on all unearned incomes above £500.[13]

But Maxton's conduct – his independent line, his attitude towards MacDonald and, especially, his suspensions from Parliament – was beginning to draw more serious criticism. In December 1927, Snowden resigned from the ILP complaining about the direction of its policy and stating that the ILP had "served its purpose". Criticism came from Scotland also as Maxton and his supporters were blamed for disappointing municipal election performances. In a letter to Tom Johnston, MacDonald complained that local election reverses where Glasgow had done "so poorly" revealed a "bad state of mind" within the Scottish Party, and demonstrated the need " to shut off a lot of our hot air".[14]

McNeill Weir, a Clydeside colleague of 1922 but now MacDonald's Parliamentary Private Secretary, joined the attack on the Clydesiders complaining in an article in *Forward*, "Do Rows Help Labour?", that their conduct was equivalent to "disloyalty". Blaming Neil McLean, Stephen and Buchanan, he wrote of "a grotesque and infatuated egotism" which had produced "the fantastic fooleries that our enemies base their constant taunts of Labour disaffection and socialist disunity".[15]

McNeill Weir's article had refrained from directly criticising Maxton, but Maxton wrote to concede that "I created the disturbance which he criticises", and asked that McNeill Weir withdraw his "untrue and unkind" attack on his three colleagues. When one of MacDonald's old friends, George Kerr, passed on the piece to the leader, acknowledging that "Maxton is too big and that Weir is too afraid to tell them off", MacDonald replied saying that "the whole lot should have been mentioned including one which did not appear in public and which was largely responsible for the whole affair".[16]

Stiffened by the support of MacDonald loyalists, McNeill Weir stepped up his attack on the Clydeside left. Claiming to be "astonished at the overwhelming volume of approval and support" for his first article, McNeill Weir now singled out Maxton for special criticism in a further piece for *Forward*.

Maxton knows what I am attacking began early in 1923 ... I suggest he cannot deny the following:

That for months past the press has been proclaiming an open socialist revolt etc.

Time and time again a tiny handful of the party have flouted the party's decisions and contemptuously ignored the advice of the party.[17]

1927, which had begun with Maxton promising a huge campaign to win Labour to "Socialism in Our Time", had now ended with Maxton on the defensive and appearing to be isolated even in his Scottish stronghold. A new, and bolder, initiative to win support for his position seemed now to be required.

26

The Cook-Maxton Manifesto

The Cook-Maxton manifesto, issued in June 1928, was the most dramatic attempt to win the Labour Party to the ideas of *Socialism in Our Time*. It had modest beginnings, in a House of Commons committee room where the core Clydesider group was joined by an ILP journalist friend, John Scanlon, and the Communist leader, Willie Gallacher. The proposal that emerged from the meeting was that Maxton should join forces with Arthur Cook, the miners' leader, to issue a manifesto to appeal both to the trades unions and the Labour Party.

Maxton had worked closely with Cook since 1926. The two had toured the Highlands together with Pat Dollan in that autumn. For three years Cook's talents as a leader had impressed Wheatley and Maxton. In a newspaper article, Wheatley described how in 1926 he had "seen young men and women literally kiss Cook's garments".[1] For Maxton, Cook was "the greatest figure in the Labour Movement during the past three years". During the miners' strike, Cook, Maxton told a radio audience, had "fought practically as one man to prevent the starvation of the miners and their wives and families".[2]

Two events contributed to the preparation of the manifesto. Cook was about to be expelled from the TUC General Council for his opposition to talks with employers' organisations and his refusal to treat General Council discussions as confidential, and the Labour Party had just issued a new policy statement, "Labour and the Nation", which, in Maxton's view, contained "too much in the way of rhetorical flourish and too little in the way of solid legislative proposals". Of its 63 paragraphs Wheatley was later to say that 60 were capitalist and three socialist. There was only one event worse than not returning a Labour Government under MacDonald, Wheatley said, and that was having one. A Labour Government elected on such a manifesto, Wheatley told Scanlon, would "set the movement back twenty years".[3]

The main aim of the campaign was to broaden support for "Socialism in Our Time" beyond the narrow confines of the ILP. The previous few months had held out little promise. In the House of Commons Maxton had been accused of bloodymindedness by his ILP colleagues and at the ILP's Scottish Conference in January, Maxton's own version of "Socialism in Our Time" had ben substantially watered down. Maxton's version was the radical one including a "living wage", the nationalisation of land, banks and the railways and controls over imports and exports. Dollan saw it as a policy for little more than a minimum wage, and minimised the ILP's differences with official Labour policy. Maxton had lost the vote. A similar defeat followed at the national ILP conference in April.

The Cook-Maxton manifesto, elaborated later in a pamphlet entitled *Our Case*, outlined Maxton's political strategy for winning popular support for "Socialism in Our Time". It took an uncompromising class view of society opposing those who believed that "the party is no longer a working-class party but a party representing all sections of the community". For Maxton, capitalism and socialism had nothing in common. The basis of socialism as a political creed was, he wrote, that society was divided into two classes in constant struggle. Only a fully active and politically conscious working class could bring radical socialist change. The concern was that there had been "a serious departure from the principles and policy which animated the founders", and that "much of the energy which should be expended in fighting capitalism is now expended in criticising everybody who dares to remain true to the ideals of the movement".

Nobody concerned with the manifesto thought that revolution was round the corner. "I want to be quite plain and straightforward," Maxton said, "that if you took a vote of the working class today between 'Socialism in Our Time' by Maxton and Cook and the 'Inevitability of Gradualism' by Ramsay MacDonald and Thomas, they would get the majority easily. That is why Cook and I are going right to the masses who hold the power."[4]

He was not asking people "to leave their present political associations", he explained in an interview in the *Glasgow Eastern Standard*. The reason for the initiative was that "the Labour Movement is practically dead. We are trying to bring it back to life. That's all. In the old days there was a goal to reach and we felt that every meeting, every pamphlet, every vote concerted and every seat won was a tangible and positive step nearer the goal. Today nobody believes that anything makes any difference."[5]

After his radio debate with a Tory, Ernest Benn, many listeners had written to Maxton "demanding a Labour Movement that could show a fighting spirit". His was "an attempt to inspire the people on a national scale with the spirit we had on the Clyde during the war when the Clyde Workers' Committee was in being. In those days a man felt sure Labour was worth striving for."

The manifesto did grave damage to the ILP. First reactions were of surprise. Emrys Hughes was "left in doubt as to what Cook and Maxton meant" with a manifesto "full of vague generalities". It was "a violent, vigorous and entirely futile display of desperate shadow boxing".[6] Maxton's old friend Patrick Dollan was angriest of all and led the assault on Maxton at one of the most heated meetings the ILP National Council had held. Dollan's motion, that there be no cooperation with the Cook-Maxton campaign, was narrowly defeated but it won unanimous support in Scotland. "Speaking as Chairman of the Divisional Council in Scotland," Dollan told the National Council, "he regarded the manifesto as the most serious interference with ILP organisation and standing that had happened in his time."[7]

The problem as Dollan saw it was that Maxton's connections with Cook and his open invitation to other groups seemed to invite what the ILP had spent years avoiding: an open association with the Communist Party and its front, the Minority Movement. Maxton denied this: he strongly resented the idea which he detected amongst some of his colleagues that he was "a disguised Communist" intent on furthering "the interests of the Communist Party". Both the Minority Movement and other Communist organisations had pressed Maxton to allow them to adopt the proposals and publicise them in their newspapers. "This he had definitely turned down to avoid starting new movements and factions."

Dollan's view was different. The ILP Chairman had called conferences outside the ILP which had included "extreme elements". Dollan also stressed "the extreme difficulties which had beset the Glasgow movement in withstanding Communist Party attacks", and believed that the Chairman had innocently associated himself with these events. Nevertheless they represented a major setback to the party in Scotland.[8]

The Cook-Maxton campaign opened on July 8, with a meeting in St Andrew's Hall, Glasgow, so crowded that an overflow meeting had to be organised. Maxton's themes were the changes now taking place in capitalism and the need to reverse the conservatism of the Labour leadership. He confessed to being "unhappy and discontented" at events around him. Capitalism, far from breaking down, was regrouping in monopolies and was "entering a new phase of trustification". Ramsay MacDonald's reaction had been to moderate the policies and impose upon the working class a kind of conservatism. Because MacDonald had the majority now, the campaign was necessary. From the accounts of Gallacher, Scanlon and Paton, who had attended the rally, the speech did not engender the enthusiasm expected. Maxton had been more restrained than usual, careful to avoid personal attacks on the Labour leadership and to counter accusations that he would damage Labour's electoral prospects, and Cook had disappointed as he read out what one onlooker recalled was "a typewritten dissertation on Marxism".[9] Perhaps both Maxton and Cook were uncertain about the political response to their initiative. Wheatley left in rage, tearing up the cheque he had promised to help finance the remainder of the campaign.

Further rallies were held in Manchester in July, in Newcastle, Derby, Nottingham, Cardiff and Bristol in August, and in Halifax and Leeds in September. Supporters were asked to pledge a shilling, or more, to the campaign. David Kirkwood acted as Treasurer of the campaign and a study of his balance sheets shows that large numbers of people attended the meetings. Many congratulatory letters to Maxton survive. Following requests for further details, Maxton and Cook published their pamphlet, *Our Case for a Socialist Revival*, written mostly by Maxton. The main theme was that the Labour Party had to change course.

> The Labour Party should scrap its existing programme and develop a vigorous socialist programme. It should retain the federal basis and allow scope within its ranks for all working-class political parties and all members of these parties. In doing so it would avoid not only the danger of a split but would call forth the enthusiasm of the rank and file.[10]

The Cook-Maxton campaign received little practical help from the ILP and none from Scotland. The Scottish Divisional Council unanimously "disagreed with the spirit and purpose of the document". They complained about the collection of funds and about the financial appeal made in *New Leader* for subscribers. One problem was that the Glasgow meeting had been organised privately. Maxton later explained "the reception of the manifesto in Scotland among the people to whom he had a right to look for support was so hostile that he engaged the support of two old friends and old members of the ILP, John Wheatley and John Cruden, and with the support of these had proceeded to organise the meeting".[11]

When condemned for "private enterprise" by the Scottish ILP his explanation was the same. The offence, caused by the private organisation of the Glasgow meeting, was unintended, but "local ILP leaders were hostile and therefore it became necessary to appeal over their heads to the rank and file". Dismayed by this excuse, Dollan responded that "it was unlikely that there will be any more unofficial campaign meetings in Scotland".[12] Dollan was wrong – meetings were held in Lanarkshire and Edinburgh – but Scotland as a whole played little part in the campaign.

Maxton and Wheatley were threatened with "court-martial", not just by the ILP but by the Parliamentary Labour Party. A special meeting of the PLP was held and Maxton and Wheatley were summoned to it. Clynes, Thomas and Henderson all attacked Maxton and Wheatley, Clynes saying that if the two MPs differed with the party they should leave. Henderson asked why Cook and Maxton were appealing for one million promises of a shilling when the Labour Party was in financial difficulty.

The Clydesiders were on weak ground. Wheatley asked simply why they had been singled out for trial. Maxton refused to make an apology and would make no promise on his future line of action. A motion to condemn Maxton and Wheatley fell but a motion implicitly criticising them succeeded. It reaffirmed that the Parliamentary Party meetings and the Conference were the appropriate vehicles for policy discussion and expressed the hope that criticisms of differences would be expressed in this "constitutional way". Only 11 opposed it. Most of them were Clydesiders.

The Cook-Maxton manifesto had failed to win even the support of the ILP. Its failure at the Labour Conference in Birmingham was predictable. A three-day debate on Labour's new policy document, *Labour and the Nation*, had been arranged. MacDonald introduced it, wound up the first day's debate and dealt with the detailed amendments later in the week. Maxton spoke on the first day. Socialism, he said, could no longer be approached by "a long slow process of gradualistic, peaceful Parliamentary change". With capitalism in crisis, the Government should introduce socialist measures "at tremendous speed". Wheatley went further. *Labour and the Nation* would leave socialism still to be implemented. The slogan should be "socialism is your only remedy". MacDonald retaliated by questioning their support for Parliamentary democracy. A young MP, Herbert Morrison, also went on to the attack after Maxton had asked that Conference give its MPs day-to-day guidance:

> Well I hope that the Whips give it to him and when the Whips have given it to him I hope he will do what the Whips tell him. If he does not do what the Whips tell him I hope that the Parliamentary Party will deal with him.[13]

Support for Maxton and Wheatley was so small that the programme was adopted without a vote and the amendment on "The Living Wage" was defeated by 2,780,000 to 143,000. Wheatley was to blame it on "the card machine vote" which gave "no indication at all of the throbbing enthusiasm for socialism evident at the Conference". The reality was that the trades unions were anxious to protect their rights to free collective bargaining and believed "The Living Wage" programme to be an unnecessary interference.

On the Sunday after Conference, Maxton addressed a crowded meeting in the Olympia Theatre in Glasgow. His speech, the *Glasgow Eastern Standard* predicted, would decide "whether the clashing elements can be fused into a harmonious whole or an open rupture would take place".[14] Maxton made clear his loyalty to the Labour Party but said it would be "no use if he hoisted the white flag the minute he got a black eye. The fight would go on still", but it was a fight for the incorporation of specific commitments in the *Labour and the Nation* programme. In accepting his defeat Maxton outlined his four immediate demands: more nationalisation, the five shilling family allowance, the living wage, and price controls. "The task before them was to see that out of that long general statement was taken a strong socialist programme."[15]

Both he and Wheatley argued that their role now was to ensure the few radical elements in *Labour and the Nation* appeared in the manifesto for the next Labour Government. "If our enemies think that Maxton and I or any of our friends are going to leave the party they are as far wrong as they usually are in things political. But we do intend to use our influence in the movement to keep it on the direct road to socialism." The duty of socialists was "to concentrate on the selection from the Birmingham programme of the socialist items and make them as far as possible the programme of the next Government".

Maxton claimed to have received promises that there would be progress on the ILP's "Living Income" proposals, and on family allowances, unemployment relief and the nationalisation of the Bank of England. It would, said Wheatley, "only be a short time until the socialist spirit again dominates the Labour Movement".[16]

To some extent their optimism was justified. Throughout 1928 and 1929 pressures grew on MacDonald to adopt a more specific socialist programme. In January 1929 Tawney, who had drafted most of *Labour and the Nation*, warned Arthur Henderson that if the Labour election programme was to be of any use it had to have something concrete and definite about unemployment. "The pages on that subject in *Labour and the Nation* are not up to scratch." MacDonald, however, was to stand out for vague commitments rather than specific promises.

Yet Maxton's private initiatives brought disagreements within the ILP in Parliament to a head. From 1925 onwards the ILP Parliamentary Group had operated with few Group meetings and day to day control in the hands of a small executive committee which Maxton and the Clyde members dominated. When Parliament resumed in October 1928 pro-MacDonald members of the ILP met secretly to discuss changes in the operation of the Group and, when there were calls for a detailed discussion of future strategy, a full meeting of the ILP members was convened. About 80 Labour MPs attended two stormy sessions in the first two weeks of December at which Maxton was carpeted.

Shinwell accused Maxton of "guarded hostility" towards the Labour Front Bench and for presenting "a competing policy" to that of the Labour leadership. One MP, Dr Arthur Salter, held Maxton personally responsible for "the destruction of the ILP". Another complained that Maxton had forced divisions in the Commons merely to embarrass his Labour colleagues. Most of those present criticised him for attacks on Ramsay MacDonald and for his associations with Arthur Cook. Oswald Mosley, who defended Maxton's general behaviour, was scathing about the "extraordinary difficulties" caused by the Cook-Maxton campaign.

The discussion was frank and open. Both Wheatley and Maxton readily conceded their difficulties. ILP members, they said, had to operate with "a dual personality" loyal both to Labour and the ILP. Maxton felt he had been made "a villain of the piece" and was "like a Cabinet Minister under attack". The whole problem of his leadership had been "shot across with the problem of the conduct of the Scottish members". Ever since he came to Parliament he had been criticised for his work as a backbencher but the activities of the Clydesider brigade had "nothing to do with the ILP NAC".

Under further attack Maxton responded, listing the tasks he had set himself as Chairman and the problems encountered. His job, he said, was to propagate "Socialism in Our Time". The ILP, he explained, had sought a new role after the Labour Party had introduced individual membership in 1918 and adopted its socialist constitution. Some had thought the ILP should be a research body, and others an organisation primarily interested in foreign affairs, but it had been decided, under his predecessor, to campaign for the policy of "Socialism in Our Time". "In all the discussions that had taken place about the new programme of the ILP he had played a minor part in the decisions." The programme had been "completed and accepted before he had become Chairman". Its novelty was its concrete proposals and its emphasis on speed in creating socialist change. It was therefore inevitable that they would criticise MacDonald.

No Mandate for Socialism

Maxton had been defeated at the Labour Conference. His bold initiative in "Socialism in Our Time" had fizzled out. The ILP was split. Maxton was undismayed. His strengths – his capacity for simplifying and dramatising political concepts and his ability to enthral political audiences were now familiar to him and the failures of 1928 were not, for him, final. Though he had failed to win over the Labour Party in one compelling great leap forward, he could still work within it to achieve singly on specific issues what could not be won in a great national campaign. In a series of speeches, newspaper articles and House of Commons interventions in the new Parliamentary session, Maxton called for detailed policies to tackle the problem of unemployment. This would only be achieved by the return of a Labour Government with specific measures in its manifesto. As Maxton later explained, he had accepted "the defeat which we received in the democratic vote of the working-class organisations of the country" and since then "worked strenuously to bring about the electoral triumph of Labour even though I do not agree with the policy accepted".[1]

At the ILP's Conference the following spring Maxton propounded a fiscal solution to the unemployment problem. The tiny minority of the very rich would pay far more in tax on their predominantly unearned income. By one bold stroke an additional £250 million could be raised to fund an employment programme. Being Maxton he had a vivid phrase for it: "A hundred money-lenders shall not tyrannise the state."[2] Labour's Shadow Chancellor, Philip Snowden, was furious. A moment's examination of such a suggestion, he said, would expose it as "an utter absurdity". It would "eliminate the supertax payers altogether" mainly because such draconian taxation as Maxton proposed could not be sustained by any section of the population, however rich.[3]

The General Election came in May. Labour's manifesto, in the hands of MacDonald and Snowden, was exactly the sort of document that Maxton had feared. It was even less specific than the Liberal manifesto of Lloyd George which promised to "conquer unemployment". In the circumstances, the ILP felt justified in producing a manifesto of its own. This represented the Maxton view. The people could choose capitalism or socialism but not both. Socialist change could be achieved by nationalising the banks, railways and mines with Government control over import and exports and the implementation of the living wage.

In his own personal manifesto for the electors of Bridgeton, Maxton was even more specific. He wanted increased unemployment benefit, larger widows' pensions and a commitment to minimum wages in industry. Family allowances should be introduced, hours of labour regulated, and educational maintenance allowances provided to encourage pupils to continue in school.

By 1929, Scotland, and Bridgeton, was little better housed, or fed, than when the Clydesiders had come to Parliament. Scotland had needed 250,000 houses: throughout the 1920s only 89,000 had been built. Scotland's infant mortality was now a third higher than that of England. With rising unemployment, a tenth of the population were dependent on the Poor Law.

The Bridgeton Labour Party, under whose banner Maxton fought, had itself been racked by the long standing internal conflicts of the Labour Party. Although sectarianism and factionalism affected the Labour Movement throughout Scotland, Bridgeton had been particularly troubled. In 1925 the party branch had been closed down after refusing to ban Communists from membership. An official party investigation had discovered "an individual section of 15 men sending 10 delegates of a Communistic type held the balance of power".[4]

For two years the constituency party officially did not exist, and then an attempt was made to reorganise it in accordance with the Labour Party constitution. Bridgeton demurred, insisted on maintaining its Communist links and affiliated itself to the National Minority Movement. In the municipal elections that followed the prohibited rump contested the Calton division of the constituency, fielding a Communist against an ILP candidate who also claimed to be the official Labour nominee. A gratified Conservative took the seat.

As if ideological troubles were not enough the constituency party was split by religious issues and over the question of temperance. Independent Catholic candidates dislodged ILP nominees from the education authority in 1928, and the local ILP had only narrowly defeated a call for the resignation of Bridgeton's town councillors who had granted public house licences in breach of party policy.

Because of his national standing, his strong personal following and his Parliamentary influence, Maxton retained a loyalty among the diverse factions. Despite their mutual mistrust both the recognised and the unrecognised constituency organisation renominated him.

In the early months of 1929 Maxton was himself under investigation by the Scottish Labour Party authorities for a catalogue of misdemeanours, and his own endorsement as a Labour Party candidate was in jeopardy. In addition to being accused of accepting nomination from a proscribed organisation, he was also charged with support for "confiscation" proposals, asked to explain his association with the Anti-Imperialist League (which had been "specifically condemned" by the Labour Party), and called to account for "publicly" encouraging the Leith by-election candidate of 1927 "to defy the Labour Party". The Scottish Executive also noted that he had sponsored the *Sunday Worker* newspaper which had been "officially condemned" by the party. In March he was asked for "an undertaking of loyalty for the future", and in April his position was referred to the party's Organisation Committee for consideration.[5] Only when the election campaign was over did the party formally agree "to drop the matter".[6]

Maxton spent only £75 in election expenses. He had always opposed what he called "electioneering which amounts to petty bribery" and would have nothing to do with the new techniques of "photos and catchphrases". His campaign consisted of an election address sent to each home, followed up by a round of outdoor meetings. Maxton's Tory opponent, a friend from his days at Glasgow University, provided an amiable competitor unembarrassed by any hopes of success. The campaign was quiet, uneventful and free from the rancour and mudslinging that occurred in many other Glasgow constituencies.

In the run-up to the election Maxton campaigned round the country speaking widely throughout Scotland but his star, *The Scotsman* reported, was waning. Fewer constituencies invited him and some complained of his "indiscipline" for example in refusing to support an official Labour candidate in Govan where he backed instead his old friend Neil McLean.[7]

When the votes were counted Maxton had increased his majority, taking more than 21,000 votes. Although for the first time ever Labour became the biggest party, it failed to gain an overall majority, taking 289 seats to the Conservative's 268 and the Liberal's 58. MacDonald once more sought to attempt to govern without a majority.

It was a decision that found no favour with Maxton. Above all socialist advance required a Labour majority providing a "mandate for socialism". None had been given.

Two aspects of the results did please Maxton. One was "the big Labour advance". The other was "the return of so many fine socialists with a record of service to the movement". The margin of disappointment had not been large and there was a possibility that by-elections might produce a majority over time and ensure that the Government survived for a full five years. He would watch the Government "in the most friendly spirit". He was not asking for the implementation of "Socialism in Our Time" but for action to deal with unemployment and poverty.[8]

His support for the new Government was therefore always conditional. There would, he said, be "active and hearty support" on one condition, "a determined attack on the poverty of the people". Election promises had to be honoured and "the dread of starvation" removed. The precondition for loyalty from the Clydesiders was the proper treatment of the unemployed.

Surprisingly, MacDonald had Maxton under consideration for a Ministerial post. One colleague of Maxton's explained that Maxton was now more in accord with MacDonald than he had been for several years and had been called into consultation on party policy – with the hint of high office being offered. The truth is probably somewhat different. Now that Wheatley was less of a threat, MacDonald feared Maxton more and therefore felt conciliation necessary. "MacDonald always considered Maxton a kind of rival because of his oratory," Shinwell explained later, and he recalls receiving about this time a letter from MacDonald, "criticising Maxton because he was afraid Maxton was going to get the leadership of the Labour Party".[9]

In a pre-election list of possible Ministerial appointments, Maxton was a second choice for Postmaster General – with Wheatley pencilled in for the Ministry of Labour. By the time the results were declared, Arthur Henderson, soon to be made Foreign Secretary, backed Wheatley, but Snowden, Thomas and MacDonald believed they could afford to keep both out.

It was Wheatley's omission that was to be the main focus of public comment. *The Daily News* called his exclusion "a piece of audacity" on MacDonald's part. *The Daily Express* saw it as a declaration of war on the left and the *Daily Record* believed that Wheatley's recent statements had cost him office. But the question of whether Wheatley, or Maxton, should have been offered office is almost certainly an academic one. Wheatley's paper, the *Glasgow Eastern Standard,* explained that the Clydesiders "believe in nothing short of courageous socialist measures" and rejected "a policy of futile moderation" which "would ultimately discredit Labour".

In fact Maxton and Wheatley were to oppose any ILP members taking office. Shinwell was to be offered a job in the War Office and told his ILP colleagues about it. Patrick Dollan was insistent that at least one ILP MP should be in the Government, and after "a long discussion it was decided that I should accept any position that MacDonald offered". "Maxton was against it. He said, 'Come on to the back benches, we'll deal with them'."[10] In fact, Maxton and Wheatley had already mapped out their role. The *Glasgow Eastern Standard* reported their view that if the Government engaged in "a laggard crawl", Maxton and Wheatley would "speed things up".[11]

There was never any question that Maxton and Wheatley would be passive supporters or would refrain from using the House of Commons as a forum to put forward their own ideas. As Maxton made clear in an interview in the *New Leader*, there were "certain matters of vital importance to the ILP". But he would "choose the appropriate circumstances and conditions for our action". He would not bring the Government down but he would select occasions when "I can best further our aims without causing embarrassment to my colleagues on the Government".[12]

These views were echoed by Kirkwood, Wheatley and Brockway at the first meeting of the Parliamentary Labour Party, Brockway arguing the new Government should introduce its socialist programme and stand or fall by it. By all accounts, Wheatley's intervention was devastating. The country, he said, was entering one of its periodic slumps. Wages would fall, social services would be restricted and a reduction in living standards was inevitable. The Labour Government would be blamed for these cuts if it administered capitalism. The Labour Party should wait until it had an absolute majority. For MacDonald, who replied, this was "mere romanticism. The Labour Government would show the country ... that it knew how to govern".

Brushed aside in the Parliamentary Party, Maxton now sought to press his case with an amendment to the King's Speech. His motion called for children's allowances, higher wages and industrial reorganisation. Almost immediately he came under fire. Shinwell, now a Minister, and Patrick Dollan, criticised him for failing to consult the ILP but Maxton, whose supporters controlled the Executive of the ILP's Parliamentary Group, pressed ahead. He was dissatisfied with the general wording of the passage in the speech about jobs. It had stated only that it would be "the foremost endeavour" of Ministers to deal with unemployment. Maxton promised to be "very patient" and to give Ministers "time" but he insisted on precise proposals for helping the unemployed and he laid down what were to be his terms for supporting the Government:

I am going to promise the Cabinet active hearty support and work on one condition and on one condition only, that they will arrange the affairs of this country that no unemployed man, his wife or child, should have any dread of starvation or insult. That is a small thing to ask. The machinery is there. It is not socialism . . . the whole machinery of public relief is there, jolting, jangling, working inefficiently. The Government have it in their power now to make it work efficiently so that I can say to any constituent of mine, "You cannot be starving. You are bound, at least, to have a bare livelihood". I say that this, at least, must be done while the Cabinet are working out their wider schemes of statesmanship.[13]

28

The Leader of the Opposition

"Has any human being benefited by the fact that there has been a Labour Government in office?" This was the question posed by Maxton in the summer of 1929, only weeks after the Government had taken office. There was, he told the ILP Summer School, no value in remaining silent. He was ashamed to go to his constituents even after making "adequate allowance for the difficult circumstances" under which Labour governed. He had never been prepared to wait for centuries for socialism, nor wade through blood to achieve it. If he had been Prime Minister, said Maxton, he would have ensured adequate unemployment allowances and raised the school leaving age. He would also have recognised Russia and admitted Trotsky into Britain. He cited the example of a dispute in the cotton industry as one where the Government should have used its Emergency Powers to bring the industry under public control. In a debate with Shinwell, Maxton explained that silence now meant only acquiescence to all that the Government did.[1]

Already Maxton's colleagues had been more outspoken. The Government, Kirkwood complained, had "done nothing for the working class and in consequence we are not prepared to stand by it". In the columns of the *Glasgow Eastern Standard*, Ministers – even old colleagues such as Tom Johnston – came under attack, accused, inaccurately, of reducing the wages of workers on relief schemes, and of rebuffing pleas to help the poor.

Maxton kept up his attacks over the autumn. They had "waited five months," he said in October, "and it was a long time for a man to go without an income". The Clydesiders were not asking for the impossible. They had "declared it would be foolish to expect the Government to deliver socialism, but they did say that the Government had it in their power to stop starvation". Labour Ministers and Liberals believed that conditions could be improved only after industry had recovered whereas the Clydesiders believed

222

that industry would recover only when workers' conditions were improved.

The first revolt came on the Unemployment Insurance Bill, introduced by the new Labour Minister, Margaret Bondfield. Maxton and his supporters vehemently opposed a new clause which debarred benefit to those "not genuinely seeking work", and a proposal which postponed the award of benefit to the newly unemployed for the first six days out of work. The ILP sought a three-day delay. But the main opposition was to the proposed scale of benefits. The allowance for the unemployed man was to be set at 17 shillings. Maxton suggested £1 (he had called for £2 at the election) and reminded the Labour Party that as long ago as 1924, the party had suggested 45 shillings for a family with three children. Under the Bill, they would receive only 32 shillings.

The amendments were Maxton's "minimum demands" and in putting them he had expected wide-ranging support for his position. These minimum demands were not new. Some had appeared in *Labour and the Nation*, and others were contained in the joint Labour Party-Trades Union Congress report on unemployment benefits prepared in 1924.

The first meeting of the ILP Parliamentary Group, attended by 40 MPs, supported Maxton and asked him for a further report. At a second meeting, 51 MPs were present and it was unanimously decided to press for amendments to the Bill.

But only nine of the ILP Group voted with Maxton when the matter was debated at a full meeting of the Parliamentary Labour Party. The meeting decided that amendments not approved by the Parliamentary Consultative Committee were to be forbidden. Maxton informed the meeting "on behalf of the minority that they felt so keenly on the matter that they must retain liberty to put down amendments on the Order Paper".

The ILP hastily convened a group meeting. 68 MPs attended and Maxton was outvoted, by 41 to 14, with 13 absentions. The meeting went on to veto Maxton's amendments to the Bill. Maxton dissented, saying that the ILP in the country wanted amendments to the Bill, and promising to submit his own anyway. Within a week 66 ILP MPs had signed a memorandum expressing confidence in the Government. As Maxton later explained, he had had a clear mandate from the ILP National Council and from three successive meetings of the ILP Parliamentary Group. "Then the 66 'manifestors' came out and within two or three days the army had all vanished. You have shoved me up against the guns and when I looked round there was nobody there."[2]

When Maxton spoke to his amendments on the Second Reading he accused the Government of betraying its own promises to the unemployed. He won a minor victory over the "not genuinely seeking work clause". Labour Exchange officials now had to prove the claimant had refused or failed to apply for a job, but the rest of the legislation was passed.

The cohesion of the ILP Group had been shattered by the episode. Even its existence was now at risk. A crisis meeting of the National Administrative Council was convened at which Patrick Dollan demanded a special conference to decide whether the ILP should oppose or amend Government legislation in the Commons. Dollan lost the vote, by 10 to three, and he took the issue to the ILP Divisional Conferences. He was, he said, not prepared "to allow even the Chairman of the ILP to do as he thinks in Parliament". Maxton must be "as amenable to party decisions as Mr Ramsay MacDonald".[3]

There followed press and public speculation about Maxton's intentions. "Join the Communist Party," a heckler challenged Maxton at a demonstration held in January 1930. "Nothing I have seen from outside the Communist Party can drag me inside it,"[4] Maxton told the heckler. He was elsewhere charged with attempting to form a fourth party and there was even speculation that if Maxton was expelled from the Parliamentary Labour Party 40 would go with him. Neither Communism nor a new party were in his mind. He explained to the Scottish Conference of the ILP that his campaign on unemployment benefits did not amount to "a party within a party but the coming together of members to resist a compromise with the Liberals". He had not, he said, acted in a foolish or irresponsible manner but was putting forward the ILP policy. Although he could have put the Government out of office, he understood the Government's Parliamentary and financial difficulties and was merely asking it to stop starvation throughout the country.

Maxton turned the attacks on his party spirit by describing the behaviour of his Parliamentary colleagues. With a clear mandate from the National Administrative Council, he had carried three successive meetings of the ILP Parliamentary Executive. Their further support should have been unquestioning. Instead they had turned tail and run. In his own words, "you have got to treat your responsible leaders in a more responsible way than that".

In his home territory at the 1930 Scottish ILP Conference Maxton lost the vote, narrowly, by 103 votes to 94. Dollan prepared for further victories at other Divisional Conferences.

The Minimum Demands campaign, as Brockway, now an MP, conceded, was "the first step in the course which led to disaffiliation of the ILP from the Labour Party".[5] More than 100 Labour MPs signed a Round Robin which protested at Maxton's leadership of the ILP, and for the first time Ramsay MacDonald allowed his membership to lapse. The ILP, he told a colleague, was "possessed of the notion that it ought to run the Parliamentary policy of the Labour Party" and was "losing its grip".

Sure of the rightness of his policy, Maxton had no intention of backing down. During February, he accused the Cabinet and J. H. Thomas, the Employment Minister, of taking "the wrong road", and warned that without a reduction in unemployment Labour would lose the next election. In February he called for a socialist Budget, pensions of 30 shillings at 60, the raising of the school leaving age, and the abolition of the means test. The aim was to withdraw young and old from the labour market and ease unemployment.

When the ILP National Conference met in April, Maxton demanded the full loyalty of his membership. Already the ILP Executive was proposing to tighten its conditions for membership of the Parliamentary Group. Essentially members were to be required to accept the policies of the ILP Conference and those contained in "Socialism in Our Time". Maxton insisted on this but conceded that a transition stage was necessary, at least until the next General Election. They did not propose to exclude members from the Group simply because they disagreed with him, or his supporters, but they did propose to exclude those who had never accepted the declared policy of the ILP Conference.[6]

Maxton's speech was a ringing declaration of the need for action from the Government on unemployment. The ILP supported "Socialism in Our Time", he said, a policy which distinguished it from gradualism and Communism. The ILP wanted control of industry and the immediate increase in purchasing power. Wage reductions were "disgraceful" at a time when lack of home demand was the most remediable problem in the economy.

In the debates which ensued Maxton's case was endorsed. In successive divisional conferences, despite Dollan's campaign, he had claimed victory after victory and now Dollan's final attempt, at the National Conference, was defeated by 357 votes to 53. When a vote of thanks was passed, Maxton broke down. For him the last 10 months had been very hard work, not only because of the intensity of the campaign but because it had involved differing in public with some of his oldest friends. The outcome after months of battering criticism was an enormous relief. "I feel at this conference the ILP has decided that our objective is the achievement of a socialist commonwealth and not mere political expediency and opportunism. I am satisfied that what we are doing as a movement will be for the great good of humanity not at some dim and distant day but in our time."[7]

Having carried the ILP Conference Maxton might have expected some advantage in Parliament. The problem was that not only the ILP Conference but also the Parliamentary Labour Party sought to control the ILP MPs. In Parliament Labour prevailed. In June, after a series of acrimonious meetings, the Parliamentary Labour Party resolved that no MP could vote against the Labour Government. ILP amendments which attempted variously to report dissidents to their constituents, refer legislation first to the PLP and free MPs from the Whips when pledges had been made to constituents were all defeated.[8] Selection discipline too was tightened. Prospective Labour candidates such as Bob Edwards, a future Party Chairman and still an MP in 1986, were rejected because they were Maxton supporters.

The vast differences which now divided ILP from Labour were addressed at a series of meetings between Maxton and Arthur Henderson. Maxton agreed that the future of the ILP lay within the Labour Party and that it would accept the supremacy of the Labour Party Annual Conference. It was decided that a new formula should be prepared for agreement between the parties. When it came to the discussion of specifics there was no further progress and a split within the ILP Parliamentary Group was inevitable.

The ILP's new standing orders reaffirmed the supremacy of the ILP National Conference and when they were circulated to the party's 140 MPs only 18 accepted them. The much diminished ILP Group reorganised itself, in Brockway's words, as "a compact body with regular meetings, a small executive committee and two secretaries who acted when necessary as unofficial whips".[9] 122 MPs had been ejected from the ILP Group. It was the biggest purge ever in the history of the ILP and Maxton had presided over it. Isolated in the Parliamentary Labour Party, Maxton now decided to take his case to the Labour Party Conference.

29

"Oh the bastard, the bloody bastard"

"Oh the bastard, the bloody bastard." Maxton, paler than ever, his fist clenched and shaking, sat within a few feet of Ramsay MacDonald at the 1930 Labour Party Conference at Llandudno, provoked beyond endurance.

Officially the debate was a Conference sequel to the ILP's Parliamentary criticism of the unemployment policy of the Labour Government. Maxton, about to propose a vote of censure on Ramsay MacDonald, had instead been the victim of a manoeuvre at once both brilliant and appalling.

On the first morning of the Conference, Airship R101 had crashed in flames at Beauvais with Lord Thomson, the Minister for Air and a close friend of MacDonald, on board, Opening the afternoon debate, MacDonald, knowing Maxton would follow, devoted much of his speech to a eulogy of Lord Thomson who had been one of his personal friends, ending with the words:

> Ah, my friends, at moments like this the eternal principles which unite us, not the temporary differences that divide us, are remembered. My good comrade Maxton has known as I have known what it is to stand at the marble gates of death and see one who is nearest pass through.[1]

Brockway records the scene. "Maxton was sitting beside me, tears were on his cheek. I knew how deeply the death of his wife had affected him. My immediate thought was to offer to take his place on the platform but that was checked by a startling exclamation from his lips which made it clear to me that despite his emotion Maxton had kept his critical faculty very much alive."[2]

MacDonald's ploy was as successful as had been intended. His bitterest critic and the most powerful orator of his generation was in utter emotional disarray. Maxton moved to the platform with

227

only five minutes of Conference time allocated to him and spent two or three of them in halting tribute to MacDonald's speech. As Brockway records, "a few sentences more and I knew that the attack and the constructive case we wanted could not be made. Maxton concluded with little more than a hint of criticism and of socialist evangelism."[3] The ILP's vote of censure was defeated by 1.8 million to 330,000.

For Maxton it had been a disastrous summer, full of personal and political tragedies. Wheatley, his friend of 20 years, had died in May. Maxton had received the news by telegram in Holland, where he had been on an attempt to bring European socialist parties together in the fight against imperialism. In Glasgow, at home for the weekend, Wheatley had died suddenly as a result of a cerebral haemorrhage at the age of only 61. Maxton hurried back to Scotland to deliver a funeral oration.

No letters between Maxton and Wheatley survive, probably because none were necessary. They were in daily contact for almost a decade in Parliament together, having won seats on the historic night of 20 November 1922, campaigned together for "Socialism in Our Time", fought side by side against the lapses of MacDonald's leadership, and jointly led the socialist opposition to the first year of MacDonald's second Government.

The precise chemistry of their political partnership is unknown in detail. Wheatley was the thinker and strategist, Maxton, 16 years younger, the popular leader and orator. Wheatley had called Maxton socialism's "new god" and its "saviour", freely acknowledging his public leadership of the socialist movement. "Nine times out of ten when differences arose," a close colleague, John Scanlon, recalled, "it was Maxton who had his way."[4] Yet for Maxton, Wheatley was the senior partner and intellectual mentor, the leader's private leader. "I know Maxton always regarded him as the biggest man in the movement," concluded Brockway. "Indeed Wheatley is the only man to whom I ever heard Maxton refer as his leader."[5]

One story recounted by McGovern described how during 1929 Wheatley had phoned Maxton at his home in Barrhead to recommend a Parliamentary initiative for the next week. "What do you think of it, Jimmy?" Wheatley asked. "It seems alright," replied Maxton, and then Wheatley said, "Then you think I should go ahead with it?"

Maxton again replied, "Why do you ask me if you should go

ahead?" to which Wheatley said, "Because you are my leader." Jimmy finally answered, "Aye John I am your leader but you will discover that I am the cutest leader you ever led."[6]

Wheatley's last years had been clouded by a dispute of no great political relevance but considerable personal cost. A former Conservative candidate, his opponent for the Shettleston seat had alleged corruption in his business life. Wheatley had sued, alleging defamation. The matter was complex, involving accounts at Wheatley's printing works, and a series of legal technicalities arose. Wheatley eventually discontinued proceedings but the matter wearied him over several years, even to the point where he had been tempted to retire from the vulnerability of public life. "I am beginning to think," he told Beatrice Webb just before his death, "we politicians are all flies on the wheel." Maxton had lost a friend, an adviser and his principal political ally.

The subsequent Shettleston by-election was bitter. Maxton had wanted Dr John Buchanan, George Buchanan's brother, to be the ILP candidate, but amid allegations of irregularity in the balloting at the selection conference, the former Communist and local Parish Councillor John McGovern who had risen from grocer's manager to small businessman secured the Labour nomination.

McGovern was viewed with some suspicion. He had been associated with ultra-left groupings before joining the ILP. The veteran ILP organiser, Willie Stewart, accurately predicted that having been in many groups already McGovern would be in a few more before he finished (and later in fact McGovern was to join Moral Re-Armament). Even in 1930, during the by-election, he was accused of political opportunism. There was a Communist challenge from a former MP, the Indian Saklatava who reminded the electorate that his ILP opponent had only a few years before been "one of the most extreme anti-Parliamentarians". More important, McGovern found it difficult to gain the support of established Catholic leaders. The political organisation built up as his personal machine by John Wheatley was less than enthusiastic in its support. Previous Communist associations made McGovern unacceptable to many Catholic voters, and the Glasgow *Catholic Observer* urged Catholic electors to vote Conservative. "That was the reason why the left wing group wanted to nominate Dr Buchanan in his place," Emrys Hughes later recalled. "Although they denounced political opportunism in all its forms they wished to secure a candidate who would be most likely to conciliate the Catholic vote."

To ensure the maximum vote, McGovern promised to be a loyal supporter of the Labour Government and secured a personal endorsement from Ramsay MacDonald. It did little to assist. Rising unemployment under a Labour Government was losing the party votes. When the result was declared, McGovern won only narrowly, the Labour vote 9,000 down on Wheatley's General Election performance.

In his election campaign McGovern had distanced himself from the Maxton rebels. Now an MP he decided to throw in his lot with the left. In doing so, he did much to further isolate the Maxton group from the official Labour Party. Instead of asking the Labour Whips to organise his introduction to Parliament, he arrived to take his Member's Oath without even telling them of his plans. There could have been no clearer signal that he was distancing himself from MacDonald and the Government. For this demonstration of disloyalty, Maxton was unfairly held responsible, but he was not to blame. He had advised McGovern to tell the Labour Whips and the Front Bench of his plans to be introduced into Parliament. McGovern insisted on being introduced by Maxton and Campbell Stephen, and, as McGovern recalled, "Maxton assured me they were perfectly willing but had better prepare for the result of such action". When McGovern walked down the Floor to take the Oath of Allegiance and shake hands with the Speaker, "not a single cheer came from the Labour benches". Instead McGovern over-heard MacDonald tell J. H. Thomas, "it is one of the most disgraceful things that has ever happened in the House".[7]

Unemployment was just over a million when Labour took office. By the summer of 1930 it had passed two million and by Christmas it was to pass two-and-a-half million. As unemployment increased, disputes in the Parliamentary Labour Party about how to tackle it became even fiercer. Ramsay MacDonald held out for inertia. A small minority of Government Ministers would have preferred a programme of reflation by means of public works. Maxton and his little band on the left still campaigned for the radical elements of the *Labour and the Nation* manifesto and for family allowances, higher unemployment benefits and a programme of industrial reconstruction.

For one ILP member and Labour Minister, Oswald Mosley, the unemployment question led in turn to his memorandum to Ramsay MacDonald, its rejection by him and the PLP, and its resuscitation for the annual Conference. Rejected by the annual Conference, Mosley launched into the wilderness with his "New Party". British Fascism was soon to follow.

Mosley's first initiatives, though they had some features in common with the ILP proposals, never wholly appealed to the Maxton group, who accused him of private enterprise. When Mosley resigned, Maxton had publicly supported him – saying that he ought not to be condemned, but thanked. His actions showed a deeper sense of responsibility about the unemployed and might lead to "a new direction" in government policy. Privately, Mosley was never trusted by Maxton and although McGovern and other ILP Group members were to support his attempt to raise the issue, and later to found a new party, Maxton stood aloof. George Strauss, another Labour Minister, was probably near the mark when he wrote that Mosley was looked upon with "little sympathy by the ILP Group who referred to him with disdain".[8] As early as 1931 Maxton had labelled the New Party anti-socialist.

The Parliamentary ILP group under Maxton's leadership was only 18-strong but it was infinitely more unanimous than its predecessor. Despite Maxton's Conference defeat in October, his attacks on the Government grew stronger. The Government's Education Bill, its Coal Mines Bill and its colonial policies came under fire. The Education Bill amounted to little more than an administrative tidying up of a patchwork of local authority and parish schools. Maxton, the former teacher, saw it as a means of improving mass education and at the same time reducing the labour force by raising the school leaving age.

The coal industry, first overstretched by the war then devastated by the recession and, as ever chronically under-financed, was ripe for rationalisation, and the Coal Mines Bill sought greater national uniformity by facilitating mergers and amalgamations. Maxton saw the Bill as a missed opportunity. Both the miners and the Labour Party Conference wanted nationalisation but a Maxton amendment to effect it attracted only a few supporters.

Maxton, chairman of the League Against Imperialism from 1927 to 1929, had long been interested in international questions and in particular was committed to self-government for Britain's colonies. The International League Against Imperialism embraced Communists and socialists in Europe but factional disputes had rendered it ineffective. Maxton resigned and sought to promote a new international socialist grouping. Now, from the back benches, Maxton sought to press India's case for immediate independence.

During 1929 he had urged the new Minister for India to release all political prisoners, declare for India's right to self-government and convene a conference to draft a new constitution. When Gandhi was arrested, Maxton and the ILP complained about Government repression. In an attempt to force a debate, two ILP members were suspended from the House. When the Simon Commission reported against immediate self-government, Maxton and the ILP dissociated themselves entirely from the Government's policy.

The key issues were still unemployment and how the Government treated the unemployed. The numbers out of work which had risen to two-and-a-half million in December 1930 were now rising to two-and-three quarter million. In February 1930 Maxton had finally introduced his Living Wage Bill under the Ten Minute Rule. It was, he explained, a measure which distinguished the ILP from the gradualism of the Government. Small or isolated reforms which do not strike at the root of capitalism must fail. His was a radical measure. "The failure of capitalism can be made a great opportunity to apply socialist principles and begin the transition to socialism," he said. Others had described a minimum provison for the poor as that necessary to avoid starvation or destitution. For Maxton, the living wage was meant to provide enough for its recipients to play a full part in the customary activities of society. The Bill, he explained, "defines a living wage as sufficient to meet the satisfaction of reasonable minimum requirements of health and efficiency of cultural life, and the provision of reasonable rest and recreation".[9]

Maxton had promised the ILP Conference that he and the ILP Parliamentary Group would "raise its voice strenuously" against any inroads on unemployment benefits. In February, a commission, dominated by Labour's opponents, had been set up to review unemployment insurance. When Maxton argued it "shocking that the Labour Government should again and again support commissions ... and place on these commissions an overwhelming number of non-socialists" and divided the House over its appointment, only 22 Labour MPs joined him. In June the commission had made its interim report, and immediately the Government had introduced an Anomalies Bill. The Bill disqualified casual workers and married women from unemployment benefit. Maxton was determined to oppose it and with five colleagues put down an amendment to the Bill. A Parliamentary Party meeting which considered their disloyalty heard them decline to withdraw their amendment. A week later, Parliament was brought to a halt by their wrecking tactics.

The Clydeside members had narrowly avoided suspension on a minor issue before they began their assault in defence of the unemployed. Several tramp preachers had been arrested in Scotland on the minor and ill-defined charge of breach of the peace. McGovern called for their release, then he and George Buchanan complained to the Scottish Secretary, William Adamson, and McGovern found himself suspended. When he refused to leave the House and the Sergeant at Arms called attendants to remove him, Maxton, and other ILP members, joined in a scuffle which brought Commons proceedings to a halt.

The next day Maxton apologised to the Speaker, expressing "regret" at conduct he now believed to be "indefensible", and both Ramsay MacDonald and the Speaker accepted his apologies, MacDonald saying it was "a model" of what an apology should be, but as Maxton explained later his apology was "a question of strategy. There was a possibility that the whole group of Clydesiders would be suspended for their part in the affair and that was exactly what we did not wish, as there was coming up an important debate in the Anomalies Bill and we wanted to be in the thick of it. In fact we were the Government's main opponents of the Bill."[10]

When the Anomalies Bill came to the House, Maxton moved a simple amendment, proposing that it be dropped. Labour, he said, had opposed such measures at the 1929 election and the new cuts were "a surrender in the face of one of the meanest, ill-natured agitations that ever have taken place by the rich against the worst defences of the poor". It was "sheer irresponsibility" for Labour to support the proposals. Unsuccessful in stopping the Bill, he chose to impede it by calling 32 divisions in the course of the night. The *Guardian* called the event "a carefully planned campaign of obstruction". As Maxton told the House:

> What we have had today is a great coalition of the three parties of the state all united to save public money, to save £5m. Suppose I never did another thing in public life I am glad that I have had the opportunity of standing here tonight exposing that great united attack on the poor people to whom I have made the same promises. The Government's big mistake was to submit to the mean propaganda that was carried on by members opposite. They cannot wash their hands of it. The responsibility is permanently theirs.

Maxton had always denied press accusations that he would prefer the Labour Government to fall. When in February 1931 he had made a speech in which he appeared to call for "revolution" he had immediately qualified his remarks to say that he would not attempt to put Labour out of office, "unless he could see the opportunity of putting in a more revolutionary government. Frankly he did not see that opportunity at the moment."

It was the ILP newspaper, the *New Leader*, which in July 1931 first printed rumours about the possibility of an all-party Coalition Government. The rumours were denied by the Labour Foreign Secretary, Arthur Henderson, but it later transpired that inter-party talks had already occurred.

Right up to the fall of the Government in August 1931 Maxton continued to stress the relevance of "Socialism in Our Time" as "the only way" to save the country, and was astounded, when abroad, to find European socialist parties in a similar state of inertia.

The Labour Government discussed protection, the nationalisation of steel and a programme of public works but paid little attention to the proposals of the ILP, and could do nothing for the two-- and-three-quarter million who were now out of work. In August 1931 the Cabinet split over further public spending cuts and Ramsay MacDonald resigned. On the prompting of the King he stayed on as Prime Minister in coalition with the Conservative and Liberal Parties. Only a handful of Labour Ministers followed MacDonald into coalition, but for the second time in a decade a Labour Government had ended in disaster.

Maxton had no doubt that the catastrophe of 1931 had begun in decisions that had been made in the early 'twenties. In an introduction to a book by his friend John Scanlon on *The Decline and Fall of the Labour Government*, he summarised his view of the events that had brought the Government's collapse. Tracing the development of the Party from 1918, Maxton explained that:

> there was a tempering of the more extreme socialist demands, diminished emphasis on the working-class aspects of our movement and a strengthening of the gradualist nature of our socialist hopes ... the more extreme elements were removed from the organisation: first, the Communist Party, then the so-called ancillary organisations, then followed the persistent attempt to silence the socialist voice of the ILP. The two Labour Cabinets allowed this frame of mind by the inclusion of a large element of the upper-class non-socialists ... I have no grievance against them. For seven years I have disbelieved completely in gradualist policies and for four years the ILP has taken no responsibility for the leadership of either MacDonald or Snowden but those who have supported, who have believed, and the mass of ordinary people who have trusted have the right to think and speak in the bitterest terms of the leaders who brought a movement that trusted them into

inextricable difficulty and then deserted their army for that of the enemy.

The ILP proposals represented not social reform but the foundations of a socialist commonwealth. They were not such as would have been conceded by capitalists without a bitter struggle. They would never have been achieved by any minority Labour Government while the ordinary methods of Parliamentary procedure operated. The acceptance of "Socialism in Our Time" by the Labour Movement would have debarred it from taking office in 1929. It would have been an active honourable opposition, it would have developed a militant movement behind it in the country whilst the Tory-cum-Liberal Government would have struggled to maintain the capitalist structure.

There must be a complete stocktaking in the ranks of the working-class movement from right to left. A real working-class spirit must be revived. The National Government can do nothing but hasten the collapse of capitalism. The working-class movement must now think in terms of acquiring effective political and economic power.

30

"If you can't ride two horses . . . ."

The Second Labour Government had ended in disaster. Ramsay
MacDonald was now leading a Conservative-dominated Coalition
Government. The Parliamentary Labour Party which had
supported the rightward lurches of MacDonald until the day of his
defection was in disarray. Maxton's warnings about the inevitable
failure of the MacDonald Government had been vindicated. Yet
at the very moment when Maxton and the ILP could have seized
leadership positions in the Labour hierarchy he chose to stand aloof.

With the departure of MacDonald, Snowden and other Labour
leaders Maxton was invited to join Labour's Front Bench and
was indeed urged by some to stand for the leadership itself.
One Scottish ILP member, Gilbert Macallister, hailed him as the
next leader of the Labour Party. In a public appeal to Maxton
in the Glasgow *Evening Times* he said there would be only one
nominee of the left – Maxton – and Tom Johnston should be
appointed as his deputy.

But Maxton was interested neither in the leadership nor in
criticising the departed leader, Ramsay MacDonald. Accusations
from the Labour Movement about treachery, Maxton wrote, were
quite out of place. There was "only one thing a man can do, be
true to in his life and that is his own beliefs". The misfortune was
that MacDonald's beliefs were "unsound and his theory of society
and social development unsound". Maxton took an apocalyptic
view. "There is no end but complete collapse," he prophesied. "An
appeal to the people seems to be altogether unlikely and the
people had better begin to prepare their minds for a semi-fascist
régime the essence of which is that the popular will is denied
its proper means to expressing itself."[1]

Maxton had misread the signs and was unable to grasp the
opportunities presented to the ILP to recover its leadership of
the Labour Movement. The Labour Party establishment could
and did accuse MacDonald of betrayal: Maxton castigated the

Labour establishment for its support of right-wing policies. When in September 1931 the Parliamentary Party met MacDonald was deposed in favour of Arthur Henderson, to Maxton's complaint that "there was no attempt to define and no attempt to find out whether Mr Henderson's views on the economy were substantially altered from what they were a fortnight ago".[2]

Maxton spoke and acted as the rejected prophet unprepared to compromise. He had, he said, "spent the last five years fighting capitalism against Labour leaders on the right" who told him everything was going to be all right if they were allowed to dally along, and also against a revolutionary rebel pack on the left who assumed that revolution was nearly here. "Nothing that has happened over the last few weeks has proved my view to be wrong and nothing that has happened yet indicates that the Labour Party now in opposition accepts our view as right."

The Labour Party Conference which met the following month found Maxton in even more agressive mood. In spirit he was already half way out of the Labour Party. The new standing orders which tightened up party discipline in the House of Commons were accepted by the Conference and Maxton told delegates that he was "not certain whether he was in order to be speaking". The standing orders, he said, did not allow "the necessary minimum of liberty" and the resolution carried by Conference "in his view expelled him from the Labour Party".[3]

At the Conference Maxton was more concerned with the differences between his views and those of Labour as a whole than he was with the similarities. While he had agreed with the speeches of Clynes and Morrison they seemed, he said, "to visualise socialism as an object to be reached in the dim and distant future". Yet it was not possible "to win socialism by instalments". There could not be "an unlimited period for its establishment. They were already in the crisis and it would get worse."[4]

By now the ILP MPs were establishing themselves as a separate group within Parliament and, when a new General Election was declared in the autumn of 1931, Maxton and 18 others were refused endorsement as official Labour candidates. The 19 ILP MPs stood independently of the Labour Party but, in the rout of the left, only three – Maxton, McGovern and Wallhead – were returned under the ILP's sponsorship. In a straight fight with a National Government candidate Maxton had a reduced majority of 4,689. Buchanan and Kirkwood were re-elected under their own union sponsorship but Campbell Stephen and Jennie Lee were defeated.

Jennie Lee had won North Lanark in a by-election in the

spring of 1929 and had joined the ILP Group. Beaverbrook, the proprietor of the *Daily Express*, called her "Maxton's darling" but when she lost her seat in the General Election of 1931 she blamed Maxton. The cause of the disagreement was an amendment to the Labour Government's Education Bill which sought to give increased protection to Catholic schools. Maxton and the other Scottish ILP members supported the amendment, but despite his advice that she could not take on both the Labour establishment and the Catholic Church, Jennie Lee had opposed it. Lee was "livid with contempt" and accused her fellow MPs of "deserting not only their friend but their principles". By the time of the election in 1931 she had become "sadly critical" of Maxton.[5] She found a sympathetic ally in her close colleague and future husband, Aneurin Bevan, who also could not take Maxton seriously.

In 1931 the Liberals and Conservatives refused to stand against each other, and although Labour's vote fell by only 7% – from 37% to 30% – the absence of competition between the parties of the right and the straight fights against Labour decimated Labour representation. The election which had reduced the ILP Group to five reduced the Parliamentary Labour Party to only 52 members, fewer than it had had at any time since 1914. The new Labour leader, Arthur Henderson, was one of more than 200 casualties. Still relations between the ILP and the Labour Party were a topic of major importance. In a much quoted phrase Maxton summed up the new position of one of his colleagues. "If my friend cannot ride two horses then he should not be in the bloody circus." He was entitled to his "acrobatics" as the right wing of the Labour Party had for years been comfortably astride both Labour and Liberal mounts.

Maxton postponed a decision in 1931. It could not be postponed much longer. Ironically for two parties both officially espousing vast social and political change, the ultimate question which split the ILP and Labour was one over the nuances of the Parliamentary freedom to be enjoyed by ILP members as Labour MPs. The ILP demanded that their MPs support ILP Conference policies and "Socialism in Our Time". Labour insisted that all its MPs abided by Labour Party policies and voted as a group.

Maxton's old friend, George Lansbury, who had now succeeded to the Labour leadership in place of Henderson, was anxious for a compromise and invited Maxton to join Labour's Front Bench. Lansbury sent an invitation to the ILP's National Council meeting the weekend following the election to join negotiations to reunite the opposition. He refused, however, to allow the continuing existence of a party within a party. The National Council discussed the advantages of continuing the association with Labour, with the ILP Secretary, John Paton, warning that "the political difficulties of maintaining and developing the organisation outside the Labour Party were enormous and it might be that it would involve a risk of the complete disintegration of the ILP".[6]

Maxton disagreed, not pressing for immediate disaffiliation but saying that the ILP should not hesitate to leave if its freedom to advocate "Socialism in Our Time" was threatened. A majority which included Maxton preferred to continue negotiations and the ILP postponed its national conference so that the issues could be discussed more fully.

How eagerly did Maxton now seek disaffiliation? Certainly he felt that the threat of disaffiliation offered the ILP the strongest bargaining position in any future negotiations with the Labour Party. The best chance for the ILP's policies and for ILP members' freedom in Parliament was to bluster a little on the disaffiliation issue. That is why he was seen to endorse disaffiliation at the autumn meeting of the National Council. He repeated the tactic when he addressed the Glasgow aggregate meeting of the ILP but at the Scottish Divisional Conference of the ILP midway through November he was to warn against disaffiliation. Dollan noted that at this private meeting, which was not reported to the press, Maxton had argued for "caution and delay".[7]

In January 1932, Maxton was still seeking the strongest bargaining position in any future negotiations with the Labour Party. He told the annual Scottish Conference of the ILP that when fighting his Labour Party opponents he had always been advised to stay in and convert them. He had been ready to do that and continue to do that if the Labour Party had not said, "You will not be allowed to stand for 'Socialism in Our Time' and remain in the Labour Party". That is what they did in the Standing Orders. "I could not do it. If I had said I accept that pledge I would have had to vote for the Anomalies Bill, for the Economy Commission and for the Education Bill."[8]

Maxton told the Scottish Conference that the ILP's National Council were loath to make a decision to disaffiliate. The annual ILP Conference had been postponed not because the ILP were afraid it would carry disaffiliation but in order that the question be fully discussed. He was personally taking a stand for disaffiliation because he wanted a united working-class movement. To secure that the ILP would have to start pioneering once more as it had done in 1893. He asked them to stand for "revolutionary parliamentarianism" and to convert rather than antagonise the working class.[9]

But Maxton had little support within the Scottish ILP. Disaffiliation was defeated by 89 votes to 49. This vote, Maxton believed, "impaired" the position of the ILP Group in the House of Commons. It was "an intimation to the Labour Party that the ILP is behind the Labour Party in its attempt to crush out ILP representation in the House of Commons unless such ILP representation submits to disciplinary regulation that makes its continued separate existence silly".

But if Maxton was driven to support disaffiliation to secure freedom for the Parliamentary Group, he knew he had other more central questions to answer. What was to be the role of the ILP if outside the Labour Party? And what was to be the strategy for socialism with speed? One ILP Executive member, Frank Wise, who was determined to keep the ILP inside the Labour Party, challenged Maxton on these very issues in February 1932, forcing Maxton to respond.

> Frank Wise asks me if I have another instrument than the Labour Party for the achievement of Socialism and if I have counted the cost. The answer is "yes". I ask him if he has counted the cost of remaining inside and working another 38 years for a repetition of the fiasco of 1931.

> I believe that outside the organisation of official Labour we can have greater influence with the rank and file and bring stronger pressure on its leaders, just as Lloyd George and his Liberal Party made from outside a bigger impression on the policy of the late Labour Government than any one of the organisations affiliated to the Labour Party.[10]

For Maxton the new task was to take the message of socialism to the public halls and to the street corners. The rank and file could be won. The ILP was unpopular only with "the somewhat limited circle of the select and elect of the labour aristocracy". But the question remained unanswered: where would disaffiliation take the ILP, and where would it take Maxton?

31

"Pure but Impotent"

"I tell you what the epitaph of you Scottish dissenters will be – pure but impotent," Aneurin Bevan told Jennie Lee in 1932. "Yes, you will be pure all right. But remember, at the price of impotency. You will not influence the course of British politics by as much as a hair's breadth." Castigating her for her irresponsibility and self-indulgence he went on, "I tell you it's the Labour Party or nothing. I know all its faults, all its dangers, but it is the party that we have taught millions of working people to look to and regard as their own. We can't undo what we have done. And I am by no means convinced that something cannot yet be made of it."[1]

Such was the vehemence with which one socialist sought to persuade another, his comrade and future wife, to resist the drift of the ILP out of the Labour Party. Negotiations dragged on over several weeks of the spring of 1932, with Maxton meeting Lansbury and the new ILP Chairman, Fenner Brockway, bargaining with both Lansbury and Arthur Henderson. Maxton did not force the pace, and Brockway was "forming the impression that Maxton deliberately permitted things to take their course". No agreement could be reached, mainly because Lansbury questioned the ILP's commitment to Parliamentary democracy, and when the ILP National Council met at the Savoy Hotel in Blackpool on the eve of its Annual Conference, Brockway reported that negotiations with Henderson had been fruitless. Maxton, Jowett and Campbell Stephen were for disaffiliation and, after a time, John Paton joined them. Frank Wise, Pat Dollan and David Kirkwood were against, and they were, as Brockway recalls, a difficult "opposition". Kirkwood used to "irritate us" and Wise "lectured us from Olympian heights".[2]

A compromise was agreed, by which representatives were appointed to redraft conditions for revised standing orders making the operation of the Parliamentary Party acceptable to the Independent Labour Party. In the meantime no action was to be taken against Labour candidates by ILP organisations in the constituencies. But by a Chairman's ruling, endorsed by nine votes to two, it was accepted that ILP endorsement could not be given to candidates who signed the present standing orders. When Dollan tried to secure a compromise by proposing that where ILP nominees were not prepared to sign standing orders ILP branches concerned should postpone proceedings pending a settlement and request Labour Parties locally to do likewise, he lost by six votes to five.[3]

While the executive refused to recommend disaffiliation to the Conference, Maxton presented his own views. They were to open negotiations. He could not tell exactly what policy would be carried out in the immediate future. He was personally in favour of complete disaffiliation and had been "driven" to that position "with the greatest regret". The ILP had to recover its socialist soul. Events had proved the Labour Party was not prepared to permit socialist activity within its ranks. The ILP had therefore to start again with the working classes and to mould a new socialist movement that would succeed where the last movement had failed.

The Conference voted to remain in the Labour Party if liberty to express ILP policy could be secured. A few days later Maxton appeared to be in a less belligerent mood when he addressed the Glasgow ILP Women's Conference. Dollan wrote afterwards of Maxton's interesting statement to that Conference. Wise statesmanship on the part of the Labour Party, Maxton had suggested, should aim at securing a unified working-class movement on a socialist basis and on such a basis there would be no need to discipline the ILP. Under these circumstances, said Maxton, the ILP would impose discipline upon itself.

Dollan regarded this statement as "significant" in that he had now come to the conclusion that it was possible for the ILP to work within the Labour Party under certain conditions instead of preaching disaffiliation. But Dollan argued it was "regrettable he did not reach this conclusion when negotiating with Arthur Henderson". It was, said Dollan, "generally forgotten that agreement between the two Executives was reached in principle" in July 1930. Unfortunately "that formula has never been drafted and I have never been able to discover the reasons for the failure".[4]

When Maxton and other senior office-bearers of the ILP met the Labour Party, the most serious point of difference was the ILP insistence that the policy of the Government be controlled by the party and that individual MPs should be free to vote contrary to party decisions. The only constraint proposed by the ILP was that such MPs should be reported to their constituency parties and to their nominating organisations. But the Labour Party was "adamant", in Brockway's words, "it demanded the acceptance of the present standing orders before any consideration could be given to the ILP amendments. Looking back on this dispute I can come to no other conclusion than that it was the obstinacy of the Labour Party executive which closed the door to agreement. If there had been any real desire for agreement it could have been reached. As it was, there was no alternative for the majority of the National Council of the ILP but to recommend disaffiliation."[5]

Now that the break seemed inevitable, Maxton went on the attack, arguing in his writings and speeches that there was no alternative to leaving and considerable opportunity if the break were made. In an article in *Forward* in May, entitled "We Are Going Out", he was at his most forceful, telling ILP members that "once you're out you'll feel the better of it. You'll feel more ready to stand up on your own feet, and put up the right kind of fight for the things you genuinely believe in."[6]

The ILP could do more for socialism if it were not associated with non-socialist forces, Maxton told a Glasgow audience. The Labour Party had not been prepared to amend the standing orders, and he would not "under any circumstances sign the standing orders". Later he was to tell the ILP Conference that in the same way that the Bolsheviks and Mensheviks had split over a minor issue – the control of the party newspaper – the disagreements over standing orders reflected "a fundamental difference of policy".[7]

There were to be no further attempts at compromise. When Labour published its final statement, rejecting the case for any changes in its standing orders, Maxton and Brockway issued a rejoinder, attacking the previous Labour Government and announcing that at a special ILP Conference they would reorganise the ILP as "a completely independent force with a programme and policy appealing to all socialists who realise the necessity of a break with the past and a new approach to the future". Speaking in Scotland, Maxton went even further, attacking the Parliamentary Party as "a miserable, dispirited remnant of a great movement".[8] But the ILP Group was already looking exactly like that. Kirkwood, who opposed leaving the Labour Party, decided instead to leave the ILP and another MP, Dick Wallhead, was to follow a few months later. Of the original team of Clydesiders, now only Buchanan and Stephen remained.

The vote at the Special Conference called in Bradford for July

1932 was decisive. 241 votes were cast in favour of leaving the
Labour Party with only 142 against. The ILP voted not just to
leave the Labour Party but to leave local Labour council groups
and the Cooperative movement and to stop paying the political
levy. There was anger over the vote, and allegations that it had
been rigged. 300 branches, said Dollan, had not been represented
but Paton, the General Secretary, denied the charge of "rigging"
and attacked Dollan's "unscrupulous arguments". It had, he said,
been "a bigger Conference than usual".

The dispute over the votes did not dim the enthusiasm of
many of those who supported disaffiliation. Moments after their
decision to leave the Labour Party delegates rose to their feet,
and as supporters cheered, six red banners were waved above
their heads. *The Red Flag* was sung and Maxton was called to
address the Conference.

The occasion demanded something big. "I will try to get
a Parliamentary majority for the ILP within five years," he
promised, "but I will also try to unite the working class without
any imposition from above by non-socialists." The party was not
going into the wilderness. His aim was to be nothing less than
"a real unity of revolutionary socialist forces".[9]

Immediately Maxton set himself to publicising the case for the
new party, offering the country a new rationale for the ILP. He
conceded that "there is a fairly unanimous view that we have
committed suicide politically", but promised that within a short
period of time the country would agree independence to be "the
right road". By now he was completing a short biography on
Lenin and he told the ILP Summer School that there were three
lessons British socialists could learn from Lenin and the Russian
experience: the need for firm character, a sound theoretical basis,
and a willingness to fight back from a minority position.

Maxton had planned to visit Russia in September but because
of the new plans to relaunch the breakaway party he cancelled
his trip. Instead he concentrated his efforts on setting down a
new ILP agenda for the coming Parliamentary session, criticising
Labour for abandoning any mention of socialism in its new policy
documents. "A big struggle on the part of the workers had to
come sooner or later," Maxton prophesied in what was to become
an increasingly apocalyptic view of a coming crisis of capitalism.
The struggle never came. There was a flicker of promise when
a cotton strike occurred in Lancashire and Maxton toured the
country urging the strikers "to widen the issues",[10] but the General
Strike he predicted never came. In October the railwaymen and

transport workers had resisted wage cuts but no widespread political action ensued. When the King's Speech was introduced in October 1932, he moved his own vote of censure and called for "a Workers' Government".

But the ILP of 1932 was quite different from the ILP that had elected Maxton Chairman in 1926. The new ILP, now a minority within the Labour Movement, had itself been hijacked by a minority. A new group, the Revolutionary Policy Committee, with Communist links and opposed to Parliamentary democracy, had formed itself as a caucus within the ILP and had been at the forefront of the campaign for disaffiliation. Although it failed in 1932 to commit the ILP to a policy of revolution it was to succeed in 1933. The ILP had left the Labour Party on the issue of being a party within a party. Now, in its turn, it was compelled to tell the Revolutionary Policy Committee that it could not operate as a separate party within.

"If Maxton had wanted an agreement with the Labour Party," wrote Dollan immediately afterwards, "an agreement could have been reached. Maxton is the man who made agreement impossible . . . Thanks to the admiration of enthusiastic admirers he would rather be the leader of a small party in Parliament than a cooperator in the Labour Party." Only a small number of Maxton's colleagues stayed with him. Among those who did, Brockway saw it as "the worst mistake in my life"; Jennie Lee stayed only because she "could not bear to be branded as a careerist, as someone ready to betray old comrades for the sake of personal advantage".[11] But few stayed on, and Maxton was virtually isolated from his circle of supporters of the 'twenties. Wheatley was dead. Kirkwood had defected. Dollan was leading a new Scottish Socialist Party back into the Labour Party, and Johnston had stayed with Labour, saying that rather than have any part "in such folly: he would prefer to be out of politics and public life altogether".[12]

Out of the ILP rump who opposed leaving Labour came, in England, the Socialist League, which merged with the Society for Socialist Inquiry and Propaganda, and, in Scotland, the Scottish Socialist Party. By November 1932, the Scottish party claimed to have captured 2,000 out of the 3,000 ILP members in Scotland. It controlled *Forward* newspaper and a long bitter legal battle with the ILP ensued over the ownership of constituency and branch premises and properties in Scotland. Every Glasgow vote had been cast against affiliation and only ten ILP councillors out of a previous 60 retained ILP membership on Glasgow Council, but it took a long time for the Labour Party to rebuild its strength in Scotland. As Arthur Woodburn, then the Scottish Labour Party Secretary, recalled, "Labour Party workers were divided and the work was duplicated in many towns and villages. My job was practically to build from scratch."[13] His task was made no easier because in his view "the greatest damage was done by Maxton and the ILP whose anti-Labour propaganda had confused our own people and weakened their enthusiasm".[14]

Elsewhere in Britain the story was the same. ILP membership fell from 15,000 to 10,000 within a year. As John Paton, himself soon to resign the ILP secretaryship, concluded, "the clean break seemed to be making a clean sweep of the party members".[15]

SECTION IV: SOCIALISM IN RETREAT

32

On The Fringes

As Parliament prepared to reassemble in October 1932 Maxton wrote a ringing declaration of the tasks before the ILP – the fight for peace, for jobs and for socialism – and promised that "whether the cry of the people outside is loud or not, the ILP Group inside Parliament will make opportunities for ensuring that the cry is heard there".

For the seven years leading up to the Second World War Maxton, the party leader, was to stand at the centre of the Parliamentary stage, but Maxton and the ILP were on the fringes of real political influence. They were to be engulfed in the sectarian controversies of the left throughout the 'thirties, distanced from power, and diverted from political campaigning by factional strife, just at the time when social and economic conditions of the people they sought to represent were at their worst and demanded a united left-wing voice of power and influence.

Unemployment had risen from one to two million between 1929 and 1931 and approached three million in 1932. By July 1933 half-a-million had not worked for more than a year. Young people and older men were the worst affected. Steel production halved between 1929 and 1932. Cotton exports halved also. Worst affected of all was the shipbuilding industry which had launched a million tons of ships each year in the 1920s and in 1933 produced only 133,000 tons.

The closure of John Brown's in Clydebank typified the Great Depression. In December 1931 work on the Cunard liner 334, Britain's largest-ever ship, was brought to a halt. For almost two years it towered over Clydebank, rusting – a vast symbol of the prevalent hard times.

On the Clyde, as elsewhere, no public works programmes were available to compensate for these job losses. Up till 1931, the Labour Government and local authorities had, between them,

249

employed 130,000 on public works projects. Now most of these enterprises were to be wound up in the search for economies.

In some parts of Britain, like Bridgeton, the *majority* of the adult population was out of work. Unemployment benefit was 17 shillings for a man and 26 shillings for a married couple before 1931. Under Labour's Anomalies Act married women had been denied benefit. Under the National Government's economy measures, benefit was reduced by 10% and was limited to 26 weeks. Most controversial of all was the system of administering transitional payments for those who had run out of benefit entitlement after their first six months out of work. The maximum payment was reduced to only 15 shillings and 3 pence for each adult but to qualify for assistance a household Means Test was applied by the Public Assistance Committee, the successor of the Poor Law Guardians. Any form of income, including pensions and contributions from sons and daughters, was deducted from benefit. Savings and even household possessions were all taken into account.

In 1932 more than one million of the unemployed came within the scope of transitional benefit and were subject to Means Tests. Within a year nearly 200,000 had been taken off benefit as a result of the Means Test to save £24m. In Maxton's Glasgow 45% of claimants suffered some reduction in their benefit because of the operation of the Means Test. Many other areas were in exactly the same position.

Local councils were under pressure to modify their Means Tests to allow transitional payments to be supplemented by the rates. Almost every month Glasgow Council heard deputations from local trades unions, ex-servicemen's organisations and the unemployed workers. During 1932 and 1933 Labour seized control of nearly half the local councils in Scotland. Whereas in early 1932 Hunger Marches and demonstrations went unnoticed, in 1933 they were at the forefront of the public mind.

Maxton was at his most masterful as the Member for the Unemployed. He, and others, protested about the inadequate benefits, the reduction of benefits because of war disability pensions, and above all the ubiquitous Means Tests. The unemployed, he said, were being accused of lavish expenditure and blamed for the economic crisis.

In December 1932 Maxton debated the Means Test on BBC Radio with the Conservative MP Harold Macmillan. Macmillan, one of the left-wing Tories, defended Means Testing on the grounds that the payments were not covered by insurance contributions and had to be within the "means" of the state. Maxton responded:

He could understand a state which said, 'Our total resources are very limited: it is impossible to allow anyone to have a very high income.' But he could not understand the state which said, 'Our resources are limited: we must drive down the income of the whole working class to one dead level of poverty while other classes are left in affluence.'[1]

In March 1933, Maxton introduced an ILP Commons debate on unemployment and poverty and in his speech he sought to describe the conditions which prevailed in the country and especially in his own constituency of Bridgeton. On two previous occasions when he had been successful in a ballot to speak, he had proposed nationalising the Bank of England and introducing a Living Wage. Now he chose as his theme "widespread poverty", asserting that it could not be removed within the present framework of the capitalist economy.

Maxton was at his most incisive, taunting his opponents by saying he had been challenged to be constructive but had noticed he might not have "the complete assent of the House". The predominant reason for poverty was rising unemployment.

> Three millions unemployed is a figure and as a figure it is a little worse than two and a half millions but not so bad as seven or eight millions in other countries. But it is only a figure, it is arithmetic and the constant repetition of these figures creates a kind of mind in the politician which puts the human aspect into a secondary place.

He had waited ten years for Governments to fulfil their promises to the out-of work.

> Since I have been in the House successive Governments have gone on the assumption that they were dealing with a temporary condition of things out of which one day we were going to emerge into the bright sunshine of prosperity. We always talked and we talk still of the day when normal conditions will be restored. I cannot remember during my life any normal conditions that I want to see restored as far as working-class life is concerned. We are suffering here from a variety of that type of thinking which has always been found where people look back to some golden past. We look back today to some golden past where people were well off. I do not know when it was. I cannot remember any time

251

during my boyhood or manhood when people were really well off. There is no normal situation such as a situation of prosperity for the mass of the people.

"Normal conditions" for his constituents meant poverty. The "good old days" were "no great days for the common people". Britain was "living in a revolutionary age" and Parliament was "falling into disrepute in every corner of the world". Civil liberties were "in danger".

But Maxton was at his most powerful when he cited experiences and accounts of conditions from his own constituency. Bridgeton was full of insanitary houses, which experts said should be demolished. Homes were damp and overcrowded. Quoting the impressions of a Tory broadcaster who had visited Glasgow, he spoke of "the darkness – that is your first impression, dark stairs, dark landings and dark homes. Aged – that is your second impression. One house I saw in Dalmarnock, half of it below street level, was 300 years old. Naturally it was damp and decrepit in every way."

Maxton then read a letter from a constituent, about the squalor which confronted a family of eight, where the father was unemployed, whose income had been cut because of the Means Test, and where, despite suspected tuberculosis, one of the sons could not secure proper hospital treatment. Barely able to feed herself, the mother had declined in health and now lay on her death bed. Death would be "a mercy". "The woman," he said, "is dead all but for the opening and shutting of her eyes. The awful condition has been brought about by poverty."

Each member of the family was affected by poverty. At 26, the eldest son was unfit for work, suspected of suffering from tuberculosis and weighing only six stones. Much of the family income that should have gone towards food had been spent in securing private medical care for him. They had wanted him treated in a sanatorium, not least because treatment at home "meant an extra mouth to fill without an extra penny to do it", but he "could not get sanatorium treatment because his health was too good. Is that not a hellish condition? A mother has to feel sorry because her son has not got consumption."

The second son, aged 22, has been idle three years. The third one, age 17, is an apprentice slater, wages 10 shillings (50 pence) weekly. The fourth one, aged 15, to augment the family income, took a job going with milk, hours 6 am to 12 am, wages 6 shillings (30p). The father is a labouring man. When working his wages never exceeded £2 a week. When the Means Test was put into operation, the only son drawing any relief was reduced to 11 shillings (55 pence) per week.

He wanted to bring Parliament to "a full realisation of the terrible consequences of the things which we may do". There were, he concluded, markets of world goods sufficient to maintain the people on all continents, but people were denied the purchasing power that would return them to work. "The basic cause of the trouble is that the people are poor ... the country should be planning for plenty."[2]

His speech was, said the *Glasgow Herald*, "a personal triumph". His Labour Party adversary, McNeill Weir, described it as Maxton's best speech and the best attack on the capitalist system he had ever heard in the House of Commons. From the Conservative member who replied came the confession that "it was good on occasions that our complacency should be shattered even if ruthlessly by a speech such as that to which we listened, which opened the windows and brought home to us from one who knows the facts as well as anybody in the House the devastating circumstances of poverty in which so many of our people live".

By the end of March Maxton was attacking both Labour and the National Government over India. The age of imperialism was past. England had no right in India and should go out of it, leaving the Indian people to work out their own salvation.[3] He attacked Scottish Members of Parliament for doing nothing about unemployment. (All they had achieved, he said, was the passage of a False Oaths Bill and a Solicitors Bill.) In his new status as a party leader he sat on an enquiry into the Fascist incidents at London Olympia (he stressed his role was to listen, rather than to legislate) during the early months of 1933. But his main interest was in the Unemployment Insurance changes being put through the House. The unemployed, he argued, deserved increasing levels of benefits – and not the cuts that would result.

Where was the ILP going? In "A Thought for May Day", Maxton called on his party to, "Organise for revolution ... It is for the ILP to make the workers of Britain see revolution as the only practical policy, and to build up the revolutionary instrument which the workers feel they can use with reasonable chance of success."[4] But even as his audiences in Parliament and in the country grew larger Maxton's supporters had diminished to a tiny band, and he found himself treated less as a revolutionary threat, more as a Parliamentary eccentricity. "A set speech by Maxton in the House of Commons is like the first night of a play," Kingsley Martin wrote at this time. "There is the hush, the emotional tension. No one ever attempts to answer his dramatic vehement indictment. If what he says is true his listeners would be better dead."

For Maxton, the political wilderness meant complex Parliamentary manoeuvres merely to demonstrate the ILP existed. Beside Maxton in the Commons sat only two ILP colleagues and they were reduced to a daily ritual of booking their seats in the House. To secure one of the Opposition Front Benches, and to emphasise their status as a distinct party, it was essential to be at the House of Commons every morning when it opened.

Maxton and Buchanan, who were still living in Battersea, had to rise at five in the morning, wait at the Commons until it opened at eight, and place their cards in the Front Bench seats below the Gangway before they returned to Battersea for breakfast. But fixing what were called "prayer cards" to their seats was only to book their places. They had also to be there to take them up at the prayers at the start of the Parliamentary day. So each day Maxton and Buchanan had to be in the Commons at 2.30 and be present for prayers.

Without the support of the Labour Whips, they had not only to find seats in the House but also accommodation for their party in the Commons buildings. Neither the Speaker, the Sergeant at Arms nor the other parties had been able to assist them. A form of direct action was required and John McGovern simply took possession of a vacant room, No. 13, and refused to move. To avoid further embarrassment, Lansbury offered Maxton the room as a personal favour, without recognising his separate party. Maxton refused, but after negotiations a compromise emerged when another room was offered.[5]

The status of leader, even without a party, was, according to his old friend Dollan, all that the ILP now sought. Maxton's followers wanted "for him the style and rank of a party leader which he can get easiest by separating the ILP from the Labour Party". Whatever the real story, Maxton now settled down to a new phase of his Parliamentary career – as leader of the rump of a sect of a once great national party. Ten years before Maxton had been at the centre of a Labour Party ready to form a Government and had been tipped by many as a possible future leader. Five years before, he had been the party's most sought after propagandist with his own programme that demonstrated how a Labour Government could use power to achieve far reaching social and economic changes. Now he would be remembered by many only for the endearing Parliamentary performances of his later years where he offered no real threat to the establishment. Though still a great orator and the most impressive of the left's Parliamentary debaters, Maxton's isolation made it easy for him to be dismissed as an eccentricity. He might speak out on the great issues of the day, but he would have little opportunity to influence their outcome. Even in 1933, Aneurin Bevan's taunt of a year before that the ILP would win purity at the cost of impotence was already beginning to be proved correct.

33

United Fronts

"You haven't got the pluck," a heckler had intervened as Maxton was outlining his commitment to a revolutionary policy at an ILP rally in the Metropole Theatre. "Somebody says I have not got the guts. Will that man stand up," retorted Maxton, beckoning his heckler up to the platform. His appearance there was brief. When he rushed into the wings Maxton followed him, returning in a few minutes to say that "it was rather unfair to leave an audience of 1,000 people to attend to one man".[1]

The dispute between Maxton and local Communist Party members was bitter but Maxton's humour had not deserted him. "For the last ten years I have fought the Labour Party with my brain," he told his audience. "If I have to fight the other enemies of the working class with my fists for the next ten years, I will do it." It was a conflict that was to last throughout the 'thirties in the midst of allegations and counter-allegations, various attempted fronts – United, Workers and Popular – and Unity Campaigns.

The reasons for joint campaigns were practical rather than doctrinal, now the ILP had left the Labour Party. He saw the dangers of isolation for the ILP. Maxton, Brockway reported, "would not be content if his days ended in an isolation which, however much it satisfied his socialist conscience, did not assist the emancipation of the working class".[2]

The ILP had still more than 10,000 members and the Communist Party probably less than 5,000. While the Communist Party had established the *Daily Worker* in 1930 with a circulation of only 18,000, the ILP had the more widely read and respected *New Leader*, but the ILP lacked the internal discipline of the Communist Party and was more susceptible to infiltration. The first threat came when the Revolutionary Policy Committee established itself as a caucus inside the ILP. Its role was crucial during 1933 and 1934 in shifting the ILP further to the left.

Was there any chance of a successful united front joining the Communist Party and the Independent Labour Party? In 1929 the new leaders of the Communist Party had abandoned their eight-year-long campaign to join the Labour Party. The Labour Party, said the Communists, had ceased to be a federation and "was in the process of being transformed from a federal organisation to a party of the social democratic type". Instead, their efforts concentrated on building what they called "a united front from below", of rank and file supporters. The objective was to separate Labour Party members from their leaders and eventually to recruit them into the Communist Party.

Throughout this period, when all Labour leaders were being described by Communists as "social fascists", Maxton had been an easy target for character assassination. One *Daily Worker* cartoon had the ghost of Lenin denouncing Maxton as "unbelievably lazy . . . never able to read, let alone write a fundamental book on socialism".[3] He was called "a fakir, a twister and a liar" and "an imperialist politician". His book on Lenin was described as "fairly worthless" and "a piece of third-rate journalism". History, said the *Daily Worker*, would expose "Maxton as an ignorant swindler just as it exposed the Russian Maxtons".[4]

Even before the ILP left Labour, the Communist Party had urged ILP militants to campaign for all the party's revolutionary elements to defect *en masse* to the Communist Party. Pollitt had declared the policy as "war to a knife with the ILP". "We must," he wrote in 1932, "make a determined effort to win the rank and file of the ILP, at the same time to avoid creating the impression that there are no fundamental differences between our party and the ILP." Inside the ILP the Revolutionary Policy Committee were pursuing a similar policy, "boring from within". They suggested a joint party, a course not yet officially favoured by the Communist Party, which had refused national negotiations on joint campaigns throughout 1932.

In the search for a broader audience, Maxton and the ILP sought links with the Communist-controlled National Unemployed Workers' Movement and cooperated on the Hunger Marches and the agitation against the Means Test. The ILP had supported the Unemployed Workers' Movement's National Charter of 1931. There had also been attempts to cooperate over wages, hours, and the campaign to repeal the Trades Disputes Act, but even where there were cooperative efforts, joint action had come to little. The Hunger March of 1932 was typical. The Communists claimed that John McGovern had weakened the demonstration by trying to present its demands to Parliament himself instead of allowing the NUWM to do so.

Prior to 1933 the United Front was largely a fiction. Faced with the hostility of the Communists on the left, and Labour on the right, Maxton spent much of his time simply defending himself. He devoted a number of articles in *New Leader* to rebutting Communist claims about his views and his speeches and replying to personal attacks on his work record. All of this showed, he said, that the problem of securing a united working-class movement in this country is met with exactly the same kind of difficulty from the alleged "lefts" of the Communist Party and its subsidiary allies as from the "rights" of the Labour Party.[5]

The *Daily Worker* attitude to him and the ILP was, he said, "illuminating" in that they were unwilling to look at the facts or listen to alternative views. They were determined to "dragoon" unwilling workers into support of their theories. He did not believe the problems were insurmountable, "but before they are surmounted leaders of the Labour Party and of the Communist Party will have to learn that the workers generally are not prepared to grant them a position of papal infallibility, nor to support them in policies which the workers do not accept as their own". In united activities, he did not in any way attempt "to limit its activities to those that suited my own political philosophy nor my own political prejudices".

But during the late months of 1932, and early 1933, a series of external events made cooperation more likely. International realignments forced the warring factions together. In 1932 the Russian-controlled Comintern diluted its "social fascist" attacks on Labour leaders. Divisions between the left-wing parties in Germany had allowed the rise of Hitler. The threat of Fascism in Britain compelled a new unity on the British left. Maxton himself drew the lesson of a divided German left to express the hope that "a common danger will now produce the unity that a working-class analysis of the situation should have produced before".[6]

Early in 1933, the Communist line shifted from one of lessened attack to conciliation. In February 1933 the Left Socialist Bureau cabled both Second and Third Internationals for a conference of all socialists and Communists. The Bureau included the ILP. In March the Comintern responded and proposed "The United Front against Fascism", but the Labour and Socialist International which included the Labour Party called for joint action between Communists and social democrats in Germany and refused to recommend the formation of United Fronts elsewhere.

Maxton now sought to realise the much-discussed unity amongst groupings on the left. On 5 March the ILP NAC approached the Labour Party, TUC, Co-operative Movement and Communists and other working-class bodies to promote the unity which Maxton felt was "urgent" and could still be achieved without the subjugation of one group to another. The approach was rejected by the Labour Party. In *Democracy versus Dictatorship*, it opposed Communism and Fascism with equal vigour, a view subsequently endorsed by the Hastings Conference in October 1933 and the Stockport Conference in 1934. All cooperation with Communists was ruled to be incompatible with Labour Party membership.

Maxton was not surprised, but the British Labour Party was, he said, making the same mistake as German Social Democrats. The fight against Fascism was too important to leave until the return of a Labour Government. The rank and file of the Labour Party, including old ILP colleagues, should seek to change the policy. The ILP Conference of April ratified this view. The new policy, Maxton explained to *New Leader*, was "cooperation – not subordination".

But once again Maxton was pushed further than he wanted to go. At the ILP Conference in April 1933, the ILP decided – by the narrowest of votes, 83 to 79 – to ask how it might assist the work of the Russian-dominated Communist International. With this victory behind them, the Revolutionary Policy Committee pushed home their advantage, and went on to pledge the party to continued and increased collaboration with the Communist Party and an approach to the Comintern.

An agreement was signed between the Communist Party and the ILP on 5 May 1933. The aims of a United Front campaign were "to fight Fascism ... and to build up resistance against the attack on the conditions of the employed and unemployed workers". Joint activity was to take place "in campaigns at the factories, labour exchanges, streets and trades unions".

Even as the campaigns started, there were problems. When Maxton turned out to speak at one of the first United Front meetings in Shoreditch Town Hall, a Communist official prevented him from speaking. Pollitt, the Communist Party Secretary, apologised profusely to Maxton for this rebuff at "what should have been the starting off of one of the biggest anti-Fascist campaigns that has yet been launched in the country. None of us should do anything that prevents the utilisation of every ounce of influence and power that all of us can bring to bear in developing the United Front against Fascism."[7]

"We slipped into a United Front with the Communist Party," concluded Fenner Brockway, "without considered attention ... Maxton, Harry Pollitt, J.R. Campbell (or Willie Gallacher) and I had frequent consultations. Pollitt was a skilled and persuasive negotiator. He went out of his way to give the ILP even greater prominence than the CP. He suggested an ultimate amalgamation ... the coming together of the two parties on an equal basis." Maxton was, Brockway recalled, "more cautious, not committing himself to Pollitt's plan, but admitting that he would not be content if his days ended in an isolation which, however much it satisfied his socialist conscience, did not assist the emancipation of the working class", but, as Brockway wrote, "we signed an agreement for cooperation in 'day-to-day' activities in practically every sphere".[8]

Maxton's political views had changed since the cataclysmic experience of 1931. That event, and the rise of Fascism in Europe, led committed democratic socialists, such as Harold Laski, Stafford Cripps, R.H. Tawney and even Clement Attlee to question the capacities of Parliamentary democracy. They feared that constitutional socialist change was too vulnerable to anti-democratic forces and some questioned the possibility that socialism could be effected by constitutional means. Marxists had always doubted the importance of the ballot box and Parliament. Although Marx had suggested that the vote foreshadowed the political supremacy of the working class,[9] Lenin had described Parliament as little more than "a loudspeaker" for the Labour Movement.

Just after the defeat of the 1931 Labour Government, Tawney had suggested how implementing a socialist programme would now become "a pretty desperate business". There could, he suggested, be "disaffection in the army" and a socialist Government would provoke "determined resistance".[10] In *The Crisis and the Constitution*, Laski had suggested that evolutionary socialism had "deceived itself into believing that it can establish itself by peaceful means within the ambit of the capitalist system". Later, Cripps had written in *Can Socialism Come by Constitutional Means?* that "the ruling class will go to almost any length to defeat Parliamentary action if the direct issue is the continuance of their financial and political control". Even the mild-mannered Attlee took the view that Parliament could be subverted. "It was no use ignoring the fact," he wrote in his book *The Labour Party in Perspective*, published in 1938, "that in the last resort a government must be prepared to defend its authority if challenged by force."

Perhaps the main point at issue was how a democratically elected left-wing government enjoying popular support would act if its will was thwarted by anti-democratic forces of the right. For some socialists the conclusion was obvious, that the institution of Parliament creating social change in the interests of the majority would have to mobilise mass extra-Parliamentary support in the event of a right-wing threat. Theirs was a statement which distinguished between extra-Parliamentary action in support of Parliament and anti-Parliamentary action to subvert it.

Shorn of its Parliamentary credibility and widely infiltrated by far left factions committed to extra-Parliamentary activity, the ILP reached different conclusions. A special report was prepared for the ILP's Derby Conference of 1933. It reduced the importance of Parliament. Parliament, the ILP said, could not be the main instrument for the destruction of the state of which it was the political expression. Thus the ILP's best-known Parliamentarian, in introducing the report, propounded the view that Parliament was a weapon of "diminished responsibility in the struggle".

The Annual Conference instructed the National Council to prepare a fuller statement on "the new policy of the ILP". The country could not simply vote its way to socialism, that report said. Only the overwhelming mobilisation of the working class could extinguish capitalism. The statement argued that "in order to maintain its power in circumstances of increasing difficulty the capitalist class will adopt various devices striking at democratic practice which however constitutional, will be in essence Fascist". In retaliation the ILP had to ensure "the organisation of the working class for the achievement of a revolutionary socialist programme".[11]

Maxton defended the ILP's change of course. The Labour Party "was wrong" in directing the minds of the workers to Parliament as the means of liberation, with the trades unions and cooperatives as subsidiary agents in an electoral fight. Again it was wrong in its basic principle that the capitalist system of society could be reformed out of existence.

> The new policy of the ILP eradicates these errors. It sets socialism as its one and only goal. It recognises that the achievement of socialism must be attained by the successful prosecution of the workers struggle. It encourages that struggle at every point where it is at present proceeding but it does not place Parliamentary representation as the chief purpose of the party's activities.[12]

The left had returned to many of the arguments that split them in 1919. Maxton himself was to be subjected to much criticism, especially as he not only claimed to believe in the report but said that he "had something to do with drafting it". He was attacked from the left by Trotsky for believing socialism was possible within national boundaries, and from the right by those who claimed he had renounced any support for Parliamentary democracy. He replied that Parliamentary and electoral work were not being rejected and should be "more virile than ever", but there was a need for workers' councils, "either for the sake of putting through that social revolution ... or for the sake of resisting any attempt to crush a working-class movement altogether". The creation of a strong working-class movement was so "urgent that I have pushed the United Front proposals".[13] "The honest course was to tell people that Parliament in itself could not be an instrument of revolutionary change."[14]

Maxton's initial enthusiasm for the party position was soon to be qualified as his personal views emerged in a series of newspaper articles and speeches. The political struggle, he said, should be taking place "at every point". Parliamentary representation could not be the chief purpose of the party's activities and workers' councils were necessary in the active struggle for working-class objectives. He had been accused of doubting whether socialists could ever win a mandate, but this was "the most mischievous of statements". While Parliament had played little part in Russia or Germany, because these countries "had neither the representative nature nor the long history of the British Parliament, Parliament is likely to play an important part in revolutionary happenings here". However, the mandate that socialists were seeking "must be something more than an electoral mandate, and must find other expressions than merely putting a cross on a ballot paper".[15]

Where precisely did Maxton stand? He had always believed that, without a sustained and active political campaign amongst working people, Parliament alone would be ineffective in pushing forward a socialist programme. If it was to succeed, a Parliamentary strategy required the additional pressure of direct action. Yet he realised that the hitherto inviolate right to vote offered British socialists avenues not open to their comrades in the Italy and Germany of the 'thirties.

Maxton had always believed in a form of workers' control. Now there was an additional argument for workers' councils. They would constitute a counter-threat to the anti-democratic extra-Parliamentary movements of the right. The better organised the

British workers, the better the guarantees against subversion by a disaffected army, Blackshirt thuggery and international cartels.

Maxton was no Communist. He rejected democratic centralism in its entirety. He never fell prey to the view that a vanguard could make revolution on behalf of the working people of Britain and appreciated that in modern Britain democratic centralism was redundant. "There will be no revolution in this country until revolution appeals to the mass of the people as an intelligent and commonsense thing to do." Then socialism would "be very near indeed".[16]

Nor did Maxton believe in "orders from the top", an essential feature of Russian practice. He had written a strong attack on this in *New Leader* early in 1933. He had rejected the Communist "desire to impose from above a discipline by a party caucus upon those who are willing to co-operate for common objects but are unwilling to be dragooned into an acceptance of theories (and the application of those theories) with which they are in disagreement". There had to be tolerance. People had to be involved in creating the socialist society of the future, hence his continuous appeal for mobilising the rank and file. No amount of pressure for central command and authoritarian leadership could induce Maxton to renounce either his independence or the independence of those who supported him.

The new line on workers' councils and on the United Front irrevocably separated the ILP from the Labour Party. The Labour Party Conference of October 1933, at Hastings, rejected any United Front. Instead it adopted a detailed statement, entitled *Democracy versus Dictatorship*, in which it argued against both Communism and Fascism. There was no point in Labour even talking to the Communists. "Past experience goes to show," the document stated, "that such negotiations in individual countries may unfortunately only too easily be turned into manoeuvres by the Communists with the result that they help to poison the situation and increase the mistrust in the Labour Movement instead of diminishing it." Maxton castigated Labour for its failure to adopt a bold policy, urging the ordinary Labour Party members to resist their leaders.

The death of the National Government MP and sitting Member for the Kilmarnock constituency provided a by-election, and hence an electoral test for the new-look ILP, which went into the contest with Communist support. The ILP candidate was John Pollock who had a strong claim to the seat, having contested it as a Labour candidate with ILP support in 1932. His principal left-wing opponent in 1933 was the Rev James Barr, the Labour candidate and a former ILP colleague of Maxton's. Maxton told the voters that unlike the Labour candidate, Pollock would "be able to stand freely and without fear in Parliament for the things that the people of Kilmarnock told him to stand for".[17]

A few days before the by-election *Forward* ran a cartoon depicting Ramsay MacDonald shaking hands with Maxton and saying, "Thanks, Jimmie! You are doing the National Government a good turn; if the ILP candidate takes enough votes from Barr – Lindsay's in." The cartoon was entitled "The United Front: Down with the Labour Candidate". The prediction was accurate. Lindsay, the National Government candidate, won, with Labour second and the ILP third, a thousand votes behind. Yet again a natural left-wing seat had been lost because of the divisions within the left. *Forward* suggested that MacDonald might reward Maxton with a seat in the Lords. Although Maxton was blamed for the loss of the seat, he in turn blamed Labour since it had failed to respond to his offer of a United Front.

34

Member for the Unemployed

The first large scale Hunger March had taken place in 1922. There had been more marches to London in the late 'twenties, demonstrations to the Trades Union Congress in 1931, and local marches, rallies and demonstrations, all organised by the National Unemployed Workers' Movement, throughout the early years of the 'thirties.

The Hunger March against the Means Test arrived in London in October 1932. 2,000 marchers were involved. The petition had been presented with a million signatures to the House of Commons. They protested against the Means Test and the 10% cut in unemployment benefit.

On this occasion joint action between the ILP and other left-wing groups, including the National Unemployed Workers' Movement, had been impossible. McGovern had wanted to present the national petition to the House of Commons on behalf of the Unemployed Workers. Their leaders, Wal Hannington, Harry McShane and others refused.

Throughout 1932 and 1933 Labour made gains in local authority elections and pressure from both the councils and the unemployed built up to secure better benefits. When Labour swept to power in Glasgow at the end of 1933, the ILP faction on the council were instrumental in forcing increased benefits and higher scale rates were introduced. In Greenock the local council had raised benefits and modified the Means Test. A Court of Enquiry was set up which sat in August 1934. It was turned into a Labour propaganda exercise. The Auditor discovered that the principle of merely relieving destitution had been transformed into a principle of adequate maintenance. Evidence from families suggested that family life was threatened by unemployment, that the long-term unemployed were demoralised and that the Government's recommended scale rates were below that necessary for physical efficiency. Political pressure forced the Government to back down.

A private Scottish Office study, carried out in 1934, conceded most of the Labour argument. It found that the physical condition of the unemployed was "a prelude to a more serious organic breakdown if conditions prevailed over a longer period". The unemployed, they found, had few household goods and personal possessions, lived in poorer quality homes and ate an inferior diet.

The ILP was involved in the organisation of the 1934 Hunger March. Other marches had led to violence and arrests. Harry McShane, one of the Communist Party organisers, recalls that the 1934 March "was very peaceful because of the cooperation we received from the ILP councillors and men like Aneurin Bevan and James Maxton". 2,000 Hunger Marchers came from all over Britain and arrived in London in February 1934. John McGovern marched with the Scottish contingent, only ill-health preventing Maxton from taking part in the march. He was, however, able to address the London demonstration and he led the march to No. 10 Downing Street. Maxton asked Ramsay MacDonald to meet the unemployed, but after a quarter of an hour in Downing Street, was spurned. MacDonald was visiting the British Industries Fair. "It was nice to be able to have a fair," Maxton remarked, "even if there were no industries." Telling the crowd that if constitutional doors closed others would open, he promised to take the fight into the House of Commons. There, a motion that MacDonald receive a deputation was defeated by 270 votes to 52 – but not before Maxton had attacked the Prime Minister for calling the marchers "extremists" and warning he would "keep these men marching and agitating so that they would remain virile citizens rather than become the crushed creatures which the Unemployment Bill would make them". "Pride," Maxton told MacDonald, "came before a fall."

> ... had they been rich brewers or bankers or wealthy people, they would have been received with open arms, but the National Government and its Head evidently intend to put the poor in their places in slave camps.[1]

Maxton had in fact written to MacDonald asking him to meet the demonstrators and in his reply MacDonald sought to minimise the damage. "Nothing would give me greater pleasure than to gratify you wholeheartedly in the first request you have made," MacDonald replied. "But you know quite well it is impossible." He would be prepared to meet any MPs but none of the march organisers. Maxton, said MacDonald, should be aware of "the record" of "the chief promoters of the march".[2] When the Budget of April 1934 restored the cuts, Maxton told the House that the recent unemployed march had played "a not unimportant part".[3]

Meanwhile, inside the ILP, there was deep revulsion to the moves towards cooperation with parties on the left. The Communists now advocated a United Working Class Party, and the ILP applied for but were refused membership of the Moscow-dominated Comintern International. But despite another appeal from Maxton, and a meeting between him and Henderson, the Labour Party had once again resisted any involvement in campaigns alongside Communists. In February 1934, the ILP wrote to the Labour Party, the TUC and the Cooperative and Communist Parties asking for "an immediate consultation between representatives of all sections of the working class so that we may plan common action". A survey of constituency activities had been set up and in December 1933 John Paton had reported that, "the analysis of the reports shows that the policy of isolated cooperation with the Communist Party has completely failed to bring general support from the other organised bodies"[4].

At the ILP's Scottish Conference Maxton had a rough ride. He criticised some speakers because "some of their views were too close to the line of thought of the Labour Party for his liking". The Labour Party he could no longer believe in. The ILP should work on the assumption that they could create a real working-class movement in Britain. In a vote, the Scottish ILP agreed to support a limited association with the Communists on specific campaigns.[5]

When the National Administrative Council considered Communist cooperation, they had before them in February 1934 details of the replies to a questionnaire. Of their 353 branches, only 137 had replied, and the replies reflected a division of opinion. Only 45 cooperated with the Communist Party. Another 65 had done so on a limited basis. In most cases, it was in the anti-war movement. Only 58 were for continued cooperation with the Communist Party in its general activities. 66 of the branches would support "limited cooperation on specific issues as they arise". 86 branches were against discontinuing cooperation with the Communist Party entirely but 30 supported that line. All in all not more than 1,200 members had been involved in replying. 400 were against any cooperation. And the majority were against general cooperation and wanted to restrict it to specific issues.

The Secretary's view was that "the majority were in favour of cooperation with the Communist Party on a specific basis but there was a small majority against cooperation in general acitivities".[6] Later Brockway could be more honest. "The result was startling," he wrote. "Two thirds of the party were participating in the United Front uneasily if not unwillingly ... in the Lancashire ILP there was open revolt; in South Wales the minimum of effort was made; from all over the country letters of criticism began to reach Head Office."[7]

The National Council of the Party recommended the 1934 Conference drop "day to day" cooperation with the CP – instead it proposed that United Front activities should be limited to specific issues. The committee decided that to build a revolutionary socialist movement, cooperation on "specific objects" as agreed from time to time required the involvement of every branch, but the extent of that cooperation "must depend upon local circumstances and leaves this to the discretion of the branches". The motion was passed by seven to four.[8]

As Brockway recalled it was "with a feeling of relief" that the majority of delegates accepted the recommendation. In his address as Chairman, Maxton regretted the failure of their efforts especially with the Labour Party to secure a United Front of all working-class organisations but said the ILP still urged close cooperation. In time, the country would recognise there was a real "workers' force" made up of different sections, each with its own philosophy, programme, policy and method, but all prepared for the maximum attainable amount of cooperation. No feeling of party pride, and party egotism, would prevent them, he said, from cooperation in the fullest manner with every working-class section on these immediate issues.

Maxton himself was still in favour of limited cooperation with the Communists. In his notes for his annual lecture to the ILP Summer School in August 1934, he conceded that the Communist Party, while "blatantly revolutionary, very generally puts its case in the way most calculated to rouse antagonism but it is a useful antidote to the Labour Party which has been all things to all men". He admitted that while "relations in the United Front have been very uneasy, (the ILP) must recognise that the Communist Party has been responsible for publication of much first-class literature which has given us bigger conceptions of how working-class struggles should be carried on ... What CP has done is to insert into our ideas that the struggle must be kept going all the time."[9]

Towards the end of 1934, a meeting at the House of Commons

between Maxton, Brockway, Campbell Stephen and McGovern of the ILP and Pollitt, Gallacher, Kerrigan and Springhall of the Communist Party laid down conditions for the continuation of the United Front. This depended on Communist assurances that it would stop interfering in the ILP's affairs.[10] Future cooperation, said Brockway, depended on neither party interfering in the internal affairs of others. Moreover, the Communist Party had to state whether it would oppose Labour or ILP candidates in elections, and there should be no attempt to unify the ILP and the Communist Party until the next Annual Conference had discussed the matter.

But the ILP was still plagued by entryism and Communist and Trotskyist penetration. In 1934 the Communist League of Trotskyists attempted to merge with the ILP. The statement by members outlined their aims:

> The building of a new party would be painfully slow. The possibility of a speedier way of establishing an effective revolutionary party is provided by the ILP which despite its past mistakes represents a potentially revolutionary force.[11]

What was Maxton's position on cooperation then? He would work with other organisations as long as his freedom of manoeuvre was not lost. Arthur Woodburn, a Scottish Labour official, probably got it right when he said, "Maxton was too wily a politician to obey Communist Party decisions when he would not accept Labour Party ones."[12]

Maxton at Fifty

For 13 years Maxton had been a widower, for most of that time living in a Battersea flat shared with Buchanan and Stephen. It was an arrangement that lasted because it worked well, offering economy as well as social support for the three MPs. According to one friend, "Stephen cooked, Buchanan washed up, and Maxton dusted." Occasionally Mrs Buchanan descended from Glasgow to do the sort of cleaning that was beyond their scope. Otherwise they were self-sufficient in their four-roomed fourth-floor flat, avoiding the isolation of life in cheap hotels, exchanging ideas and gossip, drinking vast amounts of tea – all virtually abstained from alcohol – and, in Maxton's case anyway, smoking too much.

The communal arrangement came to an end when, in his fiftieth year, with his son Jim now thirteen, Maxton decided to marry again. Little is known of Maxton's private life in his years of widowhood, probably because there is little to know. His relationships with women appear to have been of a platonic kind. "Jim Maxton has no darlings in the sexual sense, poor fellow," wrote the ever inquisitive Lord Beaverbrook in 1931.[1]

Madeleine Glasier had worked with Maxton for twelve years. She had a degree from London University, was an active member of the ILP, and was utilised by him as researcher, shorthand writer and typist. Although the two had spent much time together in political work, Maxton's decision to remarry was unexpected and the engagement came as "a great surprise" to many of their friends. The marriage was to be a happy one. They shared many interests, including politics and detective fiction.

Maxton had been off ill from November and was advised to cancel all his political engagements until the end of January. One day, during this period, Maxton was sitting at lunch in the White Heather Café in the Strand, then a favourite meeting place for Scots in London, It was shortly before Christmas and Maxton mentioned that he had to go shopping in the afternoon to buy some presents for his friends. "And one of the presents will be for you," he said to Madeleine. "Well I hope you buy something sensible," remarked Madeleine. "It will be something sensible and while I'm on the subject you'd better be thinking what finger you're going to put the ring on."[2]

They were engaged in December 1934 and married in March 1935. Maxton spent the morning of his wedding day debating the Scottish Housing Bill, and then went to Battersea Registry Office for a simple ceremony. Secrecy was such that Maxton's flatmate, George Buchanan, was told only at midday. "I am going out but not for a cup of tea. I am going out to be married and if you tell anybody about it one second before one o'clock I will never speak to you again."[3] The ceremony duly took place and afterwards Maxton, his new wife, her sister and his brother, had tea together. The bride and groom then left by car for a brief weekend honeymoon in the New Forest. The little political community in the Battersea flat came to an end.

Maxton returned from his honeymoon to wage war on the new Poor Law regulations.

Up to 1934 unemployment relief was dispensed by Poor Law Authorities and labour exchanges. The new proposals centralised unemployment relief under the Unemployment Assistance Board. New relief scales were also set and when they were announced in December 1934 (the Act was to receive Royal Assent in February), many of the unemployed could look forward only to being worse off. Protest was widespread with large-scale demonstrations in Scotland, Wales and Yorkshire. Popular pressure eventually forced the Government to back down.

In the midst of the demonstrations, Lansbury moved Parliament to delay the implementation of the Poor Law changes. Maxton supported him.[4] Once again Maxton spoke for the industrial masses saying that the working people were more stirred by this issue than by any other political matter during the past five or six years. The deep feeling was not because Mrs So and So had got two shillings less than she expected, or because John Smith had been put on a lower level. There was among the working people of this country, he concluded, a feeling that a tremendous injustice had been done to people who were already down in their depths. The Government were faced with a serious emergency. If he were to consider only the narrowest and immediate political interest he would have said: "Let it rip; let it go; let the discontent spread; let the whole thing boil over." However, he had recognised that millions faced injustice and deprivation and he must speak on their behalf.

271

Not surprisingly, the Parliamentary battle was lost. Immediately Maxton sought a united countrywide campaign with the Labour Party, but, as Maxton was to report to the Communist Party when he addressed their February Conference, Labour had refused even to discuss cooperation. [5]

But then Maxton made what appeared to be a controversial proposal. To the Communist Conference Maxton had expressed his hope that a joint conference might be convened of the ILP and Communist Party "to establish in this country a United Communist Party that will represent every revolutionary throughout Great Britain". Immediately afterwards he had qualified his remark implying that he had only a federation of groups in mind. It was "not a fusion with the Communists but the formation of a Workers' Party to which members of all Labour, Socialist and Communist organisations can belong without sinking their identity".

The proposal brought fresh controversy. Later in April 1935 he told his own ILP Conference that the workers of Britain were "looking to the United Front of the ILP and the Communist Party to lead their agitation and actively voice their discontent. The time was not too far distant when it would be practical politics for a new workers' party to take shape in this country." Speaking about a new workers' party, Maxton said:

> I cannot say that I feel, as Pollitt has expressed it, that we are ready for the unification of the ILP and the Communist Party. But I do feel that already things are shaping so that the possibility of the formation of a new working-class party in this land with the ILP and the Communist Party as its central core is not in the far distant future but is very near us.[6]

The Communist Party Secretary, Pollitt, explained that he was "absolutely against Maxton's idea of a workers' party".[7] Maxton again had to backtrack, saying that talk of a new party was a "misunderstanding"[8] and that he had not suggested he would form such an organisation.

Maxton had hoped to achieve greater unity in the fight at home against poverty and abroad against Fascism. He had little faith in the Labour Party, he told the ILP Conference in April. When he left the Labour Party he had hoped that the ILP could fight "courageously and freely" for the working class, and that it would compel Labour to abandon reformism. The first had happened, but the second had not been realised. But rebuffed once again in his attempts at greater unity amongst the parties of the left outside the Labour Party, Maxton continued to speak out against the horrors of war and of poverty, which he had sought to make the basis of a unity campaign in Parliament. He had once again taken up the question of the condition of Scotland's housing alleging that, when he did so, he had been threatened by officials of the Glasgow Property Owners Association.[9] In the Budget debate, he again complained about the absence of any help for the unemployed. He warned of the dangers to peace in the steady rising defence budgets of the major powers, and he asked the Government to listen to the voice of the German people rather than the voice of Hitler.

Maxton was 50 in June 1935. Addressing the ILP only a few weeks before his birthday, he spoke of his first 30 years in politics as an apprenticeship. The really important struggle lay ahead. An outside view is available from a birthday profile of Maxton which appeared in the *New Leader*. It quoted the views of Professor Harold Laski, to whom Maxton was an evangelist who wanted to see everything he preached realised immediately.

Maxton continued to strive for some accommodation with the Labour Party. If a united front proved impossible, an electoral agreement would at least be useful. The objective of the new negotiations he proposed in August of 1935, he told the ILP Summer School, was "to avoid conflicting candidatures" with a view to removing the National Government. The consultation "must not involve any compromise in policy or limitation of freedom where candidates are returned to Parliament".[10]

Negotiations, he felt, were made more urgent by the events in Ethiopia. Fascist Italy, in a search for the return of the grandeur of Rome, had attacked the virtually medieval kingdom of Haile Selassie. Since any British action would simply signify a competition between two forms of imperialism, in September 1935, Maxton and the ILP issued a manifesto opposing any form of British military intervention. War would see British workers used as "capitalist fodder" for British imperialism. Maxton went on to demand the recall of Parliament. The people of Britain did "not want any national efforts diverted into anything military". Sanctions he also opposed.[11]

By now Maxton was concerned about the danger of a general war in Europe towards which he felt Italy's invasion of Abyssinia was a step. In 1934 he had complained about the "upward curve in arms spending", which suggested to him that hopes of peace were being thrown aside.[12] He had also vigorously protested that each new set of Defence Estimates was a "confession of failure", moving Britain "further and further" from any resolution of the problems of war. Maxton's perspective was dominated by the memory of the Great War. He told an anti-war meeting in Glasgow that in 1919 it would have needed a tank to take one man who had been at war back to another. It would have taken machine guns, he said, to compel wives and mothers to allow their husbands and sons to enlist again. His fear was that as 20 years had passed memories had become dulled.

But Labour's own internal divisions over the rearmament question made any alliance with the ILP unlikely. Labour's leader, George Lansbury, was a pacifist who opposed both war and sanctions. At the 1935 Labour Party Conference his views cost him the leadership. He was hounded out when Labour adopted a policy of support for League of Nations sanctions.

There was therefore no chance of any electoral agreement. The Labour Party put up candidates against even the sitting ILP MPs. Woodburn, the Scottish organiser, later defended this action as "necessary, otherwise they would have spread themselves over the whole of Scotland losing us perhaps many seats".[13] Maxton found this decision "vindictive and dictatorial".[14]

Worse than the continued Labour hostility was the renewed opposition of the Communist Party to the ILP. The programme of joint cooperation had been abandoned at Communist Party insistence. The Communists were now seeking affiliation to the Labour Party and at the election generally supported Labour candidatures in preference to those of the ILP. Only Maxton and the two other sitting ILP MPs were exempt. Maxton saw this as a betrayal. His response was to redefine the ILP MPs as "a group of militant fighters with a clearly defined socialist objective whatever government is in power". The enemies were poverty, war and Fascism.[15]

Maxton's own seat, Bridgeton, was secure and his majority in 1935 exceeded 8,000, the official Labour candidate losing his deposit, with only 594 votes. Buchanan and McGovern were both returned, and Stephen, regaining his Camlachie seat with the slenderest of majorities – 884 votes – rejoined them at Westminster.

In Bridgeton the contest had lapsed from its previous civility. Maxton's final rally had to be abandoned when he was howled down by right-wing opponents singing the National Anthem and *Rule Britannia*. The chairman, Maxton's minister brother-in-law, Rev John Munro, was ignored and police officers present were equally unsuccessful in controlling the interruptions. Maxton was statesmanlike, urging the audience to disperse in peace. "I do not want any human being in Bridgeton to be hurt tonight and I do not want anyone to be arrested"[16], but privately he was not unhappy with what had happened. He had been under attack from the Catholic community over schooling in the area, and as he explained later to Bob Edwards, "I could have controlled the meeting. I didn't. I had a quarrel with the Catholics over schools, and I deliberately allowed the Orangemen to close the meeting down. The news went round like wildfire that I had been howled down by Orange demonstrators. The whole Catholic community voted for me." Such were the sectarian calculations that socialist politicians had to make in the Glasgow of the 1930s.

Throughout the country the ILP secured only 139,000 votes, 80% of them in Scotland. It was a dismal performance but one that Maxton thought worthy of "congratulations. This was the election at which we were to be obliterated. We come out of it increased in numerical strength and actual representation."[17] Maxton blamed the Labour Party for the return of the National Government. Would it ever learn, he asked? It was half-hearted on reconstruction at home and utterly divided on the war question. Its leader Lansbury had resigned and his replacement, Attlee, he saw "only as a stopgap".

Three years after leaving the Labour Party, the ILP had lost one-third of its card-carrying membership. This was now only 6,000. Joint activities with the Communist Party had virtually ceased despite the calls for "a united Communist Party". The ILP responded with yet another new statement of aims, calling for "workers' councils under the leadership of the revolutionary party". The ILP now aimed "at using the existing governmental institutions – parliamentary and municipal – to the utmost. They can be of value for agitation purposes and for winning concessions from the capitalist class."

But increasingly the ILP had become a forum for conflicting viewpoints rather than a party with a coherent policy. Maxton had always viewed the ILP not as a full-blooded Marxist-Leninist vanguard party but as the true, yet unheeded, conscience of the Labour Movement. Others saw it differently. In particular, far left groups viewed the ILP as ripe for infiltration, to be used and then discarded. The departure of one such group was followed by the arrival of another when in 1935 the Revolutionary Policy Committee left and the Trotskyists began to organise within the ILP for a new Fourth International.

Maxton and the leadership of the ILP responded by bringing

275

in a conference ruling that unofficial internal groups were "bad in principle". It was passed by a majority of only three. As one historian of the period concluded, the ILP was "not organisationally or intellectually equipped to become revolutionary. By its democratic constitution, it had to accept what point of view a well-organised minority could enforce at any particular time. In its attitude to revolution as in its other policies, the party constantly vacillated."

Was there any chance of a reconciliation between Maxton and the Labour Party in 1935? Oliver Baldwin, the socialist son of Stanley Baldwin and an ILP supporter, had had conversations with Arthur Woodburn. When he told Woodburn that the ILP "wanted to work with the Labour Party", Woodburn made an offer.

> I offered that if Maxton would protect me by a private letter giving me the necessary assurances I would invite Maxton publicly to come in to the party again. This would have made it an act of grace on their part and the responsibility would have been mine. I said we would kill the fatted calf if this happened. All that Maxton said was that the Labour Party had plenty "fatted calves" for returning prodigals.[18]

Woodburn acknowledged that Maxton's "popularity was such that he would have automatically been elected to office" once he was working as a colleague, but was "driven to the conclusion that James Maxton preferred the privileged position in Parliament of being the leader of a small party without responsibility. This gave him a right to seek the front stage in every debate. He spoke as one of the four leaders. He did not seek power or responsibility which would have been a handicap to his oratory."[19]

36

Fighting Fascism

Maxton's politics were rooted in Glasgow and the Clydeside, but he was a committed internationalist whose support for liberation struggles in India and elsewhere was in the internationalist traditions of the ILP. At home, in the 1930s, the Parliamentary battles were fought for the unemployed. Abroad, the socialist struggle was against Fascism. Throughout the previous 20 years Maxton had travelled widely in Europe. He had hiked round France, Germany and Holland in a European trip before the Great War. His honeymoon of 1920 had taken him to the Continent. In 1923 he and John Wheatley had visited the Ruhr and then challenged the Labour Parliamentary leadership to offer a less harsh policy on reparations, and in 1930 and 1931, he had attended conferences of European socialists where he had been amazed at their impotence in the face of mass unemployment and the Great Crash.

Maxton's interests extended to India. He and Fenner Brockway had called on the Second Labour Government to move faster towards its independence. In this campaign he had made contact with Gandhi and other leaders of the Indian campaign for independence.

For a brief period, in 1927 and 1928, Maxton had been the Chairman of the League Against Imperialism, but had been deposed when he failed to follow the Moscow line and append his name to an article which gave general support to the Comintern.

In almost all his efforts Maxton could call on the general support of many socialists inside and outside the Labour Party, and the wholehearted support of his own party, the Independent Labour Party. In 1936, over his attitude to sanctions against Italy over Abyssinia, Maxton stood virtually alone.

The Abyssinian crisis had already removed one leading socialist leader, George Lansbury, the pacifist leader of the Labour Party. Accused by Ernest Bevin of "hawking his conscience round the

277

country", Lansbury had been forced to resign. According to Bevin, "Lansbury had been going around in saint's cloths for years. I set fire to the faggots." During 1936, Maxton, too, was to resign from the leadership of his party, although his return was not long delayed.

Before the 1935 election Maxton had argued that war in defence of Abyssinia would "not be worth the life of a single British worker". Back in Parliament in the early months of 1936, he scorned the idea of sanctions. The ILP, he said, were "100% against them". Sanctions were "not a substitute for war, but a preliminary to it".[1] When, in the event, sanctions were established, he argued against any extension of them. "Could any of these additional sanctions have been applied without having men under arms, and ships and aeroplanes ready to go?" Maxton asked.

The ILP stood alone in its opposition to sanctions, deserted even by the Communists. Relations with the Communists had deteriorated to the point that the Communist Party was not even invited to send a fraternal delegate to the ILP's 1936 Conference. Maxton's Presidential Address was a simple admission of his isolation. It was "distressing" to find that the ILP in its anti-war policy at this stage held itself almost as solitary as on previous occasions. He told the Conference, "He would be prepared to go to tremendous lengths in the way of recommending the party to sacrifice its independence for the sake of getting one great, broad, united front against war but when he looked around at this moment he regretted to say he found it impossible to discover them." As a result the ILP was "unable to any extent to influence the course of international events".

Maxton was in a minority even in his own party. Some ILP members – including Fenner Brockway and the Trotskyist faction – favoured what Maxton considered the abstract doctrine of workers' sanctions. Within the party's inner Executive (which consisted of the MPs, John Aplin and Brockway) Maxton had been arguing that the policy of "working class sanctions" could not be distinguished publicly from League of Nations sanctions and would simply create a psychology for war against Italy. This decision was accepted by Brockway only until the Annual Conference and when at the 1936 ILP Conference Brockway and the Trotskyists' leader C. L. R. James opposed the Inner Executive position, Maxton lost the vote by 70 to 57.

Maxton immediately informed the Conference that he and the Parliamentary Group would have to reconsider their position, and at a special meeting of the National Council Maxton resigned as Chairman and as a member of the council. He and the MPs were unable conscientiously to carry out the party policy. They would act independently on this issue while hoping to carry out ILP policy in other respects.

As Brockway recalls, Maxton's statement "fell like a bombshell. I had to make a quick decision: should I stand out and split the Party or compromise temporarily in the confidence that fuller discussion would bring unity? I had no doubt that if Maxton's statement was repeated to the Conference a split would be inevitable. Nor had I any doubt about the dimensions of the split: faced by the prospect of losing Maxton and the Parliamentary Group, the majority would rally to them, leaving those who took my view a futile and isolated section. I saw the policy of the Party not as complete but as developing. I saw there was little hope of building up a revolutionary Socialist party in Britain except through the ILP."[2]

The loss of the ILP's leader and best known figure was for Brockway, and the ILP at large, too great to contemplate and ways were found to consult the entire membership on the issue with the hope of retaining Maxton. "I decided on compromise," Brockway recalls, "and when James Carmichael proposed a ballot of the membership I agreed at once, though without any illusions about the result. I knew it was inevitable that the vote would be influenced more by the desire to retain Maxton and his colleagues than by the political issue. I myself drafted the compromise resolution and moved it at the conference the next day."[3]

In the plebiscite that followed Maxton prevailed with a three to two majority. The National Council then issued a detailed programme on peace. It confirmed the ILP's absolute opposition to all capitalist and imperialist wars.

Maxton, involved not only with the Abyssinian question but also with the campaign against unemployment and the Means Test, now found time to reflect on the condition of his much diminished party. The Conference of 1936 had heard how one-fifth of the branches had failed to pay any fees and how the majority had failed to contribute to the election fund. Three branches in every four had not paid their full party subscriptions. Maxton believed that one of the explanations of the party's decline was that for three or four years the theoretical side of their activities had become too dominant. Theorists, he said, had to bring their theory into practical operation.

Maxton saw the ILP less as a repository of Marxist truths than as a propaganda organisation for the systematic exposure of the evils of unemployment and its consequence, poverty. During 1936 and 1937 Maxton returned to these themes. In Parliament he had called for the abolition of the Means Test, claiming that National Government spokesmen had promised changes to win votes at the General Election campaign.[4] Scotland was worst off, the worst housed country in Europe, he told the Scottish teachers' conference and this prevented children benefiting from education.

Ramsay MacDonald had lost his Parliamentary seat to Shinwell at the 1935 General Election. When he attempted to secure re-election as the Member for the Scottish Universities, Maxton's response was to call for the abolition of this "reactionary" method of representation. Maxton also entered the controversy over the abdication of King Edward VIII. In December 1936, he called for a Republic and proposed that the House of Commons reject the Abdication Bill. The monarchy, he said, had outlived its usefulness. The ILP was determined to build a classless society. The abdication crisis illustrated the importance of changing an outmoded system of government. It would be foolish, he said, "if we do not seize the opportunity ... to establish a completely democratic form of government that does away with the monarchial institution and the hereditary principle".[5] Only six other MPs joined him in the Commons vote that ensued. Maxton was later to step up his attacks on the monarchy, voting against the 1937 Civil List and saying that it was "utter rubbish" to deny pensioners and the unemployed extra money when the Royal Family was to receive it.[6]

Once again the dominant theme of Maxton's speeches was the conditions of the poor and the unemployed. When, during 1936, new regulations on unemployment benefit were introduced the Clydesiders engaged in a now typical Commons demonstration. First Maxton told Conservative MPs that "but for the Grace of God" they too would be on the dole. Then Buchanan savaged the Home Secretary, Sir John Simon, as he explained Government policy.

Maxton explained to the *New Leader* that "during the whole course of the debate my ILP colleagues and I had felt anger and disgust as speaker after speaker rose on the Government side – young men well educated, well groomed, well fed, who had obviously been well treated by society from birth onwards, and used their abilities and Parliamentary position to put up a case which had the effect of denying to their less fortunate brethren – the unemployed – the few extra shillings that could make life half-tolerable for them."[7]

Of the clash between Buchanan and Simon, Maxton reported,

"I was having the greatest of difficulty in keeping myself down, and if Buchanan had not let loose I would have been into it before the speech concluded." Buchanan's reward was suspension, with McGovern following him out shortly afterwards. Maxton acted as a teller as only 50 Labour MPs voted against Buchanan's suspension and just 11 against McGovern's.

The Clydesiders' anger was in a just cause. The household Means Test Maxton regarded as invidious. "It played havoc in working-class homes," said Maxton. If teenagers found work the household income decreased. Parental authority was diminished and families were split up. All the time the unemployed were being branded as idle, and their support regarded as a costly extravagance and the root of the economic crisis. It was "patently a dishonest piece of political propaganda".[8] The poverty problem had to be "attacked at its foundation".[9]

Throughout the later months of 1936, another political project occupied Maxton's mind. He would not rejoin the Labour Party, but he had always pledged to work for unity among left-wing socialists. In this he had a new ally within the Labour Party in Stafford Cripps, the Labour lawyer who had served in the 1929-31 Labour Government but who had, like Maxton, come to doubt whether Parliamentary democracy, without a mass movement of the left, could successfully oppose Fascism in Britain. From their private discussions, and from negotiations between Cripps and the Communist Party Secretary, Pollitt, came the proposal for a Unity Campaign.

The Unity Campaign brought together the left of the Labour Party, the ILP and the Communist Party. As it opened with round-the-country demonstrations in January 1937 Maxton was to write that "never in my thirty years experience have I seen such a successful series of demonstrations". He saw in it the left-wing unity that he had hoped for ever since he had broken with the Labour Party in 1932. For the first time, he said, he could see a united front "wielding tremendous influence in the country".[10] The greatest hour of danger to the workers was, equally, pregnant with magnificent opportunities. The maximum possible campaign effort was needed because inactivity would result in the country either drifting to war or being overrun by Fascism.[11]

Although Maxton was a central figure in the Unity Campaign, this most ambitious of the various unity attempts was not his or even the ILP's initiative. More than anyone else, Stafford Cripps had made it possible, smoothing over the differences in a series of contentious preliminary meetings between the ILP and the Communist Party. The Communists had initially aimed for a popular front, embracing non-socialists as well as socialists. Maxton's ILP, incapable of bringing itself to support any arrangement with groups opposing socialism, had hesitated. Its 1937 Conference had insisted on a workers' front exclusive to socialists, and on this occasion the Communists compromised.

There was another related but evidently irreconcilable area of disagreement between the ILP and the Communists. Maxton and the ILP Executive were increasingly concerned about the fate of the Russian dissidents and wanted to exclude Russia from the "Peace Front" envisaged by the campaign. Brockway recalls that "Cripps and Mellor proposed that the 'Peace Front' be limited to democratic countries and the clause was amended to read 'states in which the working class have political freedom', but this did not satisfy us – we were in favour of a pact only between working-class governments. On the subject of Russia's fight for peace we were adamant: we did not regard its foreign policy as either socialist or peace-making."[12]

Eventually Cripps produced a compromise. Maxton agreed in public to a final draft accepting the Soviet Union as both free and peace-loving. Privately he and the ILP recorded their reservations in a letter to Cripps. Such were the agonies of unifying the left in the mid-1930s.

The Unity Manifesto launched on 18 January 1937 called for the return of a Labour Government, the unity of all sections in the Labour Movement and for the Labour Party to take a lead in securing such a unity. Without unity, said Maxton, "we would drift into war and be overcome by the power of Fascism".[13]

For Maxton the campaign had two fundamental objectives. The first was to recapture the ideals and spirit of earlier periods. The second was to awaken the political consciousness of working people. But Maxton had a third, private, objective which was to use the campaign as a test of whether or not the Labour Party could accommodate socialists such as him. Brockway admitted to being surprised by this. Maxton had been, he says, "the most isolationist" of all ILP leaders but had told Brockway that, if the Unity Campaign succeeded in convincing the Labour Party that it should open its doors to the Communist Party and the ILP, he would regard it as "evidence that attitudes had sufficiently changed to justify reaffiliation".[14]

On this he had to face a public reservation expressed by his own National Council. When the campaign had been discussed by the Executive, the members accepted the principle of affiliation but in Brockway's words "defined it more closely saying that the ILP looked to the Unity Campaign to create a spirit within the Labour Party which could give reasonable hope of its democratisation and of freedom to express socialist policy".[15]

Speaking in Glasgow, Maxton repeated the Executive's position while saying there was no future for Labour without the Communists and other elements. The ILP's condition for returning would be that the Labour rank and file "so change the Labour Party in structure and outlook that it would be possible for honest men and women to work amongst them".[16]

The Unity Campaign featured some of the best speakers the movement could muster. A vast and overflowing meeting in Manchester's Free Trade Hall on 24 January gave the campaign a spectacular start. The platform, bringing together Mellor, Cripps, James Maxton and Harry Pollitt, was certainly a formidable one. With the aid of the other principal signatories of the Manifesto – Harold Laski, George Strauss, Aneurin Bevan, H. N. Brailsford, John Strachey, William Gallacher, Fred Jowett, Fenner Brockway, Tom Mann, Jack Tanner, Arthur Horner, Palme Dutt, G. R. Mitchison, and Frank Horabin – a series of mass meetings were organized all over the country on a scale that dwarfed anything known for years. Cripps called the Manchester meetings "the most remarkable experience of my short political career", and he spoke of Maxton as the real leader of the Labour Movement. Elsewhere the response was just as enthusiastic. 8,000 turned up in Glasgow. Overflow meetings had to be held. 13,000 Unity Pledge Cards were signed.

The numbers and the initial enthusiasm were misleading. Although Maxton reported to the ILP Conference in 1937 that, as he had always hoped, the rank and file were now asserting themselves, the campaign never had a serious chance of success. The unity sought became even more fragile as the ILP angered Communists by criticising the treatment of dissidents in Soviet Russia. In Spain the parties were literally at war as the POUM, backed by the ILP, and Communists, backed by the British Communist Party, shot at each other in the streets of Barcelona.

While the Communists and the ILP fell out, further and irreparable damage occurred when the Labour Party declared members of the Socialist League ineligible for its membership and then, when the League was dissolved in May, banned Cripps and other party members from appearing on platforms with the ILP and the Communist Party. The end was near.

By June the National Unity Campaign was dead. Threatened

with expulsion if they continued to associate with the proscribed Communist Party and the ILP, Labour leaders regrouped into the Labour Unity Campaign. Maxton was forced to withdraw from a Unity meeting in Hull. As he explained in a letter to George Strauss, "the responsibility for my absence does not rest with me but with the executive of the Labour Party. They have said that if you associate with Harry Pollitt and myself in the campaign for unity you will be expelled from the Labour Party. That seems to me to be a narrow, shortsighted and dictatorial attitude."[17]

37

Spain

All his political life Maxton had been thought of as a pacifist. His objections to the First World War and his consequent imprisonment were well known. His recent campaign about intervention in Abyssinia reinforced this impression, but strictly speaking, his pacifism was qualified. He was prepared to fight revolutionary wars but not capitalist or imperialist wars. Capitalist wars could not be abolished by military action in the trenches but only by industrial and political action at home.

The Spanish Civil War tested Maxton's philosophy to its limits. When challenged in Parliament in October 1936 over fighting Fascism in Spain, Maxton had said he was prepared to go. His case was that, with Italy and Germany on the side of Franco, the Government's policy of neutrality was tipping the balance against the properly constituted Government. The National Government had not given Republican Spain their moral support, and yet, as he told the Commons in December, if Spain was to become a Fascist outpost on the Mediterranean, Britain's problems would multiply.[1]

In August of 1936 Maxton had sent his colleague John McNair to Spain on a fact-finding tour. The Spanish workers needed "above all the assurance that whatever capitalist governments will not do, we, as a workers' party, are prepared to help them to the utmost limit".[2] On McNair's return from Spain in October both addressed a rally at Shoreditch and, inspired by Maxton, a campaign began to raise money for medical supplies. The ILP was able to equip and send motor ambulances. McNair returned to Spain in November with McGovern and stayed there for nine months.

Maxton's view and that of the ILP was, in Bob Edwards' words, that "the future of human freedom for the peoples of Europe was being drawn on the map of Spain". In the Civil War that ensued, one million men and women were to die, including 500

of the 3,000 British volunteers. Half Britain's volunteers were to
be wounded.

For Maxton and the ILP passing resolutions, and donating
cash, were insufficient. From September 1936 a steady stream
of British volunteers travelled in small groups over the Pyrenees
into Spain. Edwards was captain of the ILP contingent. During
the first months of 1937, they did a twelve-week stint on the
Aragon Front, taking part in the capture of Mount Aragon and
Saragossa. "We spent much of our time training members of
the Spanish Militia how to take cover and we were constantly
trying to persuade them that to walk upright and bravely into
an offensive was not necessarily the best method," Edwards
recalled later.

Edwards was joined in his contingent by George Orwell, who
had by then applied to join the ILP. Orwell too had been a pacifist
and according to Bob Edwards, had, during 1935, submitted
a manuscript on pacifism which was "long and absolutist in
character" for the consideration of the ILP. The two met again
in December 1936 on the Aragon Front during the Civil War.
Homage to Catalonia, Orwell's best selling account of the Spanish
Civil War, was to follow.

As ILP members fought alongside the Republicans, Maxton
stepped up his propaganda effort on the Spanish people's
behalf. Writing in January 1937, Maxton argued that the overt
intervention of Germany and Italy required a British response.
Five months ago, he wrote, it might have been argued that it
did not matter to Great Britain which side won in Spain and
that a policy of intervention was the one calculated to limit
the extent of hostilities and to hasten the restoration of peace.
Franco had practically unrestricted aid from the two Fascist
powers, Germany and Italy, while Britain had done nothing to
help the Republicans. Worse than that, the Government had in
effect tacitly supported the Fascists. Their "class prejudices were
with Franco".[3]

Maxton followed this up with an assault on the Government
in Parliament. Non-intervention had actually been an act of
discrimination against the Spanish People's Government. If Spain
had been ruled by a right-wing government, it would have been
accorded all the rights normally accorded to foreign powers.
Maxton's intervention in the debate dwarfed other contributions.
The speech, the *Guardian* said, showed "perfection from the
technical point of view. After this brilliant example of the art of
debating the other speakers seemed to be amateurish."

Once again the Labour Party was split. Maxton accused them of vacillation,[4] but within Spain, the anti-Franco forces were also divided, with a neo-Trotskyist organisation, POUM, fighting against the Communists for control in Catalonia and the Basque areas. Maxton's sympathies were with POUM. In June 1937 POUM was declared illegal, its leaders imprisoned, and the ILP contingent hunted down by the Communists. One Scots ILP member, Alex Smillie – a grandson of the miners' leader Bob Smillie – was arrested, and later died in a Communist jail in Valencia.

Maxton conceived a plan designed to help the Basques. Bilbao was under Fascist blockade. Maxton and Brockway planned to purchase a boat, crew it with volunteers and take in much-needed food. It was *Boy's Own* stuff.[5] "The ILP will break the blockade," said the press. The proposal caught the public's imagination and £6,000 was raised in one week.

Meanwhile another ILP colleague Bob Edwards was acting as an intermediary for the Spanish Government and managed to negotiate a deal with a British shipowner to arrange the shipment of food supplies. Edwards bought the boat, promising that the Spanish Government would pay up when it reached France, and the ILP fundraising effort was not required. The money raised was sent for food supplies. An ILP home was set up for Basque children with what was left, but the ILP could legitimately claim credit for forcing the negotiations which brought the relief.

Now Maxton decided to go to Spain. Originally he had had doubts about the trip, both on account of his health and because he had believed he could do more good for his comrades in Spain from London than he could do there "handicapped as I would be by language and other difficulties".[6] He went and was glad he did. His health held out almost to the end of the trip and the difficulties of language did not prove insuperable.

Maxton got off a night train from Paris to Toulouse to face his first ever trip by air "over the snowy peaks of the Pyrenees and I can't say I like the look of them from up above. In less than two hours we came down at Barcelona. The plane got oil and petrol and we got coffee . . ."

Their destination was Valencia, crowded with twice its normal population as rebel forces closed in. There were difficulties with accommodation, and formalities such as reporting to the British embassy, but the main business of the trip, which was to find and succour the POUM prisoners, came first. "We started on the job at once."

Maxton saw the lawyers engaged for the defence, and had

audiences with various officials, including the Attorney General who was responsible for conducting the prosecution. The defendants themselves he saw twice, once with guards present, once without.

In his report in the *New Leader* Maxton was circumspect about the government's intentions towards the POUM men: ". . . no one takes the espionage charges seriously and there is no desire to pass vindictive sentences for the May events in Barcelona, which will be the substance of the charge against them."

The Communists were less circumspect about Maxton. During his visit he was denounced by the official Valencia press as a Trotskyite and even a Fascist ("I think they are making a very profound error").

By the end of his visit he was able to confirm the release of four POUM prisoners and some members of the International Brigade. Maxton's experience in Spain seemed to confirm his own thesis of politics. The people had taken much power and had done much with it. There were "no signs of war weariness or lack of confidence in the ultimate success of the struggle against Fascism". Workers' control of the transport in Barcelona, and other services, was "doing great work".[7] There was unity amongst the workers, but not amongst the politicians, mainly because of the vicious and devious policies being pursued by the Communist Party of Spain.

Abroad Maxton enjoyed the status of a minor statesman. At home his party apeared to be dying on its feet. Maxton's ILP had already suffered badly from its split with the Labour Party.

In 1936 and 1937 branch affiliation had fallen to only 233, compared with a 1933 figure of 452. The financial position had been just as bad. In 1931, income from subscriptions had been £1,445, falling to £329 in 1934. The first eight months of 1937 brought in only £98. The party's situation was so bad that the National Administrative Council was told on 13 November 1937 that "the point must be reached where we must cease to function as a party".

A paper was prepared setting out the merits and disadvantages of Labour Party affiliation. The ILP was now a "conscious political unit" with a "clearly defined line". In support of affiliation were the arguments that this would produce greater contact with workers, an opportunity to increase party membership, and extended circulation for *New Leader* and party literature. The disadvantages were the identification with the reactionary view of the Labour Party, the limitation of freedom including that enjoyed in Parliament and the danger of fostering vulnerable illusions as to the effectiveness of the Labour Party as a bastion against Fascism. Necessary conditions of membership of the Labour Party, as stated in the paper, were that the ILP:

    a. Remains an organised unit;
    b. Retains its newspaper and literature;
    c. Voices its own policy;
    d. Voices its own policy in Parliament;
    e. Criticises LP policy "in a comradely way".

As the ILP drew away from the Communist Party, it found itself once again having more in common with the Labour Party, both Labour and the ILP having opposed Popular Fronts including non-socialists. At the 1938 ILP Conference a resolution was carried by 55 to 49 "to approach the Labour Party for the purpose of securing the maximum common action against the National Government, united action on class issues and an electoral understanding"[8]. At the National Administrative Council in July and August 1938, representatives were authorised to continue negotiations with the party.[9] This was all the more important because of 220 branches only 124 had paid fees.

Maxton was approached by Stafford Cripps, who had told him that he had been authorised by Mr Attlee, the leader of the Parliamentary Party, and George Dallas, a Scot who was then Chairman of the National Executive (1938-39), to encourage discussion. According to the ILP Secretary, McNair, "the initiative in seeking negotiations came from the Labour Party and not from the ILP".[10] Maxton reported this to the National Council and at the Manchester Conference it was decided that the Council should commence exploratory talks. A committee consisting of Maxton, Campbell Stephen, John McGovern, Fenner Brockway and John Aplin was nominated to meet representatives of the Labour Party. A meeting duly took place with the Labour Party Executive in one of the committee rooms of the House of Commons.

Despite known differences of policy, the great majority of the Executive were in favour of reaffiliation. Only one Executive member was opposed in principle and the ILP's Scarborough Conference approved negotiations for conditional affiliation.

The following points had been submitted to the Labour Party as a basis for re-affiliation:

1. A united effort to secure the defeat of the National Government and the return of a Labour Government.
2. A united campaign in the country on agreed issues.
3. United action in Parliament on agreed issues.
4. An electoral arrangement for by-elections and the General Election and mutual support for the candidates of the two parties on the understanding that each party has the right to maintain its own policy on issues where agreement has not been reached.
5. The right of both parties to participate in conferences called by either party when such conferences are extended to working-class organisations beyond the party itself.

No further meetings took place but it became known that only four members of the Labour Party Executive had voted against ILP affiliation in principle and 16 had voted in favour.[11] Further correspondence was carried on during 1939 which confirmed that the ILP could reaffiliate on the conditions laid down but with the one vital limitation that ILP Members of Parliament would not be permitted to vote against the Labour Party.

Maxton was not prepared to accept that limitation. In private conversations with McNair, he took the view that the ILP "would very soon be thrown out if it attempted to implement its socialist convictions. He had no desire to stand in the way of other men but the shadow of war was looming and his conviction was that the ILP must retain its freedom."[12]

But when one ILP member decided to rejoin the Labour Party, Maxton was dismayed. George Buchanan had come to Westminster with Maxton, had shared digs with him, first in Pimlico, and then in Battersea, and been one of his closest colleagues. He too had been suspended in 1923 and he had followed Maxton in the "Socialism in Our Time" campaign, joined the rebellions during the Labour Government of 1929, and acquiesced in the decision to leave the Labour Party in 1932. In April 1939, in the midst of the ILP discussions on re-affiliation, Buchanan applied to rejoin the Labour Party. It was, McGovern recalled, "one of the greatest blows dealt to Jimmy Maxton". Until he had rejoined, Buchanan had kept his intentions quiet. "I don't mind what any man does," Maxton told McGovern, "that is a matter for his conscience but you would think that after a lifetime's association, common decency would urge a person to act like a man and inform his colleagues of his decision."[13] Of the original Clydeside MPs who had travelled to London with Maxton on that November Sunday of 1922, only Campbell Stephen remained within the ILP.

Maxton, however, continued to hold out for independence but by a small majority the National Administrative Council decided to recommend rejoining the Labour Party if agreement could be reached. A special conference to decide the issue was called for September 1939 in Leeds. Because of the outbreak of war, the conference never took place.

38

Munich and War

In August 1934, Maxton had warned that the world had only five years to defeat war and Fascism. His views on war and armaments were well known. Only collective disarmament agreements, with Britain leading the way by unilateral disarmament, could ensure peace. The mass slaughter of the Great War, to which he had been a conscientious objector, still haunted him and many of his generation. In 1934, he had warned the Commons that implicit in "the upward curve" of arms spending was a resignation to war. Hopes of peace were being thrown aside as "a fatuous dream".[1]

In the years that followed, Maxton's warnings grew more stern as the growth of European Fascism made war more likely. Ever since the reoccupation of the Ruhr, the expansionism of Hitler's Germany had threatened Europe. The subordination of Austria occurred early in 1938 and Czechoslovakia became Hitler's next target. On a pretext supplied by the Sudetenland Germans in Czechoslovakia Hitler demanded vast territorial and military concessions which Anglo-French guarantees appeared incapable of denying him. When war seemed inevitable Chamberlain flew to Munich and conceded to Hitler virtually all he asked. The day after their meeting Chamberlain returned to London with "a scrap of paper" which he said ensured "Peace in Our Time".

Maxton had promised Chamberlain support in his search for peace even before the Prime Minister's party had left for Munich. He did not endorse any specific peace terms but expressed support for any endeavour which sought to avoid war, but when other parties stood to applaud Chamberlain and Attlee in the Commons, the four members of the ILP had remained in their seats.[2]

Chamberlain returned from Munich to a hero's welcome, but before the Parliamentary debate on the affair, Brockway and another member of the ILP Executive, John Aplin, urged Maxton not to endorse Chamberlain's agreement. At that stage Maxton would not commit himself. Later, in the course of the debate, he congratulated him. Reminding Parliament that the last war had been the war to end wars, he said he was against war then, now and always.

> The last war lasted four and a half years and produced none of the results it was fought to achieve. It destroyed the lives definitely in battle of 10,000,000 men. How many lives should we have lost in this war? We have seen the Japan-China war and the Spanish war lasting two years. There have been estimates assuming that war on the scale envisaged here would have lasted twice as long and having regard to the tremendous intensification of war dealing instruments is it foolish to assume that 50,000,000 people would have lost their lives on this occasion? . . .
> . . . In my own home town I saw trenches being dug and I pictured dignified and sensible human beings rushing into them to escape some foul death of the skies. I could see it not only in London but in Berlin: I could see it in Prague and in Paris. I could see the terrible degeneration of humanity and that if we survived we were going to live only if we could make ourselves completely callous to all these horrors. What sort of new world is to come out of that? What is democracy going to get out of that? What sort of new social order is to come out of that?

He did not believe Chamberlain had achieved peace, nor could he as long as capitalism and the Empire bred conflict, but the country welcomed the agreement he had signed.

> The only way in which world peace can be secured is by the common people of the world stating in no uncertain terms their determination to have peace, their determination to construct new forms of social order which shall not have the power ideal as their aim and object but the ideal of human brotherhood and fraternity. That is my socialist conception, and anything that I can do throughout the world, in Britain or in Germany, to bring that general conception to a point where it becomes practical politics will be done. I congratulate the Prime Minister on the work he did in these three weeks and in saying that, I do not accept his social philosophy. I do not accept the political philosophy of those who sit behind him. I do not believe that political philosophy can lead to anything but misery for humanity and I will use every effort I can to employ the breathing space that has been vouchsafed to us, not merely to make this action safe, but to make the world safe, the world secure, the world prosperous and the world happy.

It was, says McNair, who heard it, "a great speech", and even

Brockway who opposed Maxton's line conceded that it was even "more moving than Maxton's speeches as a rule ... he had put his whole being into that speech".[3]

The ILP did not support the Government in the vote on Munich nor did it back Labour. Instead it put down an amendment distancing itself from the Government's general policy. Maxton's view, expressed at a Glasgow anti-war demonstration, was that he did not oppose giving credit to Chamberlain for his efforts at the eleventh hour but he did not exonerate Chamberlain from responsibility for the eleventh hour that had just occurred.[4]

Inevitably it was Maxton's congratulatory remarks about Chamberlain that gained media attention, both on the BBC and in the newspapers. Worse still, John McGovern went even further than Maxton, concluding his speech with a eulogy of Chamberlain ("Well done, thou good and faithful servant"). Brockway immediately called for a meeting of the ILP Executive. What the Parliamentary speeches lacked, he believed, was a revolutionary socialist analysis. Maxton should have denounced the pact as unjust. Capitalism inevitably led in war to the slaughter of millions or in peace to the slavery of millions.[5]

Even before the Executive met on the Thursday, Maxton, on his way to the Commons, saw on newspaper billboards the statement, "Maxton Repudiated by the ILP". Maxton had arranged to meet the London regional executive of the ILP that afternoon. Instead, as the newspaper reported,the London ILP had condemned him without a hearing for what they claimed was a flagrant breach of party policy. Behind this Maxton saw the disloyal hand of Brockway.

Many of his colleagues, Jennie Lee for one, had said of Maxton that there was "no hard metal in him"[6], but on this occasion Maxton was stung into action. He immediately demanded the unequivocal support of his colleagues in Parliament, Stephen and McGovern. Maxton's pride was hurt, recalls McGovern. "This was the first occasion that either of us had been asked for personal backing and we gave an assurance of 100% agreement." At the Executive meeting that evening the usually tolerant Maxton was unusually tough. As Chairman he first asked all Executive members for their views. Then after a speech by Fenner Brockway's daughter roused him to "boiling point", Maxton hit back. He had sought to give the honest views of the party. He felt particularly hurt at the disloyalty of his General Secretary, Brockway, and he objected to a public repudiation of his leadership from a small clique in the London section.

For weeks now I have been the knockabout for every bird of passage who has only been in the party for a few months. I have been attacked, repudiated, insulted, and kicked even by those I have defended in the past when defence of their action seemed quite impossible. An attempt has been made to crucify me.

With these words, McGovern recounts, Maxton broke down completely and cried "like a child". Campbell Stephen turned on Brockway and his daughter: "You are a lot of bloody hounds." It was this, McGovern later wrote, that led him to conclude that the ILP "had within itself the germ of its own destruction and from then onwards I supported a move for our return to the Labour Party".[7]

The meeting gave Brockway permission to dissociate himself publicly from Maxton's position, although Maxton asked him to think it over for 24 hours. In the event Brockway and John Aplin issued their statement the next morning saying that the Munich agreement was merely "an imperialist truce" that imposed "terrible suffering" on the Czech people. Maxton was unrepentant. He was to be equally aggressive when he defended his conduct at the ILP Conference four months later, but by now ILP branches were responding to Brockway's statement, some calling for Maxton's resignation, others demanding his expulsion from the party. Emotionally and physically exhausted by the fracas, he and Madeleine left the country on a two-month cruise. He was "very weak and low in spirits", recalled McNair who was now working alongside him: "To be misunderstood by his friends was more than he could bear and he had what amounted to a physical breakdown."[8]

The cruise which took Maxton from Southampton to Madeira and then to the Cape was a pleasant interlude, although, as Maxton wrote to his son from Madeira, "we are still waiting for the warmth, the sunshine and the calm". The Maxtons travelled by a Union Castle liner, enjoyed "a new environment and meeting new people". "We've spent our time sleeping, reading and eating," he reported to his son.[9] Ever the enthusiast Maxton so threw himself into social events that he was appointed in charge of sports. Among the ship's passengers were Mormons on their way to missionary work in South Africa. It was difficult to discover what they were going to preach, Maxton recalled. When they told him that polygamy had now been rejected, "there did not seem much left but an advocacy of an austerity of life. Judging by what I saw of the Europeans in South Africa they were going to have a thin time getting converts on that basis."

The Maxtons reached Port Elizabeth on Christmas morning. They were met by the South African Labour Party and Maxton was asked to address the Institute of International Affairs. He would have found "a street corner" meeting more "appropriate" and he rejected a series of impressive invitations to speak in Durban and Johannesburg, restricting himself to addressing only two meetings. He was on holiday. He had not sought to study the political situation but the problems of South Africa were, he told *New Leader* on his return, "so obvious as to hit one in the eye".[10]

Maxton returned to Britain at the beginning of February 1939 to announce that he would not stand for the Chairmanship of the ILP, simply reminding people that a year ago he had made clear his intention of standing down. Interrupted and heckled at the Scottish ILP Conference, he announced he did not "regret a single word" of his Munich speech, and he rounded on his critics in public. Chamberlain was not a Fascist, as many ILP members were claiming. His own expulsion was being sought by men who had been in the ILP for only three years and whom he had defended against expulsions on the grounds they would learn over time. It was a first and candid admission from Maxton that his tolerance of a Trotskyist faction had gone a long way to destroying the entire party.

Nor did Maxton make apologies about Munich to the Annual Conference of the ILP. He had been shocked by the concentration of some colleagues on eternal controversy instead of public activity and he had been hurt by the actions of the Secretary, Fenner Brockway, who would not even take 24 hours to consider his action. The real issue remained the threat of war and the need to seek to avoid it. The tragedy was that there was "no clear international voice that can make itself heard coming from the united workers of the world".

> So far as I am able I will use what time is left to me to stave off, dodge and evade a large-scale war in the hope that somewhere and somehow some spark of working-class spirit will be set alight and the workers of the world will refuse to be marched to the slaughter.

Once again Maxton was exonerated by the ILP Conference. The attempt to refer back Maxton's Parliamentary report was defeated, as was the proposal to expel Maxton from membership of the ILP.[11]

Maxton's campaign for peace continued. He opposed the Defence

Loans Bill, declared working people could alone stop the war and claimed that British preparations for war were weakening the progressive forces in Germany. He claimed the Commons now resembled how it must have been in the days preceding August 1914. He warned that war now would be "a mass horror that will make the last show appear like a pleasant Sunday afternoon gathering". People should be brought to realise war's "utter futility". The sad truth was that Maxton had nothing to offer. He had no positive proposal, no fresh initiative, nor even any political weight. He could only *hope* that war could be avoided.

With the invasion of Poland, he appealed for common sense. As Chamberlain prepared to declare war on 2 September, Maxton made a last-minute plea to delay the decision and demanded that if there was to be conscription of labour there should also be conscription of wealth. Maxton had a rough ride. When a Labour MP said that "the Poles are dying in order to save you, you bloody pacifist", McGovern called him a "drunken lout", and reminded him that it was not MPs who would be fighting the war but their constituents.

War was by now inevitable. On their way to a Sunday morning session at the Commons, Maxton and McGovern heard the air raid sirens for the first time and knew that it had begun.

"Will they arrest Maxton?" asked the *New Leader* in a front page headline of November 1939.[12] Many anti-war campaigners were to be imprisoned during the war, and, as Maxton told the House of Commons in November 1939, his anti-war views made him an obvious candidate for detention. Maxton was opposing the Government's new Emergency Powers Regulations, which gave the Government powers to detain opponents of the state and to censor newspapers and the media. It was, said Maxton, "a charter to put into prison anyone who was politically objectionable". Although Sir Samuel Hoare conceded a number of amendments, Maxton persisted in his principled opposition to the Bill.

Maxton's anti-war stand in 1939 was even more unpopular than his stand against war in 1914. He was not a pacifist, he explained to the House of Commons, but this was a war that he did not believe Britain should have entered. The ILP, he explained to a Summer School in 1942, was not a pacifist party either. Although there "was a marked minority of pacifists in the party and [they] always welcomed them if they are socialists", the distinctive policy of the ILP was that it was anti-war.[13]

Little political progress was made by the ILP in the first months of the war. In December 1939 Bob Edwards polled 4,214 votes in a by-election at Stretford, but lost to a Conservative majority of just under 19,000 and Maxton had to admit that after six months of war-time activity by the ILP "we have no success to record". A Communist had stood against Edwards and in March 1940 when Maxton spoke in the debate on the seizure by Russia of Finland he distinguished the ILP's position from the pro Soviet speeches of the Communist MP William Gallacher. But while he argued against the futility of war, Maxton could only repeat his assertion that war could have been avoided and that working people throughout Europe should insist that "this mutual slaughter must cease". When the Germans invaded Norway and Denmark in April, Maxton expressed his sympathy for the two Scandinavian peoples.

The ILP took its campaign into the country, with Maxton's sister Annie taking the opportunity provided by a by-election in East Renfrewshire to stand as an anti-war candidate.[14] She polled reasonably well. At this time a number of leading politicians and establishment figures were pressing for peace by negotiation. The owner of the *Daily Express*, Lord Beaverbrook, was one of them and he was impressed by the support that the ILP had in Scotland. "We have our various peace movements here, none of them amounting to much," he wrote to a friend in March 1940. "Only in Glasgow and the Clydeside generally have they any real hold. This is the stronghold of the ILP, whose leaders, McGovern, Maxton and Campbell Stephen, are men of force and integrity, as well as being pacifists."[15]

Beaverbrook invited Maxton and his colleagues to dinner. McGovern records that Beaverbrook offered the party a minimum of £500 for every by-election it fought, but when McGovern wrote to Beaverbrook after the Renfrewshire by-election asking "if you are still of the same mind", he was rebuffed. Although Maxton met Beaverbrook for lunch in June, the press lord had already joined the Government. He could not follow up his offer of March, he explained by letter, because "the whole of civilisation has changed since that time".

What had in fact happened was that Chamberlain's Government had fallen. Its Norwegian expedition had been a disaster. Chamberlain had been pilloried in the House of Commons and Churchill had been installed, with Labour support, as Prime Minister. Beaverbrook was Minister for Aircraft Production. Maxton's response was to move the motion of censure against the new Churchill Government, and to force a division in the House of Commons. He even asked Churchill to recognise the

ILP as the official Opposition – something Churchill might have been happy to do but for the hostility to the proposal of Attlee and the Labour Party leaders who joined the Coalition.

Towards the end of 1940, casualties were mounting. Maxton was gloomy, despairing at yet more useless slaughter. In June the frequent air raids on London had begun, and he wrote to his son about how deeply the bombing affected him and the impotence of politics in the face of it. On one occasion, Maxton chain-smoked his way through 16 hours of an air raid, bemoaning that "I cannot see a new world coming out of all this destruction".[16] The Chamber of the House of Commons was bombed and it was Maxton who was responsible for the suggestion that the elected MPs meet in the Chamber of the House of Lords. But, isolated in Parliament and in the country, Maxton could say or do little that was effective. He was reduced to generalities amounting to "no ultimate good can come from the war". In December 1940 the ILP called for a peace conference in an amendment moved by John McGovern. Speaking in the debate, Maxton called for statesmanship in the pursuit of peace but when Attlee challenged him Maxton, for once, lost the argument:

> Attlee: Did Maxton hold that peace was right at any price or did he believe in the principle of social justice of which he spoke? Would he give his life for the principle of social justice?
> Maxton: I would answer that these things are not achieved by war.
> Attlee: That is no answer. The Hon. member is suggesting that the Government should put forward certain terms of peace. If he agreed with them would he support them? (Mr Maxton: Certainly.) And if it came to a conference, and Herr Hitler refused to listen to what was called the voice of reason, and rejected Mr. Maxton's ideas of liberty and social justice what would Mr Maxton do then? Would he fight or would he give way? (Cheers and cries of 'Answer'.)
> Maxton: The Rt. Hon. gentleman puts a hypothetical question. (Laughter). If the Rt. Hon. gentleman and the Government accept my suggestions, I and my friends will not be found wanting.[17]

Maxton had, for once, been bettered in debate. If he would fight against Fascism in the event of an invasion of Britain, why would he not fight Fascism to prevent an invasion of Britain? "In these circumstances is it not much better to tie them down across the Channel and thereby prevent them from invading this country?"

The attack went on. Attlee had great respect for people who held the absolute pacifist conviction, although he did not agree with them. Maxton, said Attlee, always took an attitude of complete irresponsibility. His irresponsibility was part of his charm. He had never taken the line of facing bitter and hard things. In his amendment he had faced none of the difficulties. Why did he not go to Hitler and ask him to come to a conference? Other people had appealed to Hitler. A better pacifist than any in the House, the late George Lansbury, a great apostle of peace, went to see Hitler and Mussolini but he got nothing from them. It was no good being blind to the type of people with whom they had to deal.

Maxton had lost the argument and McGovern recalls how "Campbell Stephen and I twitted Jimmy for weeks for falling for such an obvious dodge and for giving away our case. He knew that he had unintentionally held the anti-war movement up to ridicule."[18]

The ILP amendment had called for the Government to state its peace terms and to support an International Conference to end the war by creating a new international social order. While Maxton clearly lost the argument in the Commons, and complained, perhaps unfairly, about the press coverage the amendment received, he claimed to have won it in the country. Hundreds of letters were sent to him in support, and the *New Leader* reported the "ILP MPs overwhelmed with congratulations". On no occasion during his Parliamentary career, Maxton said, had he received so many letters supporting any action he had taken. The Nazis, he concluded, could only be smashed effectively by the German people.

The ILP maintained its anti-war and anti-Labour stance. At their Conference in April 1941, the ILP refused to re-affiliate to the Labour Party – Maxton said that to ally with Labour would force him to be a supporter of the Coalition – and launched a new campaign against the conscription of women. But isolated by the war, the ILP increasingly turned its thoughts to the reconstruction of British society. In October 1941 he challenged the Archbishop of Canterbury over promises the clergy had made about social reconstruction. "Why wait until after the war for social reconstruction?"[19] Maxton asked, and in November Maxton and McGovern introduced an amendment to the King's Speech in which they called for socialist change. In December 1941 he was, as he told the Commons, "in the unusual position of welcoming a Bill" – one to extend school meals for pupils in Scottish schools.

1942 opened with an Edinburgh by-election in which the ILP put up Tom Taylor as a candidate. The ILP polled badly. When six months later a by-election was called in Hamilton, the ILP opted out. From the autumn of 1942, the party would stand only in by-elections where it was "possible to secure a reasonable vote". But as Maxton later explained to an ILP Summer School, pro-war sentiment was so strong that the ILP would only win by-elections if they promised a bloodier war than Churchill. "We are not prepared to say it," he replied, "because we do not want to kill more Germans than Churchill – we want to end the war."[20]

Throughout the war Maxton's thoughts were mainly on measures that could be taken to change conditions at home and abroad. He was afraid that even if Britain won the war, the fruits of victory would elude the working people of Britain. He wanted absolute guarantees that India and the Colonies would be liberated, a theme taken up by the ILP Conference of 1942. A new ILP campaign, "Socialist Britain Now", was launched calling for an end to the war by the creation of socialism. It called for a United Socialist State of Europe, European economic and political unity, and the creation of minimum social standards nationally and internationally.

When the Commons debated the ILP's amendment to the 1942 Address, Maxton and Attlee clashed once again, with Maxton this time the winner. He spoke in favour of decent wages and conditions for the miners, who had threatened strike action, and asked why constituents of his were expected to "rear gladiators on thirty shillings a week". Maxton spoke of conditions at home. Attlee replied by speaking only about conditions abroad. This time Attlee looked foolish – but only seven joined Maxton in the vote.[21]

During 1943 the ILP considered a lengthy paper prepared by Fenner Brockway on its future strategy. The ILP's political allies included pacifists, and "left" Labour MPs, Brockway stated. They could not, however, work with the Peace Pledge Union. It wanted peace at any price, which was not the ILP policy. The ILP's strategy so far had been to support the Labour Party "on issues other than the war itself if it will go into opposition and fight vigorously for the working class and socialism". The aim was to "collaborate with militant trades unionists outside the ILP". They would not make the mistake again of working with Trotskyists whose aim was "to destroy the ILP which it regards as a centrist obstacle to a revolutionary socialism", but they could work with the new Commonwealth organisation formed to fight by-elections.[22]

If the ILP Conferences of the 'forties were both smaller and less important than their Conferences of the 1920s, Maxton had lost none of his oratorical talents. Addressing the 1943 Conference he again proved how he could bring an audience to tears and then as quickly reduce them to laughter. An address which began with Maxton as defiant as ever ended with his listeners cheering at his humour. He told them: "If the Government want to throw anybody into prison, young people who have accepted my views or followed my advice, let them turn their guns on me, let them throw me into prison or ... better still my good friend John McGovern."

Yet in their search for a wider audience and allies, most ILP members now wanted a new arrangement with the Labour Party. Some wanted to re-affiliate immediately, a course which Maxton opposed. A compromise view was supported by the ILP's National Council which recommended that the ILP should rejoin Labour as soon as Labour broke from the Coalition. Labour remained unenthusiastic. When the ILP moved its traditional motion of censure against the King's Speech in November 1943 they were joined by only nine Labour MPs.

39

Final Days

In November 1943 Maxton celebrated 21 years as a Member of Parliament. At a reception for him in Glasgow his friend James Carmichael said that Maxton was conventionally described as "a failure" but this was only because he had retained his faith in both socialism and working people. In reply, Maxton said that he could have held government office "if I had joined the queue".

> I went into politics for something different. I went into politics for the very different purpose of trying to free the world from poverty and to establish social equality. I should not have hoped to achieve any of these aspirations by taking office under the governmental conditions which had prevailed in this country.[1]

21 years in Parliament had taken their toll. Maxton, never physically strong, experienced a gradual deterioration in health through 1944. Abdominal symptoms had compelled him "frequently to leave the bench in the House of Commons, leave the game of golf and hurriedly leave meetings".[2] He was examined by a Glasgow ILP friend, Dr McAloon, who suspected cancer and urged him to see a specialist. Maxton delayed the necessary examination and X-rays until late August and shortly afterwards told an ILP audience in Ayr that he was going into a Glasgow hospital for observation and treatment.[3] After two major operations, bulletins described his condition improving from "as well as can be expected", to "fairly comfortable", and then "very satisfactory".[4]

After two months in hospital he returned to his Barrhead home in the last week of October 1944 to convalesce. His recovery was to be only temporary. He was suffering from cancer of the stomach and the surgery could at best delay the outcome. Dr McAloon confided to John McGovern that Maxton "would only buy two years of life – two years at the very most".[5]

303

Maxton returned to political activity. Just as the war ended, he was present at the Independent Labour Party's Conference during which his party voted, by the narrow margin of 89 to 72, to re-affiliate to the Labour Party. In the first speech following his absence Maxton told the Conference that the Labour Party's rise from 1900 had been "phenomenal". Churchill, he believed, would soon be driven out of office. But his main theme was that "human courage could banish war, hatred and hunger". All the courage of the airmen, and the navy, and the army, should be devoted to "ending the unnecessary power which blights mankind, and the massacre of war itself and the hatred and hunger which follow it".[6]

When Maxton returned to the House of Commons on 19 April 1945, Churchill crossed the floor to welcome him back. *The Times* reported that he was "greeted with general cheers as he took his seat".[7] In the second week of May, just as the war in Europe ended, Maxton spoke at his first rally in Glasgow, and typically called for measures that would avoid "a third Armageddon".

Germany surrendered on 7 May. The Coalition broke up and the General Election campaign began almost immediately. Maxton's theme for Bridgeton was that "a new world of plenty must be the reward of the people". Housing should be built "at top speed". Pensions and benefits should be "paid on a generous scale". "My influence by speech, by vote, by argument, and in counsel," he said in his manifesto, "will always be directed towards the end of securing the complete abolition of poverty in all its hideous forms." Previous Parliaments, he said, had never had a majority prepared "to tackle the big problems in a big way with unlimited faith and courage. It is greatly to be hoped that the General Election, which in my view has been too long delayed, will give us a Parliament of the kind required."[8]

The Labour landslide astounded almost everyone, including Maxton to whom the result was "totally unexpected". He had thought that Labour's break with the Coalition had come too late to establish a distinctive alternative. "Even now I don't believe that Labour so much won the election as that Churchill and his most vocal colleagues lost it."[9] But victory, he counselled, was only the beginning of Labour's problems. He warned the ILP Summer School at Bangor that the Tories would attempt sabotage.

Surprisingly perhaps, Maxton had nothing but praise for the new Government. Attlee was of "clean, upright character" with "undoubted brainpower", and compared "more than favourably with many of the Prime Ministers that I have known personally during more than thirty years". The King's Speech was "not a bad selection of the first tasks to be done", although he regretted that old age pensions were not a priority. Foreign affairs were being approached with "common-sense and with some regard at least to the general principles of the Labour Movement". His major criticism was of the handling of the Dock Strike, but he was sure that the ILP's "general decision will be to help in every way to make the Labour Government a success".[10]

Maxton's return to the fray was brief. In the summer and autumn of 1945 he was ill again. He knew what was going on. "The truth is that I am jiggered," he told McGovern. "There is not an ounce of energy in my body and I just want to lie in bed. I feel that this cancer bug has got me in its clutches and will never let go."[11]

But if any considered that Maxton had mellowed with age and illness, and that his political passion had evaporated, they were to be disappointed. In the first censure debate on the Government in December 1945, Maxton returned to speak and flayed the Tory opposition. He wanted Labour to succeed.

> Nobody who has a decent sense of his own country would want to see a Government fail that has only been two months in office. I want them to succeed and to do things for the people of this country that have never been done before. If they fail the curse of hundreds of thousands of men who have laboured and sacrificed to put them there will rest on their heads and rightly so. But should that day come the power will not shift from the Labour to the Conservative benches but to an even more fundamental quarrel than even Mr Churchill wishes for.[12]

It was a speech described by a young journalist, Michael Foot, as "so devastating to the Tories that their silence became almost audible . . . to the Labour Party his words were so generous and sincere that no one at that moment could fail to have wished that he was still a member of the official party".[13]

In August 1945 the role of the ILP had been effectively downgraded from that of alternative party to that of a pressure group for political propaganda – exactly the option for the ILP which, throughout the 1920s, Maxton and his colleagues had resisted. Its aim was now "to maintain and extend its propaganda, educational facilities and its literature" to make socialism "a burning issue" within the Labour Movement.

But would Maxton, even in what he knew to be the last months of his life, consider rejoining the Labour Party? He stood alone as a Glasgow ILP MP, the only one of the original Clydesiders who had stayed with the ILP. He had promised the ILP Summer School of 1944 that while his prejudice was against rejoining Labour, he would reconsider his position after Labour left the Coalition. Labour had not only left it but had trounced its former Coalition partner. Maxton still held back.

There were a number of reasons. One of them, Maxton confessed to McGovern, was that "my wife and sister are very hostile to the Labour Party and I do not want to start a controversy in our family circle".[14] But knowing his death was near Maxton was content to remain the titular leader of the party he loved, although fearing for the worst. "Our party is a small party," he told John McKimmie, his ILP agent in Bridgeton. "It is too small to satisfy the ambition of some of our folks."[15] To McGovern the death-bed message was the same. "I think that the ILP will go down as it is steadily losing its finest stock and has a small unstable element left that has no united policy. I feel that I must go down with it."[16]

Public appearances were to be few and far between in the first few weeks of 1946. Maxton's last recorded talk was a radio appeal he made on behalf of the Victoria Royal Infirmary in Glasgow. For the next few months he was to be confined to his home in Largs. He almost certainly knew he was a dying man, but he refused to stop smoking. When Brockway visited him during the spring of 1946 he found Maxton "reading Tawney, still smoking cigarettes, still that winning smile lighting his blue eyes, still flicking back his long black hair, but he knew he was to die".[17] The week before his death, as his cancer moved from stomach to liver, he asked Dr McAloon, his doctor and friend, if his death would be quiet and peaceful. "I would not like to go off my rocker or suffer extreme pain before passing over," he said.[18]

Having borne his illness with great courage Maxton died peacefully at Largs on 23 July. He was 61-years-old.

A few weeks before Maxton died, Winston Churchill had written to him. "I have been thinking a lot about you lately," Churchill said. "I always say of you, 'The greatest gentleman in the House of Commons'." On hearing of his death the House of Commons stood for a minute's silence, a tribute almost unique for a backbencher who had never held government office. The Speaker called it "a special and exceptional tribute in memory of a very remarkable and lovable colleague".[19] Newspapers which had condemned him while he lived now paid warm tributes as he died. Maxton, said the *Daily Mail,* gave Parliament "a moral authority". The *Birmingham Post* said that "it was a point of honour to appreciate Maxton's burning sincerity in his championing of the underdog". The *Daily Telegraph* spoke of "his scrupulous fairness and his strict principles". The *Daily Mirror* recalled that "no politician commanded more abounding respect". "No one ever doubted his sincerity," concluded the *Daily Telegraph,* "in the storm or calm of debate."

Maxton was mourned not only in Britain but in every continent where the Labour Movement had friends and allies. Through the Governor of Bombay, Gandhi expressed his condolences to the family, having spoken "with great pleasure of his acquaintance and of his talks with him".

The funeral service, the family decided, was to be a celebration of Maxton's life, and not an occasion for political propaganda. "No mourning," said the short funeral notice published in the *Glasgow Herald.*

Thousands lined the route to the red-brick Glasgow crematorium at Maryhill. There were, one ILP observer found, "women pushing prams, boys with cycles, men in boiler-suits and women with their shopping bags and grubby slum children clutching little bunches of wild flowers which they gathered by the roadside as they went along".[20]

Inside the crematorium, members of the Glasgow Orpheus Choir began the ceremony with *All Through the Night*, one of Maxton's favourite songs.

The funeral oration was delivered by Sir Hugh Roberton, a socialist and life-long friend of Maxton, best known then and now as the founder and leader of the Glasgow Orpheus Choir. It was "the greatest trial and the greatest honour of my life", he later wrote.[21] His address reads oddly today: at once couthy and sanctimonious, heartfelt and marmoreal. Perhaps only the beginning bears quotation now, but it suffices:

James Maxton was a great man. He was more, he was a good man, a just man, a true man and a man without malice.

40

Maxton the Socialist

Throughout his career, whether on a street corner or in the Commons, Maxton had sought to make socialism the common sense of his age. In the industrial unrest of Glasgow during the Great War and after 1918, in his battles with Ramsay MacDonald and the Labour establishment of the 1920s, and even in his isolation in the 1930s, he saw his role as that of propagandist, a crusading politician rather than a career politician. He was, he admitted, "more concerned with the propagation of a new order called socialism than with the day to day routine of law making or national administration".

Maxton never considered himself a potential party leader, or a future Prime Minister. In the 'twenties many saw him as an alternative to Ramsay MacDonald and Ramsay MacDonald himself, Shinwell recalls, always considered Maxton "a kind of rival". Instead Maxton thought of himself as an agitator for socialism. "The leader who may be the best man for one stage of the journey," Maxton frankly conceded to Jennie Lee, "is not necessarily the right leader for the next stage."

Maxton's indifference to high government office led opponents to charge him with indolence. "Vanity unsupported by a capacity for hard work is at the root of the trouble," Ramsay MacDonald concluded in 1929. Other political adversaries spoke of his spending hours reading only cheap detective fiction. "He could have achieved the highest office but for indolence, a defect about which he was perfectly frank," Shinwell concluded. Others who worked with him held similar views. "Maxton was by nature lethargic," one ILP Secretary, John Paton, remarked, "disliking responsibility and committee work." Yet the sheer volume of his propaganda work belied this. Perhaps W. J. Brown summed up Maxton best when he said, "his impatience with detail leads to the superficial comment, 'If only he would work'. If ever he did in the sense meant by the criticisms, his special genius would be destroyed."

Maxton was a visionary. Without Maxton, one colleague told an ILP Conference, "there was a temptation to moderate our policy and our point of view". His idealism had a political purpose, wrote W. J. Brown in 1930. "In domestic politics there is an irresistible tendency of parties which begin as revolutionary to lose their revolutionary spirit and to prove themselves when they attain power little different from the parties they supersede . . . To arrest this drift a special mind is required. Maxton's significance in political terms is that he possesses it in a pre-eminent degree . . . It must be a mind which thinks in large broad outlines and not lose itself in detail . . . it must be a character which is immune from the lures of office and negative to the invidious temptations of society . . . It must be a soul whose standards of value are formidable."

When Maxton embarked on his political career in the first years of the century, there were only a handful of Labour Members of Parliament. When he died they commanded a Parliamentary majority. In the early 1900s the Labour Movement, both unions and Labour Party, struggled hard simply to exist. In 1946, when Maxton died, it was the foremost institution in the land. Yet socialists saw in its rise to power a simultaneous erosion of its original idealism. The determined rebels of the 1920s had given way to the dark-suited grey men of the Labour establishment. When Emrys Hughes returned to Glasgow 30 years after the St Enoch demonstration of 1922 and visited the old meeting places – the theatre halls that were filled every Sunday, the cafés that blossomed in heated discussions about coming struggles, and the Labour committee rooms that were social centres for communities – he found "all the colour and life and vitality seemed to have gone out of politics and apathy prevailed . . . the crusading socialist movement was as good as dead".

Hughes' obituary was, and remains, premature, but on at least one level Maxton had failed and would have been the first to admit it. He had set out to transform the ILP from a high-minded pressure group into a crusade for proletarian emancipation, from a propaganda society into an instrument for the overthrow of capitalism. He ended his career as a leader without a party. If a successful socialist politician is one who advances the fortunes of his or her political party and progressively uses political power to transform society, Maxton enjoyed little success. Other less impressive backbench MPs have steered crucial Private Members Bills through the House of Commons. Maxton had not even one of these to his credit. The party whose cause he championed for

40 years could, with justice, be accused of committing political suicide for the sake of ideological purity. "Why don't you get into a nunnery and be done with it?" Aneurin Bevan had taunted Jennie Lee in 1931. "Lock yourself up in a cell away from the world and its wickedness, my Salvation Army lassie." Like most of Maxton's supporters who defected with him in 1932, she later returned to the Labour Party and considered her decision to leave the worst mistake of her political life.

Yet James Maxton's journey through the politics of the 'twenties and 'thirties must be viewed in its context. Capitalism appeared to be approaching its final collapse. Mass unemployment and deprivation had created huge inequality and injustice in Britain. Yet at the very moment when events cried out for a radical political response, the British Labour Party seemed immobilised, frozen by the enormity of the challenge. The failure of capitalism and its consequence, the opportunity for socialist change, did not energise Labour but paralysed it. To the Labour leadership the crisis of capitalism was simply an excuse for postponing socialist change. To Maxton it was a unique opportunity to implement it.

Maxton's view was straightforward. "Socialism in Our Time" offered a non-violent road to full employment, social equality and public control over the economy. He knew that socialism could not be achieved by the palliative adjustments and spineless compromises that characterised MacDonald's leadership but he knew also that Labour had to stand against the ultra-left and its belief that change must inevitably be violent. Until 1917 revolution was discussed in the abstract. Afterwards many on the left were prepared to go the Russian road. Maxton, more than anyone, appreciated that, and the consequent necessity for a coherent, effective, yet still Parliamentary democratic socialism which took account of British conditions. Hence the vehemence with which he tried to promote "Socialism in Our Time".

He had a credible programme which was vindicated in its essentials by the post-war Keynesian revolution. He brought to it vast personal appeal and brilliant rhetorical skills. Yet he and his ILP failed dismally.

One reason was that the economic crisis of the 1920s and the 1930s, far from increasing the possibility of radical change, diminished it. Though for the ultra-left the unemployed were an army already mobilised and simply waiting the summons to attack, mass unemployment had not radicalised working people. The unemployed were demoralised and isolated by their poverty from those still in work, refugees within society rather than a force ready to attack it. MacDonald told the unemployed to wait and hope, further diminishing their political potential. Between the frustrated incendiarism of the ultra-left and the time serving passivity of MacDonald, Maxton offered a middle way. Maxton blamed both the ultra-left and the Labour right. He took account of the effect of unemployment on the morale of the unemployed but sought to give Labour a policy that would exchange their despair for hope. Yet his alternative, a Government-led reflation that would help the poorest most, failed to capture the support of the Labour Party.

Why did he fail? His failure was also that of the ILP. A party of activists, it was strong on enthusiasm and skilled in propaganda but outside Scotland and perhaps Lancashire it had never recruited the mass support of the trades union movement in the way the Labour Party did in 1945. Only rarely did the ILP succeed in convincing the trades union delegates at Labour Party Conferences. With only a few exceptions, it never enjoyed the support of the most prominent trades union leaders of the time. Outside Scotland, only a few ordinary trades unionists joined its ranks.

In the 1930s the ILP paid an even greater price for its isolation from rank and file trades unionists. Elsewhere in the organisations of the Labour Movement, the trades union connection averted what Tawney called "the deadly disease of dogmatic petrification" and saved British socialism from "the sterility which condemned to impotence a party severed from its working class roots". In its later history the ILP was so far from the realities of mass politics that it became, for long periods, an adventure playground for successive invasions of ultra-left theorists.

If the 1920s witnessed the rise of the Labour Party, the 1930s saw the collapse of the ILP. Now powerless in the country, Maxton was patronised in the House of Commons. "The ruling class in this country have various ways of dealing with revolutionaries," wrote Kingsley Martin in 1933. "Where it cannot buy them off its usual method is flattery. But Maxton has refused the aristocratic embrace – he makes a rule of never dining with rich men – so they have found another way. They have made a House of Commons character of him. He is their raven-haired pirate, a Captain Hook who waves his finger but who everyone knows is really the most lovable of fellows. They treat him as an institution and entertainment. It is a point of honour among them to appreciate Maxton's burning sincerity. Are they not tolerant? Does anyone doubt that they understand the working

311

class point of view? His presence in the House, they tell you, 'raises politics to a higher plane'. Of course he is hopelessly impractical ... but how sincere, what an idealist."

Yet Maxton represented an important and identifiable tradition in the early history of socialist movements. In the pioneering days of the 1880s Hardie had been influenced by both Marxism and the Scottish radical and Christian traditions: in the early years of the twentieth century Maxton too had sought to combine elements of Marxism with the influences of Christian teaching and Scottish radical thought. More than anyone else John Maclean had been Maxton's gateway to Marx, and Maxton was to write that Marx was "the impregnable rock on which the working class laid the foundations for a new social order". The influence of Marx was, he said, "perhaps greater than any other individual" and "it was essential for men and women who were going to play a responsible part in the workers' struggle to fully understand the Marxian point of view as regards working-class politics".

"Our ethical standards are largely defined by economic considerations," Maxton told the capitalist apologist Sir Ernest Benn during a radio debate in the 1920s when he warned him that the first duty of socialists was to rid society of "the dominating minority, the few acting as rulers and controllers of the destinies of men". But if Maxton was influenced by Marx – William Gallacher unfairly said that "Maxton's knowledge of Marx was nil" – he was an incomplete Marxist. In an ILP lecture on "The Nature of Capitalism" in August 1937 he warned of the dangers of "supernaturalising" and "canonising" Marx. Britain, he felt, should map out its own home-grown road to socialism, and in Maxton's case much of his beliefs sprang from the Christian principles of duty and service and not a little perhaps from a middle-class social conscience. "I always feel guilty when I have something denied to the majority of my fellows," he once explained.

In any struggle to reconcile hard-headed socialist analysis with practical down-to-earth social service, service for Maxton would come first. Indeed when he spoke to students at Glasgow University in March 1928 on the theme "Socialism is Life" and argued that the working class "had been left to plough their difficult furrow with little help from the intellectuals of the universities", he reminded students of what he considered their "evident duty". It was "to put something extra into the common pool" in return for the advantages in opportunity and leisure that they enjoyed. Socialists were both revolutionaries and servants of the people. "The capacity for anger – anger against a strong, cruel system

– is a necessary part of the socialist make-up," Maxton told the ILP Conference in a stirring Chairman's address in 1927.

> It is that feeling in our hearts that is the basis of revolution. But at the same time as that passionate anger swells up within us, what socialist worthy of the name does not feel in his heart a tremendous pity, a tremendous desire to relieve immediately the sufferings of the victim? That human love, human sympathy, human understanding is equally an absolute necessity of the socialist make-up. It constitutes the basis of our thought. These two things do not exist apart in different men, some men only feeling the one and some feeling the other. Almost every socialist feels both.

No catastrophe or Armageddon was needed to achieve that socialist change. Socialism, said Maxton, would be achieved by "imagination, will and the courage to pool these qualities in common organisation" with their fellows. He never supported those socialists who refuse to make any compromise with the electorate. Mass uprisings, violence, bloodshed, or even syndicalism held no attractions for him. Even in the dark days of the Means Tests of the early 'thirties, when across the political spectrum democracy was under siege, Maxton held to the view that socialists would work through a national representative assembly. Through their exercise of democratic power they would bring society to the point where there was no alternative but to pass peacefully towards a socialist society. The overriding test of the progress of socialism would be how many people had become socialists. "The Government can go no faster in progress than the people will allow them to," he said in a lecture appropriately entitled "Democracy and the Spirit of Service" in December 1924.

Maxton often spoke of himself as "a Utopian fool". Mankind, he believed, was "infinitely better than the social system within which it lives". It was his faith in the capabilities of ordinary people, a faith born of his experiences as a teacher, that led him to advocate a social and economic democracy in which everyone played a part in making the decisions that mattered. The community, and not simply the capitalist, was capable of running industry and had, in the talents of working men and women, the ability to do so. He did not dispute the need for a division of labour, but there was no reason why "labourers and artisans" should not "be the social equals of the directive heads". Nor did he argue against the social importance of the exceptional talents which many people possessed. There would always be people "of outstanding capacity, musical, artistic, scientific, manual, commercial and financial, who will have the regard and respect of their fellows for the special contribution they are able to make to the common pool of humanity". That, he found, an argument for equality, and not against it. "From my observations I believe that wealth and poverty both destroy the opportunity of enjoying the best things in life by those who suffer either one or the other."

Maxton's prescription of socialism was not, he said, "activated by envy, hatred, and malice: it was simply dictated as a necessity by my common sense". Maxton, his friend Bob Edwards wrote, could not be bought. He never accepted hospitality he could not return and was unimpressed by all social distinctions. Although he owned up to his Glasgow M.A. he turned down an offer in 1930 of an honorary degree from Edinburgh University.

He had little interest in material possessions. "In my philosophy of life the pleasure to be obtained from the possession of material things is much more limited than the pleasure to be obtained from human associations," he wrote. "I want to meander through life surveying the world as I go, trying to understand it, taking that share of the work that is reasonable and just and receiving a modest share of the necessities of life."

No one was more tolerant than Maxton, Attlee said. He was, wrote his colleague John McGovern, "the soul of honour and never at any time double-crossed a colleague". Even the harsh experience of prison did not embitter him. "I was with him on the night of his release from prison," wrote Dollan. "I marvelled at his lack of complaint." Throughout his career he treated his political opponents with charm and civility. When J. H. Thomas was hounded out of office in the 'thirties Maxton defended him. Although he was deeply opposed to his politics, he felt "tremendous regret at his downfall", and when Maxton met Ramsay MacDonald in the Commons only two months before MacDonald died, they were able to exchange friendly reminiscences. Brockway described how MacDonald laid a hand on Maxton's arm:

> "Oh, Jimmy," he said, "I was staying with Sir James Barrie last weekend and he was enquiring most kindly after you." He hesitated and then added rather wistfully, "It's good to think that we can have mutual friends even if fate has separated us from each other."
>
> "Oh, Mac," said Jimmy characteristically, "I shall always have a warm place in my heart for you for old time's sake." MacDonald looked wonderingly at me. "I'm not so sure about Fenner," he said, "I'm not so sure he was my friend even in the old times."

He and Jimmy laughed and I laughed too, rather uneasily. He passed on without another word.

In his last lecture to the ILP Summer School, in 1945, Maxton had stressed the importance of the individual in society. "We must not allow ourselves to become ants in an ant-hill," he told his audience. Cold, bureaucratic, centralised state socialism held no attractions for him. For Maxton the only test of socialist progress was in the improvement of the individual and thus the community. Greater educational opportunities would not only free exceptional people to realise their exceptional talents but allow common people to make the most of their common humanity, and ordinary people to realise their extraordinary potentials.

The social equality he supported was not for the sake of equality but for the sake of liberty. A truly socialist society would free men and women from the fear of poverty, the uncertainties of unemployment and the miseries of deprivation.

It is doubtful if, with his background, and his experience, Maxton could have thought any differently. Throughout his life he had seen how poverty crippled the schoolchildren he taught and how unemployment had devastated the constituency he represented. From the first, he had understood that men and women should be treated equally. "Write me as one who loved his fellow men," Maxton once told an intending biographer. Perhaps his colleague Fenner Brockway characterised him best. Maxton, wrote Brockway, seemed to have got nearest to the solution of life's problems. He always lived his own life, yet he accepted everyone on equal terms. Maxton could be friendly to all without being subservient to any. "I think," he concluded, "the secret of Maxton's conduct was an inherent sense of human equality."

Notes

The primary sources for this study have been the *Maxton Papers* deposited by Mr John Maxton in the Strathclyde Regional Archive, Mitchell Library; the papers of the Independent Labour Party, now on microfilm and microfiche; the minutes and reports of the Labour Party (Scottish Council) and the Labour Party National Executive Committee; the Glasgow minutes of the Independent Labour Party, deposited in the Mitchell Library; and the newspapers *Forward, The New Leader* (until 1922 *Labour Leader*, and subsequently *Socialist Leader*), in which, from 1927 Maxton wrote a regular, sometimes weekly column, and the *Glasgow Eastern Standard* from 1923 onwards. The *Glasgow Herald, The Times,* The *Scotsman* and other newspapers have also been consulted.

The papers of John Maclean (National Library of Scotland), Ramsay MacDonald (Public Record Office), Tom Johnston (National Library of Scotland), Arthur Woodburn (especially his Unpublished Autobiography in the National Library of Scotland), Pat Dollan (especially his Unpublished Autobiography in the possession of Mr James Dollan), and Emrys Hughes (especially the Unpublished Autobiography) have also been drawn upon. Government papers in the Public Record Office in London and in Edinburgh have also been examined.

Chapter 1: St. Enoch Station: November 1922

1   P. Dollan, *Unpublished Autobiography,* p.50-51 Other then when stated, references to the comments of Patrick Dollan come from the chapters of his unpublished autobiography.

2   *Scotsman,* 17 November 1922. The account of the scenes of November 1922 is drawn also from the *Glasgow Herald, Forward, The Times* and from Dollan's work.

3   Quoted in *Socialist Leader,* Life of Maxton, 27 July 1946.

4   P Dollan, *op cit,* p. 51.

5   *Glasgow Herald,* 21 November 1922.

6   A J P Taylor, *Observer,* 1956 Review of J McNair, *The Beloved Rebel.*

7   P Dollan, *op cit,* pp.82-3 and 86.

8   *Forward,* 9 December 1922.

9   Maxton found the difficulties of writing about Maclean "insurmountable" and handed his material to others. He was later accused of deliberately failing to produce the book. He replied in *New Leader,* 5 June 1936.

10   The book was to contain "a number of incidents and happenings from my private diaries". It was to be "what I think of the Big Time", with reminiscences about MacDonald, Eden and others. A synopsis is contained in the Maxton Papers.

11   Letter to Editor of the *Scottish Daily Express,* 15 April 1935, in Maxton Papers.

12   Letter to Allen, 25 May 1932 in A J Marwick, *Clifford Allen: The Open Conspirator,* (London, 1964), p. 120.

13   *New Leader,* 9 April 1926.

14   House of Commons Debates, 14 March 1940.

15   P Dollan, in *Socialist Review,* March 1926, reprinted in *Glasgow Eastern Standard,* 10 April 1926.

16   E Wertheimer, *Portrait of the Labour Party* (London, 1930) p. 253.

Chapter 2: From Unionist to Socialist

1   *New Leader,* 9 December 1932

2   Certificate contained in Maxton Papers.

3   Certificate, with annotations by Maxton, in Maxton Papers.
4   *Ibid.*
5   *New Leader,* 9 December 1932.
6   *Ibid.*
7   *Ibid.*
8   *Ibid.*
9   *Ibid.*
10 *Ibid.*
11 Certificate in Maxton Papers.
12 *New Leader,* 9 December 1932
13 P Snowden, *Autobiography* (London, 1934), p. 747. Maxton wrote that "it was after hearing a speech by Snowden that I finally made up my mind that it was my duty to join the ILP and play my part in its work".

Chapter 3: Educate, agitate, organise

1   Minutes of the Barrhead ILP, contained in Maxton Papers.
2   *Glasgow Eastern Standard,* 10 April 1926.
3   E Benn, J Maxton, *Benn-Maxton Debates* (London, 1928).
4   D Lowe, *Souvenirs of Scottish Labour* (London, 1919), p. 1.
5   Minutes of Barrhead ILP, in Maxton Papers.
6   W Walker, "Dundee's Disenchantment with Churchill", *Scottish Historical Review,* 49, 1970, p. 91.
7   Testimonial in Maxton Papers.
8   Letter contained in Maxton Papers, 7 December 1908.
9   Testimonials, December 1908, September 1909 in Maxton Papers.
10 Article in *Forward,* cited in N Milton, *John Maclean* (London, 1973), p. 41.

Chapter 4: Children's Champion

1   R Sherard, *The Child Slaves of Britain* (London, 1905), p. 175.
2   Quoted in W J Ashley, *The Progress of the German Working Class* (London, 1904), p. 50 and cited in J Young, *The Rousing of the Scottish Working Class* (London, 1979), p. 170.
3   Testimonial, written in 1911, in Maxton Papers.
4   Chairman's address, April 1927, ILP Conference, *Report,* 1928.
5   *New Leader,* 27 December 1941.
6   Article by J McKimmie, in Maxton Papers.
7   W Stewart, *Wartime and Other Impressions* (Glasgow, 1933), pp. 10-14.

Chapter 5: Sowing the Seeds

1   J Maxton, "The Working Class Movement", *Scottish Review,* Winter 1914, pp. 558-561.
2   H McShane, quoted in I McLean, *The Legend of Red Clydeside* (Edinburgh, 1983), p. 176.
3   *Forward,* 4 January 1913.
4   *Forward,* 31 August 1956, cited in W Campbell, The Origins and Early Development of *Forward* Newspaper: an assessment of its impact on Labour politics in Glasgow, 1906-1914 (Edinburgh University, 1973).
5   H McShane, *No Mean Fighter* (London, 1978), p. 25.

NOTES

6   *Is David Lloyd George a Socialist When Chancellor?* Unpublished pamphlet in Maxton Papers.

7   Maxton in *Scottish Review, op cit,* p. 563.

8   Debates between Johnston and Maclean in *Forward,* 9 July 1910, 6 August 1910, 24 September 1910.

9   Labour Party, Memorandum on "Scotland", *Labour Party National Executive Committee Papers*, 3 April 1910.

10   *Forward,* 18 March 1911.

11   Diary, contained in Maxton Papers.

Chapter 6: War Abroad: Struggle at Home

1   Letter to Sissie, 25 August 1914 in Maxton Papers

2   *Ibid.*

3   Information contained in documents in Maxton Papers.

4   Letter to Sissie, 21 March 1916.

5   Letter to Sissie, 4 April 1916.

6   P Grimley, *Scottish Daily Express,* April 1935, reprinted in *The Story of James Maxton MP* (Barrhead, 1985), p. 15.

7   Letter to Mother, 31 March 1916.

8   Letter to Sissie, 4 April 1916.

9   Letter to Sissie, 18 April 1916.

10   Letter to Ada Maxton, 25 April 1916.

11   Letter to Sissie, 18 April 1916.

12   Letter to Sissie, 24 April 1916.

13   Letter to Sissie, 4 May 1916.

14   *The Story of James Maxton MP, op cit,* p. 15.

15   Reprinted in F Brockway, *Towards Tomorrow, op cit,* pp. 37-38.

Chapter 7: Prison

1   W Stewart, *Wartime and other Impressions* (Glasgow, 1933) pp. 13-14.

2   Letter to Mother, 18 April 1916. A fuller account of the trial is contained in P Grimley, *The Life of James Maxton MP.*

3   A Woodburn, *Unpublished Autobiography*, p.25.

4   Letter to Sissie, 11 May 1916.

5   A Woodburn, *op cit,* p.25.

6   Letter from Sissie, 17 July 1916.

7   D Kirkwood, *My Life of Revolt* (London, 1935), p. 137.

8   *Glasgow Eastern Standard,* 10 April 1926.

9   D Kirkwood, *op cit,* p. 155.

Chapter 8: Working on the Clyde

1   B Shaw to J R Middleton, 3 April 1917, National Executive Correspondence, Labour Party Papers.

2   F Brockway, *Inside the Left* (London 1942), p. 53.

3   Letter to Sissie, 18 May 1917.

4   Letter to Sissie, 30 July 1917.

5   Letter to Sissie, 9 August 1917.

6   Minutes of Glasgow ILP, 30 November 1917.

7   National Executive of the Labour Party Minutes 1917-1918. A study of the

relationships between the Labour Party in Scotland and the Labour Party nationally is contained in R McKibbin, *The Evolution of the Labour Party, 1910-1924* (London, 1974).

8   Letters to Sissie, 18, 19 September 1918.
9   Letter to Sissie, 11 November 1918.
10   Letter to Sissie, 13 November 1918.
11   *Ibid.*

Chapter 9: Petrograd of the West

1   Royal Commission on the Housing of the Industrial Population in Scotland, Cmd 8731, 1917-18.
2   *Ibid.* p.91.
3   Minutes of ILP Parliamentary Group, 6, 13 December 1928 in Maxton Papers.
4   Minutes of Labour Party National Executive, November-December, 1918, also cited in D Marquand, *Ramsay MacDonald* (London, 1977), p. 234.
5   *Scottish Co-operator,* 7 December 1918.
6   *Forward,* 16 November 1918.
7   Scottish Unionist Association, General Election Literature, 1918. For a fuller account of the 1918 Election in Scotland, see G Brown, The Labour Party and Political Change in Scotland, 1918-1929 (Edinburgh University PhD, 1981), pp. 26-100.

Chapter 10: Two New Jobs and Marriage

1   *Glasgow Herald,* 30 December 1918.
2   Letter to Sissie, 13 January 1919.
3   Glasgow ILP Executive Minutes, 24 January 1919. Confirmation of a permanent appointment is contained in the Minutes of 11 July.
4   *Ibid,* 31 October 1919.
5   *Forward,* 8 February 1919.
6   *Ibid,* 31 October 1919.
7   Labour Party, Scottish Executive Committee Minutes, 3 March 1919.
8   Glasgow ILP Federation Minutes, 26 March 1919.
9   *Forward,* 12 April 1919.
10   *Glasgow Eastern Standard,* 27 March 1928.
11   Letter to Sissie, 27 January 1919.
12   Letter to Sissie, 5 February 1919.
13   Marriage Certificate in Maxton Papers.

Chapter 11: "Bolshevism"

1   R Blake, *The Unknown Prime Minister: The Life and Times of Andrew Bonar Law, 1858-1923* (London, 1955), p. 412.
2   *Glasgow Herald,* 16 November 1918.
3   *Ibid,* 31 January 1919.
4   *Forward,* 25 January, 1918. Wheatley contributed a series of articles on democracy, syndicalism and socialism at this time.
5   *Ibid,* 18 January 1919.
6   Letter to Sissie, 31 January 1919.
7   *Forward,* 9 December 1922.
8   ILP Glasgow Executive, Minutes, August 1919.

NOTES

9   *Forward,* 1 February 1919.
10   *Ibid,* 28 September 1919.
11   *Ibid,* 6 July 1919.

Chapter 12: Splits in the ILP

United Kingdom *Fortnightly Report,*
ɔlic Record Office.

linburgh, 1981) pp.21-22.

on Unemployment and Distress in

in August 1920, after being told of
ɔte how glad he was that she had
(Letter, 13 August 1920).

-4606, June 1923.
2, Maxton Papers.
)22, MacDonald Papers, PRO 30 69

1922, Maxton Papers.

New Statesman, 8 February 1921.
3   *Forward,* 15 April 1922.
4   Labour Party Scottish Executive Report, 1922.
5   *Forward,* 23 September 1922.
6   P Dollan, *Unpublished Autobiography,* p.50.
7   *Scotsman,* 30 October, 1922.
8   Labour Party Scottish Executive, Minutes of meeting of Executive with
     Scottish MPs, 7 October 1922.
9   Handwritten Manifesto for Bridgeton in Maxton Papers.
10   *Forward,* 18 November 1922.

Overlaid library receipt:

Glasgow University Library
CheckOut Receipt

02/12/00
04:07 pm

S CHARLES CHRISTOPHER

have just borrowed the following items:

Maxton a biography
return no later than 09-12-00

Please keep this receipt for your own records
Borrowed items are subject to recall and may have
earlier due dates

11   Letter from F Johnston, 16 November 1922, in Maxton Papers.
12   *Forward,* 18 August 1922.

Chapter 15: The Best Broadcasting Station in the World

1   *Glasgow Herald,* 22 November 1922.
2   *Ibid,* 21 November 1922.
3   *Ibid.*
4   P Dollan, *op cit,* p. 51.
5   E Shinwell, Transcript of Interview with Bob Cuddihy for Scottish Television, p. 41.
6   P Dollan, *op cit,* p. 51.
7   Letter from Maxton to MacDonald, 7 September 1922, MacDonald papers, PRO 30 69 1166 46.
8   J Scanlon, *Decline and Fall of the Labour Party* (London, 1932), p. 34.
9   *Forward,* 8 December 1922.
10   House of Commons Debates, 8 December 1922.
11   Dollan, *op cit,* p. 19.
12   *Ibid,* p. 56.
13   *Glasgow Eastern Standard,* 23 August 1923.
14   Dollan, *op cit,* p. 19.
15   *Glasgow Eastern Standard,* 7 April 1923.
16   Scottish Home Rule Association, *Newsletter,* May 1924.
17   Information in J Scanlon, *op cit,* p. 50.
18   P Dollan, *op cit,* p. 19.
19   Scottish Trades Union Conference Report, 1923, p.87.
20   Labour Party Scottish Conference Report, 1923, pp. 34-35.
21   Labour Party Scottish Executive Committee Report for 1923-24, pp. 11-12.

Chapter 16: "Murderers"

1   P Dollan, *Unpublished Autobiography,* p. 21. The incident took place on 27 June 1923 and is recorded in House of Commons Debates, 165, 2377-4606.
2   *Glasgow Herald,* November – December, 1922.
3   Report of Scottish Board of Health, *PP,* 1923 Cmnd 1857, pp. 11-12.
4   *The Times,* 28 June 1923.
5   *Glasgow Eastern Standard,* 4 August 1923.
6   *Daily Sketch,* 9 July 1923.
7   *Glasgow Eastern Standard,* 14 July 1923.
8   *Ibid.*
9   T Graham, *Willie Graham* (London, 1948) p. 134.
10   *Sunday Mail* 9 July 1923.
11   *Daily Sketch,* 4 July 1923.
12   *Glasgow Eastern Standard,,* 27 July 1923.
13   *Ibid,* 4 August 1923.
14   *New Leader,* 6 July 1923.
15   Letter from MacDonald to Maxton, 20 July 1923 in Maxton Papers.
16   *Ibid,* 13 July 1923.
17   *Ibid,* 1 August 1923.
18   *Glasgow Eastern Standard,* 14 July 1923.
19   *Ibid,* 4 August 1923.
20   MacDonald Diary, 1 May 1923 (PRO 30 69 1753). Cited in D Marquand, *Ramsay MacDonald* (London 1977), p. 288. MacDonald's diary was intended to be "notes to guide and revive memory as regards happenings".

NOTES

Chapter 17: Taking the Slums into Parliament

1   *Glasgow Eastern Standard,* 10 November 1923.
2   Dollan, *op cit,* p. 56-57.
3   *Ibid,* p. 60.
4   *Glasgow Eastern Standard,* 20 October 1923.
5   W Bothilo, *Cancer of Empire* (London 1924) pp. 13-60. His book had first been published as articles in *New Outlook.*
6   *Glasgow Eastern Standard,* 22 September 1923.
7   Letter from Susan Lawrence, June 1923, in Maxton Papers.
8   *Glasgow Eastern Standard,* 1 September 1923.
9   *Glasgow Eastern Standard,* 19 November 1923.
10   Letter from MacDonald to Allen, 1 September 1923, Allen Papers.
11   J Scanlon, *op cit,* p. 56.
12   Dollan, *op cit,* p. 58-59.
13   *Ibid,* p. 50.
14   *Forward,* 9 December 1922.
15   Labour Party Scottish Executive Report, 1923, p.2
16   *Forward,* 1 May 1923
17   *Ibid,* 5 September 1923.
18   *Ibid,* 29 September 1923.
19   *Glasgow Eastern Standard,* 10 November 1923.
20   Western Council Scottish Unionist Association, 6 December 1922.
21   Annual Report, Glasgow Unionist Association, 1924.
22   Dollan *op cit,* p. 25.
23   Scottish Unionist Association, Executive Minutes, 9 November 1923.
24   Novar to S Baldwin, 8 November, 1923 cited in C Cook, *Age of Alignment* (London), p.116.
25   *Scotsman,* 8 December 1923.
26   Maxton to MacDonald, 22 December 1923, MacDonald Papers, PRO 30 69 746 77.

Chapter 18: In Government But Not in Power

1   E Hughes, *Rebels and Renegades,* Unpublished Autobiography. For story of formation of Labour Government see R Lyman, *The First Labour Government* (London, 1952) and D Marquand, *Ramsay MacDonald, op cit. p. 279-328.*
2   P Dollan, *op cit,* p. 25.
3   *Glasgow Eastern Standard,* 15 December 1923.
4   *Ibid.*
5   Maxton to MacDonald, 22 December 1923, MacDonald Papers, PRO 30 69 746 77.
6   Wheatley to MacDonald, 21 December 1923, MacDonald Papers, PRO 30 69 746 219-210.
7   *Glasgow Eastern Standard,* 12 January 1924.
8   Dollan, *op cit,* p.28.
9   Smillie to MacDonald, 21 December 1923, MacDonald Papers, PRO 30 69 746.
10   Wheatley to MacDonald 21 December 1923, MacDonald Papers, PRO 30 69 746 209-210.
11   T Jones, *Whitehall Diary* Vol 1 1919-1925 (ed Middlemass) (London 1969), p. 266.
12   MacDonald Diary, 24 January 1924, MacDonald Papers, PRO 30 69 1753.
13   N Maclean to MacDonald, 24 January 1924, MacDonald Papers, PRO 30 69 1443-5.

E Hughes, Unpublished Autobiography, *Rebels and Renegades*, R Lyman, *The First Labour Government*.
[14] *Glasgow Eastern Standard*, 16 February 1924.
[15] Labour Party Scottish Conference Report, 1924, p. 27.
[16] B Webb, *Diaries*, 1912-1924 (ed M Cole), (London 1952) p. 263.
[17] *Glasgow Eastern Standard*, 19 April 1924.
[18] Labour Party Scottish Conference Report, 1924 p. 27.
[19] Labour Party, Scottish Executive Committee, 7 January 1924.
[20] *Glasgow Herald*, 16 May 1924.
[21] B Webb, *Diaries*, July 1924, Microfilm, National Library of Scotland.

Chapter 19: Conscience of the Party

[1] Labour Party, Scottish Executive, 1919 Report, p. 20.
[2] *Glasgow Herald*, November 1922, contained in papers of Scottish Secretariat (National Library).
[3] *Glasgow Evening Citizen*, 27 August 1923.
[4] Labour Party Scottish Executive Committee Minutes, 13 January 1919.
[5] *Scottish Home Rule*, November 1923.
[6] *Scottish Home Rule*, May 1924.
[7] House of Commons Debates 173, 871.
[8] *New Leader*, 13 February 1943.
[9] J Scanlon, *op cit*, p. 76.
[10] E Shinwell, *Lead With The Left* (London 1976) p.86.
[11] Election Address, 1924, in Maxton Papers.

Chapter 20: New Alliances

[1] MacDonald Diary, 3 December 1924, quoted in D Marquand, *op cit*.
[2] Labour Party, Scottish Conference Report, 1925, pp. 32-33.
[3] *Glasgow Herald*, 12 January 1925.
[4] *Scotsman*, 14 January 1925.
[5] Quoted in P Grimley, *Scottish Daily Express*, April 1935, in The Life Story of James Maxton MP, *op cit*, p. 47.
[6] *Glasgow Eastern Standard*, 9 April 1925.
[7] J Scanlon, *op cit*, p. 92.
[8] *Labour Standard*, 17 December 1925, cuttings in Woodburn Papers.
[9] Glasgow Eastern Standard, 5 December 1925.

Chapter 21: Moving Left

[1] *Glasgow Eastern Standard*, 27 June 1925.
[2] *Ibid*, 1 August 1925.
[3] *New Leader*, 21 August 1925.
[4] *Glasgow Eastern Standard*, 13 February 1926.
[5] Letter from Wedgewood to Brockway, 25 November, quoted in *Inside the Left*, *op cit*.
[6] *Glasgow Eastern Standard*, 19 December 1925.
[7] Minutes of ILP Parliamentary Group, 23 November, 8 December, 15 December 1925, 12 February, 3 March 1926 in Maxton Papers.
[8] *New Leader*, 29 January 1926.

NOTES

Chapter 22: Splits and Succession.

1   *Glasgow Eastern Standard*, 8 August 1925.
2   F Brockway, *Inside the Left* (London, 1942) p. 157. Also in *Towards Tomorrow* (London, 1977) p. 69.
3   Letter from Allen to Maxton, 21 October 1925 in Allen Papers, cited in A Marwick, *Clifford Allen: The Open Conspirator* (Edinburgh, 1964) pp 100-101.
4   Cited in M Gilbert, *Plough My Own Furrow* (London, 1965) pp. 198-99.
5   Marwick, *op cit*, pp. 100-101.
6   Cited in D Marquand, *op cit*, p. 430.
7   M Gilbert, *op cit*, p. 297.
8   Letter from MacDonald to Allen, 3 November 1925 in Allen Papers.

Chapter 23: Chairman Maxton

1   *Socialist Review*, April 1926, reprinted in *Glasgow Eastern Standard*, 10 April 1926
2   *New Leader*, 9 April 1926.
3   *Forward*, 13 March 1926.
4   F Brockway, *Towards Tomorrow, op cit*, p. 70.
5   B Webb, *Diaries*, April 1926, Microfilm Collection, National Library of Scotland.
6   F Brockway, *Towards Tomorrow, op cit*, p. 76.
7   P Dollan, *op cit*, pp. 82-83.
8   *Glasgow Eastern Standard*, 22 May 1926.
9   Minutes of ILP NAC, 5-6 June 1926
10   Letters to Maxton while in hospital, included in Maxton Papers.
11   *Glasgow Eastern Standard*, 21 August 1926.
12   *New Leader*, 29 October 1926.

Chapter 24: Socialism in Our Time.

1   *New Leader*, 9 January 1928.
2   ILP Conference Report, Chairman's Address, April 1930.
3   *Glasgow Eastern Standard*, 22 August 1925.
4   *Ibid* 5 December 1925.
5   *Ibid*, 30 October 1926.
6   *Ibid*, 30 October 1926.
7   *Ibid*.
8   *Ibid*, 8 January 1927.
9   *Ibid*, 19 March 1927.
10   *Ibid*, 2 April 1927.
11   *Ibid*, 18 December 1926.

Chapter 25: The Rebel Spirit.

1   *Glasgow Eastern Standard*, 20 November 1926.
2   *Ibid*.
3   P Grimley, The Life of James Maxton MP, *op cit*, p. 60-61.
4   *Ibid*.
5   *Glasgow Eastern Standard*, 2 April 1927.
6   ILP NAC Minutes, 24-25 July 1926.

7 Wheatley to MacDonald, MacDonald Papers, PRO 30 69 1172 814-5 July 15 1927.
8 House of Commons Debates, 23 July 1927, 2135.
9 *New Leader*, 27 July 1927.
10 *Glasgow Eastern Standard*, 8 October 1927.
11 *Ibid*, 3 December 1927. His suspension came on 23 November 1917 Col 1933-34.
12 MacDonald to Maxton, 28 November 1927, MacDonald Papers PRO 30 69 1172 83.
13 *Glasgow Eastern Standard*, 15 October 1927.
14 MacDonald to Johnston, MacDonald Papers, PRO 30 69 1172 815.
15 *Forward*, 17 December 1927.
16 Kerr to MacDonald, MacDonald Papers, 2 December 1927 PRO 30 69 1437 84.
17 *Forward*, 7 January 1928.

Chapter 26: The Cook Maxton Manifesto

1 *Forward*, 19 June 1926.
2 Cited in E Benn and J Maxton, *The Benn-Maxton Debates* (London 1928).
3 J Scanlon, *op cit*, p. 111.
4 *Glasgow Eastern Standard*, 23 June 1928.
5 *Ibid*.
6 *Forward*, 23 June 1928.
7 ILP NAC, 30 June 1928.
8 *Ibid*.
9 J Scanlon, *op cit*, p.111.
10 A Cook and J Maxton, *Our Case for a Socialist Revival* (London 1928).
11 ILP NAC Minutes, 30 June 1928.
12 *Forward*, 28 July 1928.
13 Labour Party Conference Report, 1928.
14 *Glasgow Eastern Standard*, 13 October 1928.
15 *Ibid*, 20 October 1928.
16 Cited in D Marquand, *op cit*. p. 484.
17 Minutes of ILP Parliamentary Group, 5, 12 December 1928, contained in Maxton Papers.

Chapter 27: No Mandate for Socialism

1 *New Leader*, 14 June 1929.
2 *Ibid*, 8 April 1929.
3 P Snowden, *op cit* p. 846.
4 Minutes of Labour Party Scottish Executive, Minutes 1925-1929 cited in G Brown, *The Labour Party and Political Change in Scotland* p. 383 (Unpublished PhD, Edinburgh University, 1982).
5 Labour Party, Scottish Executive Committee, 18 March 1929. The matter was sent to the organisation committee for consideration (Minute, 15 April 1929).
6 *Ibid*, 10 June 1929.
7 *Scotsman* 25 April 1929.
8 *Glasgow Eastern Standard*, 14 June 1929.
9 *Shinwell Talking*, pp. 72-73. See also E Shinwell, *Lead with the Left*, pp. 88-89.
10 *Ibid*.
11 *Glasgow Eastern Standard*, 15 June 1929.
12 *New Leader*, 14 June 1929.

NOTES

13   House of Commons Debates, 229, 166.

Chapter 28: Leader of the Opposition

1   *New Leader*, 4 August 1929.
2   *Times*, 6 January 1930.
3   *Forward*, 14 December 1929.
4   *Times*, 6 January 1930.
5   F Brockway, *Inside the Left, op cit*, p. 267-8.
6   *Times*, 21 April 1930.
7   *Ibid.*
8   *New Leader*, 23 May 1930.
9   F Brockway, *Inside the Left, op cit*, 207-8.

Chapter 29: "Oh The Bastard, the Bloody Bastard"

1   F Brockway, *Inside the Left, op cit*, p. 210-211, see also M Foot, *Aneurin Bevan* (London, 1962), p.124.
2   *Ibid.*
3   *Ibid.*
4   J Scanlon, *op cit*, p. 195.
5   F Brockway, *Inside the Left, op cit*, p. 195.
6   J McGovern, *Neither Fear Nor Favour*, (London 1960), pp 65-66. A more critical account of the by-election is contained in E Hughes, *Unpublished Autobiography*.
7   *Ibid*, p. 89-90.
8   Diary of George Strass, quoted in R Skidelsky, *Politicians and the Slump* (London 1967), p. 211.
9   Interview in *New Leader*, 6 February 1931.
10   Cited in The Life Story of James Maxton MP, *op cit*, p. 66.

Chapter 30: "If you can't ride two horses ...."

1   *New Leader*, 4 September 1931.
2   *Ibid*, 4 September 1931.
3   Labour Party, Annual Conference, Report 1931, quoted also in *New Leader*, 9 October 1931.
4   *Ibid.*
5   J Lee, *My Life with Nye* (London, 1980), p. 82-83.
6   ILP NAC Minutes, November 1931.
7   *Forward*, 12 December 1931.
8   *Ibid.*
9   *Ibid.*

Chapter 31: "Pure But Impotent"

1   Cited in M Foot, *Loyalists and Loners (London 1985)* p. 26.
2   F Brockway, *Towards Tomorrow, op cit*, p. 108, also in *Inside the Left, op cit*, p. 239.
3   ILP NAC Minutes, 30 March 1932.
4   *Forward*, 9 April 1932.

[5] F Brockway, *Inside the Left, op cit*, p. 239.
[6] *Forward*, May 1932.
[7] *Times*, 1 August 1932.
[8] *Forward*, 23 July 1932.
[9] *Times*, 1 August 1932.
[10] *Times*, 10 September 1932.
[11] J Lee, *op cit*, p. 81.
[12] *Forward*, 6 August 1932.
[13] A Woodburn, *Unpublished Autobiography*, p. 68.
[14] *Ibid*, p. 76.
[15] J Paton, *Left Turn* (London 1936), p. 398.

Chapter 32: On the Fringes

[1] *New Leader*, 23 December 1932.
[2] House of Commons Debates, 8 March 1933.
[3] *The Times*, 30 March 1933.
[4] *New Leader*, 1 May 1933.

Chapter 33: United Fronts

[1] *Forward*, 4 February 1933.
[2] Brockway, *Inside the Left, op cit*, p. 249.
[3] *Daily Worker*, 18 June 1932.
[4] *Ibid*, 26 May 1932.
[5] *New Leader*, 6 January 1933.
[6] *Ibid*, 3 Febuary 1933.
[7] Letter from Pollitt to Maxton, in Maxton Papers.
[8] Also in *Towards Tomorrow, op cit*, p. 110.
[9] T Bottomore, *Marx: Selected Writings*, p. 200.
[10] R H Tawney in *Political Quarterly in the Thirties* (London 1967) p. 326-7.
[11] *Times*, 10 August 1933.
[12] *New Leader*, 19 August 1933.
[13] *Ibid*, 23 June 1933.
[14] *Ibid*, 19 August 1933.
[15] *Ibid*, 23 June 1933.
[16] *Ibid*, 19 August 1933.
[17] *Forward*, 13 October 1933.

Chapter 34: Member for the Unemployed

[1] *The Times*, 28 February 1934.
[2] Letter from MacDonald to Maxton, in Maxton Papers.
[3] *The Times*, 18 April 1934.
[4] ILP NAC, 21 December 1933.
[5] *The Times*, 13 January 1934.
[6] ILP NAC Minutes, 10-11 February 1934.
[7] F Brockway, *Inside the Left, op cit*, p. 252-4.
[8] ILP NAC Minutes, 10-11 February 1934.
[9] Notes for speech to ILP Summer School, 1934 in Maxton Papers.
[10] ILP NAC Minutes 12 December 1934.
[11] *New Leader*, 23 March 1934.

NOTES

12   A Woodburn, *Unpublished Autobiography*, p. 52.

Chapter 35: Maxton at Fifty

1   A J P Taylor, *Beaverbrook* (London 1972), p. 321.
2   *Scottish Daily Express*, 14 May 1935.
3   Buchanan's Obituary, in *Sunday Observer*, August 1946 in Maxton Papers.
4   *The Times*, 30 January 1935.
5   *Ibid*, 4 February 1935.
6   *Ibid*, 22 April 1935.
7   *Daily Worker*, 24 April 1935.
8   *Forward*, 4 May 1935.
9   *Glasgow Herald*, 8 March 1935, and 15 March 1935.
10   *Ibid*, 5 August 1935.
11   *New Leader*, 27 September 1935.
12   *Ibid*, 21 July 1934.
13   *The Times*, 22 March 1935.
14   A Woodburn, *op cit*, p. 84.
15   *New Leader*, 22 November 1935.
16   *Ibid*, 8 November, 1935.
17   *Glasgow Herald*, 14 November 1935.
18   *New Leader*, 22 November 1935.

Chapter 36: Fighting Fascism

1   House of Commons Debates, 7 April, 1936.
2   F Brockway, *Inside the Left*, *op cit*, p. 327.
3   *Ibid.*
4   *The Times*, 4 December 1936.
5   *Ibid*, 12 December 1936.
6   *Ibid*, 28 May 1937.
7   *New Leader*, 31 July 1936.
8   *Ibid*, 26 September 1936.
9   *Glasgow Herald*, 12 October 1936.
10   *The Times*, 31 March 1937.
11   *New Leader*, 20 February 1937.
12   F Brockway, *Inside the Left*, *op cit*, pp. 266-7.
13   *New Leader*, 27 February 1937.
14   F Brockway, *Inside the Left*, *op cit*, pp. 266-7.
15   *Ibid.*
16   *New Leader*, 26 February 1937.
17   Letter to Strauss in Maxton Papers.

Chapter 37: Spain

1   *The Times*, 29 January 1937.
2   J McNair, *op cit*, p. 225.
3   *New Leader*, 29 January 1937.
4   *Ibid*, 30 July 1937.
5   F Brockway, *Inside the Left*, *op cit*, p. 320.
6   *New Leader*, 3 September 1937.
7   *Ibid.*

8 ILP NAC Minutes, 13 November 1937.
9 *New Leader*, 2 April 1938.
10 ILP NAC Minutes, 13 November 1937.
11 J McNair, *op cit*, p. 268.
12 *Ibid.*

Chapter 38: Munich and War

1 *New Leader*, 21 July 1934.
2 *Forward*, 8 October 1938.
3 *New Leader*, 7 October 1938.
4 F Brockway, *Inside the Left, op cit*, p. 352.
5 *Ibid* p. 332.
6 J Lee, *My Life with Nye, op cit*, p. 72.
7 J McGovern, *op cit*, p. 129.
8 J McNair, *op cit*, p. 277.
9 Letter to Son, in Maxton Papers.
10 *New Leader*, 3 February 1939.
11 ILP Conference Report, 1939.
12 *New Leader*, 10 November 1939.
13 *Ibid*, 29 August 1942.
14 ILP NAC May 25-26 1940.
15 Cited in A J P Taylor, *op cit*, p. 404-6.
16 J McGovern, *op cit*, p. 152.
17 *Times*, 6 December 1940.
18 J McGovern, *op cit*, p. 158.
19 *New Leader* 4 October 1941.
20 *Ibid*, 29 August 1942.
21 *Ibid*, 12 December 1942.
22 ILP NAC Minutes, 27-28 February 1943.

Chapter 39: Final Days

1 *Glasgow Herald*, 3 January 1944.
2 *Socialist Leader*, 3 August 1946.
3 *Glasgow Herald*, 28 August 1944.
4 *Ibid*, 22 and 25 September 1944.
5 *Socialist Leader* 3 August 1946.
6 *New Leader*, 2 April 1945.
7 *The Times*, 20 April 1945.
8 Maxton's Manifesto for Bridgeton in Maxton Papers.
9 *New Leader*, 4 August 1945.
10 *Ibid.*
11 *Socialist Leader*, 3 August 1946.
12 *Forward*, 22 December 1945.
13 *Daily Herald*, 8 December 1945 reprinted in *New Leader*, 15 December 1945.
14 McGovern, *op cit*, p. 168.
15 Article by McKimmie on Maxton, in Maxton Papers.
16 J McGovern, *op cit*, p. 168.
17 F Brockway, *Towards Tomorrow, op cit*, p. 146.
18 *Socialist Leader*, 3 August 1946.
19 Letter from Churchill to Maxton, in Maxton Papers.
20 House of Commons Debates, 426, 1.
21 *Socialist Leader*, 3 August 1946.
22 Letter from Roberton to A Maxton, in Maxton Papers.

INDEX

174, 189 (his slogan for the miners), 208, 209, 210, 211
Cripps, Stafford (Sir), 260, 281, 282, 283, 289
Cruden, John, 212
Dallas, George, 37, 52, 56, 289
Dalton, Hugh, 182, 194, 197
Dickson, Tom, 147
Dollan, Agnes (Lady), 154, 202 (protests against Maxton's treatment of MacDonald)
Dollan, James, 9
Dollan, Patrick (Sir), 11, 18, 20, 43, 48, 75, 105, 117, 118, 122, 123, 126 (questions from Glasgow), 127, 128, 129, 140, 149, 151, 152, 156, 170 (defends MacDonald), 171, 184 (supports Maxton against Allen), 186 (praises Maxton as Chairman), 188, 189, 202, 209, 210 (leads assault on Maxton), 212, 220, 224, 225, 244 (his charge of "rigging"), 245, 254, 314 (Maxton's lack of complaint)
Duffes, Alexander, 70–71
Dutt, Palme, 283
Edward VIII, King, 280 (Maxton's call to reject the Abdication Bill)
Edwards, Bob, 9, 226, 275, 286, 287, 297, 298, 314 (Maxton could not be bought)
Elliot, Walter, (Dr), 134 (refers to Maxton's sincerity), 145, 157 (wins Kelvingrove)
Ferguson, Aitken, 156–157 (defeated at Kelvingrove)
Foot, Michael, 305 (refers to a speech by Maxton)
Franco, General, 285, 286, 287
Gallacher, William, 62, 73, 74, 75, 76, 99, 102, 208, 211, 260, 269, 283, 298, 312 (his unfair assertion re Maxton's knowledge of Marx)
Gandhi, Mahatma, 231, 307 (expresses condolences)
Geddes, Sir Auckland, 83
Gladstone, William Ewart, 32, 33
Glasier, Bruce, 53
Graham, Duncan, 134
Graham, R.B. Cunninghame, 33
Graham, William, 101
Grayson, Victor, 138
Greenwood, Arthur, 152
Haldane, Lord, 148, 152
Hannington, Wal, 265

Hardie, Keir, 32, 36, 50, 52, 53, 54, 56, 58, 59 (died of a "broken heart"), 82, 95, 123, 159 (his promise to fight for a legislature in Scotland)
Hastings, Patrick (Sir), 124, 163, 164
Henderson, Arthur, 58, 59, 62, 78, 82, 124, 169, 212, 214 (warned by Tawney), 219, 226, 234, 237 (leader of Parliamentary Labour Party), 238, (replaced by Lansbury), 241, 267
Hicks, Joynson, 133, 134
Highton, Herbert, 95
Hitler, Adolf, 258, 292, 300
Hoare, Samuel (Sir), 297
Hobson, J.A., 194, 197
Hope, John, 204
Horabin, Frank, 283
Houston, James, 56, 96
Hughes, Emrys, 147, 151, 210, 229, 309 (disappointed as he re-visits Glasgow)
James, C.L.R., 278
Johnson, Francis, 120
Johnston, Tom, 49, 53, 54, 59, 75, 103, 120, 123, 134 (shows sympathy and agreement with Maxton), 147, 152, 186 (praises Maxton as one of the great men of his time), 190, 200, 206, 236, 245
Jowett, Fred, 241, 283
Kerenski, (Russian social democrat), 83
Kerr, George, 175 (his discomfiture attributed by MacDonald to Maxton), 206
Kerrigan, Peter, 269
Keynes, John Maynard, 194, 197
Kirkwood, David (Lord), 13, 61, 74, 75, 76, 99, 123, 124, 126, 136, 141 (visits the Ruhr, along with Maxton and other MP s), 148, 171, 174, 178 (cruises with Maxton, to Northern Africa), 179, 190, 200 (charged with disaffection and fined), 211 (Treasurer of Cook-Maxton campaign), 220, 222, 237, 241, 243 (decides to leave ILP), 245
Lansbury, George, 164, 170, 171, 172 (Lansbury's Weekly), 173, 178, 179, 238 (succeeds to Labour leadership in place of Henderson), 241, 254, 274, 275 (resignation as Leader of Labour Party), 277, 278, 300